Planning Individualized Speech and Language Intervention Programs

by Nickola Wolf Nelson

Communication Skill Builders, Inc.
3130 N. Dodge Blvd. / P.O. Box 42050
Tucson, Arizona 85733
(602) 327-6021

ISBN 0-88450-790-4
Catalog No. 3099

For David
who never needed communication learning to be so explicit
and the others
who did

PREFACE

The Education for All Handicapped Children Act of 1975, P.L. 94-142, places the responsibility for ensuring provision of a Free Appropriate Public Education for all handicapped children, including speech and language impaired children, squarely in the hands of the nation's schools. Now in the early stages of full implementation, the impact of the law is only beginning to be felt.

Any of us who have been associated with the financial and emotional struggles of handicapped individuals and their families as they have been turned away from traditional avenues of public support to endure financial stress, distant separation, or little or no professional help must surely believe that this law represents a great deal of hope. However, it also presents some major challenges and potential dangers to the continued provision of quality programs to severely communicatively impaired children who have previously been served in other settings. The new law does not require that the schools actually provide each child's program, but that the schools make sure that the appropriate program, at no cost to the parents, is provided in an environment least restrictive to the child.

The Individualized Education Program (I.E.P.) planning process makes the determination of what constitutes "appropriate" service for each child the responsibility of a multidisciplinary team of individuals — especially and importantly including the child's parents and the child him- or herself — if possible. Given the need to contribute to this team process, speech-language pathologists practicing in the schools and their colleagues must take a fresh look at the variables which determine appropriate speech and language programming. Distinctions between speech and language intervention programs provided in schools and other professional settings should become increasingly less noticeable.

The task of full implementation of P.L. 94-142 seems overwhelming when one tries to imagine squeezing the comprehensive requirements of the law — designed to protect and promote the interests of handicapped students and their parents — into the "traditional," as it is often termed, school delivery model of twice weekly sessions for large groups of children. Yet the requirements of the law are no more than most of us are taught as good clinical practice in the process of our professional training.

Certainly the concern of professionals who fear that implementation of the "due process" provisions of the law will consume precious time previously devoted to direct intervention is a valid one. Well-written I.E.P.s require commitments of professional time and energy, but they also provide a way to ensure effective programming for individual children. Additionally, the specification of "special education and related services" in all of the I.E.P.s of a school district should provide powerful evidence of the need for changes in staffing patterns to comply with the specifications of the collective I.E.P.s of the children to be served.

Educators are concerned that so much time will be consumed in writing the I.E.P.s that significantly less time will be available for implementing them, particularly the "statement of annual goals including short-term instructional objectives," and the "appropriate objective criteria and evaluation procedures for determining, at least on an annual basis, whether the short-term instructional objectives are being achieved."* *Planning Individualized Speech and Language Programs* is primarily a set of short-term objective sequences designed to contribute to the development and implementation of the I.E.P. The book should also be of use to speech-language pathologists planning programs in settings other than the schools, and to students who are learning to plan programs for communicatively handicapped children. A glossary is provided for those who are unfamiliar with some of the professional terminology used in the behavioral objective sequences and explanatory notes.

The objectives are remedial in nature and are designed to assist the development of desired communicative abilities in areas where a specific disability has been identified. As such they are quite different from scales of normal development or programs which are to be followed sequentially from beginning to end.

The instructional objectives presented here have been found to be successful in the author's clinical practice in a variety of settings over the past 10 years and incorporate new concepts and procedures which have been tested and reported in the literature (see references following each discussion for individual sequences). In their present form, these objectives have been in successful use by school speech-language clinicians in Berrien and Cass Counties, Michigan, during the 1978-79 school year and have been adopted by a number of other school districts across the nation.

---

*All quotations from the Rules and Regulations for P.L. 94-142 are from the *Federal Register,* Tuesday, Aug. 23, 1977.

ACKNOWLEDGEMENTS

Initial drafts of many of the sequences were constructed at a workshop of Berrien and Cass County speech–language clinicians in southwestern Michigan. Those who participated were Diane Albright, Karen Antisdale, Dean Betz, Pearl Blaylock, Doug Borst, Nancy Bunkley, Carol Cox, Francine Damm, Kathy Daniel, Cathy Englehart, Barb Erlich, Barb Farnan, Lee Fly, Debbie Geiger, Chris Hoddy, Sue Keith, Ann Kerrigan, Jan Le Claire, Diane Lewis, Lee Lyon, Janet Mack, Sara Maxam, Marilyn McCulley, Dawn McDonald, Beth Murphy, Carol Olson, Jean Silbar, Robyn Williams, Linda Williamson, Pat Wishart, Kerry Wulf and Judy Wurtz.

Prior to the workshop I had the opportunity to become familiar with similar projects of other school districts around the state of Michigan. This was largely due to the efforts of Carol Thomas and Linda Fairchild whose committees of the Michigan Speech and Hearing Association collected sets of short–term objective sequences and published them in the Fall 1976 *MSHA Journal*. The format designed by the Muskegon Public Schools was especially influential in determining the format presented here. Berrien County Intermediate School District provided support for this project, and Sandy Porter, in particular, supplied patience and creativity in setting the objective sequences down on paper.

Some of the language intervention objectives were developed in Berrien County classrooms for learning and language impaired students which are funded with P.L. 94–142 Flowthrough grants awarded by the state of Michigan. The teachers and speech–language pathologists serving those programs are especially creative. Some of their ideas are reflected here.

Individuals with less immediate, but no less significant, input into the work presented here are my teachers, colleagues and clients at Wichita State University, the Institute of Logopedics, and the Butler County Schools in Kansas; particularly my clinical mentors, JoAnne Simmons and Elizabeth Bosley. Other professionals whose methods and procedures had a major influence on the development of the objective sequences are credited in the footnotes.

Finally, Larry and David have my loving appreciation for their continual toleration of the inconveniences that such a project creates in our homelife.

CONTENTS

x   *Contents*

INTRODUCTION

It is important when planning to use these objective sequences to have an understanding of the philosophy underlying their development. They are not intended to be prepackaged programs nor to represent the proverbial "cookbook" approach to speech and language intervention. They do assume a graduate level understanding of speech-language pathology and in most instances would be implemented directly by a qualified speech-language pathologist. Exceptions to this general rule might occur when a paraprofessional or aide is given more explicit direction for working toward certain objectives than is provided here, or when parents and teachers are actively involved in providing environmental intervention, natural language opportunities, or carry-over activities as specified. The objective sequences and recording formats were designed with the intent of being (a) broad enough to encompass different theoretical and methodological constructs, (b) specific enough to be operational, and (c) open-ended enough to allow further individualization for a particular student.

General Suggestions

The federal Rules and Regulations for P.L. 94-142 (121a.346) specify that:

> The individualized education program for each child must include:
> (a) A statement of the child's present levels of education performance;
> (b) A statement of annual goals, including short-term instructional objectives;
> (c) A statement of the specific special education and related services to be provided to the child, and the extent to which the child will be able to participate in regular education programs;
> (d) The projected dates for initiation of services and the anticipated duration of the services; and
> (e) Appropriate objective criteria and evaluation procedures and schedules for determining, on at least an annual basis, whether the short-term instructional objectives are being achieved.

The objective sequence formats provided in this book are primarily intended to contribute to components (b) "short-term instructional objectives" and (e) "appropriate objective criteria" of the I.E.P. The diagnostic summaries at the top of each sequence will also contribute to (a) "A statement of the child's present levels of education performance,"

but the formats presented here are not all-inclusive enough to be the child's total I.E.P. Probably the major function of a written I.E.P., at least in the minds of many parents, is (c) "A statement of the specific special education and related services to be provided to the child." In order to meet this requirement, it is critical that there be *one* coordinated I.E.P., which includes the five elements outlined above for *all* of the services to be provided to the child. Most school districts already have a form and a procedure for meeting this requirement, but it is difficult for the I.E.P. to be both concise enough to outline the major elements of the program in an easily retrievable manner and also provide sufficient detail in each of the disability areas, especially for students who exhibit multiple impairments. It then becomes the responsibility of each participating specialist to provide input into the child's total I.E.P. – often in the form of more detailed diagnostic reports and instructional plans.

Prior to the initial I.E.P. meeting it is critical that the student already have been evaluated in all areas related to the suspected disability. Although it is often overlooked, the speech and language evaluation is an important part of the diagnostic process for the majority of handicapped students in any category, not just those whose major handicapping condition is a communicative impairment. The evaluation should yield two types of information. First, it should provide sufficient evidence — through the use of formal and informal multiple nondiscriminatory procedures — that the student does indeed have a speech-language impairment which justifies a special education program or service; and second, it should be detailed enough to suggest major areas of emphasis for the speech and language intervention program.

Suggestions for Using These Objectives in Planning I.E.P.s

If the evaluation has been complete, and if the child does need a special program, it should then be possible to select communicative goals in one to three areas for direct speech and language intervention programming. The *Index of Goals* (page 5) for these objective sequences can be consulted to select areas of intervention to correspond with a particular student's need. The Goals are written in general terms that define "normality" in each of the 29 areas categorized under the labels *Preverbal, Early Language, Articulation, Language, Auditory Processing, Voice* and *Fluency.* They are to be considered ultimate goals rather than the annual goals which would be written into I.E.P.s. Most students would not be expected to reach the goal in any of the areas during a normal school year or the span of an annual I.E.P.

Each sequence also has a *Long-Range Objective,* or a terminal objective, printed in its heading. A number of the long-range objectives require insertion of specific target content for individual students (see particularly sequences Articulation, A–6 and A–7; Semantic Acquisition of Vocabulary, L–8. and Morphology and Syntax, L–9). For these sequences, the same long-range objective, but with differing target content, may be appropriately used in a series of I.E.P. revisions for the same student. Other students may not be expected to be able to move through a complete set of objectives to the terminal objective within a year or a shorter duration of the I.E.P. In this case, the speech–language pathologist would help to determine an intermediate step in the acquisition of desired behavior which could then be written into the student's overall I.E.P.

The *Diagnostic* categories highlighted at the top of each set of objectives are those which are especially critical for children who need that particular area of intervention. Brief notes on the results of formal or informal assessment can be inserted in the slots provided, and in some instances it may be useful also to construct a special baseline test and add its results to the heading in a pre- and post-test style format. Such procedures could be part of the I.E.P. evaluation plan.

The *Short-Term Objectives* themselves are presented in the vertical sequence which generally works best in the acquisition process. Occasionally, however, a horizontal program may be designed with several short-term objectives from the same sequence being addressed during the same session. More often, the horizontal program will be made up of short-term objectives from more than one sequence. For example, a language-impaired child may require help in acquiring a syntactic or morphological structure (L–9), new conceptual vocabulary (L–8 or L–16), and accurate articulation skills (A–6). Direct intervention sessions and support experiences could be constructed with a balance of activities directed toward achieving short-term objectives from each of these sequences.

When placing a child within a particular sequence of objectives, the speech-language pathologist should carefully consider the child's incoming abilities and existing skills in the specific area of inter-

vention and use that information to determine which objective within that sequence should be approached first. The *Date Initiated* (Date In.) can then be entered for the desired objective. Vertically, each time a *Date Accomplished* (Date Accom.) is entered for an objective on the form, the following objective may be initiated. In many instances it is helpful to continue to use activities from objectives which have already been accomplished as a warm-up to activities for training new behaviors, and to begin to introduce upcoming objectives in a probing situation prior to their actual implementation.

Since children with communicative disorders learn at different rates, it is occasionally necessary to break each objective into smaller steps for some students and possible to skip objectives for others. These are decisions the speech-language pathologist and other team members must make on an individual basis. The open columns for description of *Stimulus Content and Context* and for *Comments, Techniques and Evaluation* are also to be used in the process of individualizing a sequence of objectives for a particular student. Since these objectives are designed for the purpose of marking progress toward the acquisition of desired communication skills, rather than as prepackaged programs, it should be possible for the speech-language pathologist to adapt his or her own techniques and other published materials for insertion into the appropriate portions of each plan. For example, if a child is almost totally nonverbal or severely unintelligible, it is of course possible to substitute Bliss Boards, signed language, or other communication enhancement methods and equipment in place of the modality printed in an objective sequence.

Individualization is perhaps the most important consideration in planning for all handicapped children. Using this book as a resource, the speech-language pathologist, the child, and those who know him or her well can tailor a communicative intervention program by first selecting the combination of goal areas which will best suit the child's particular needs and, next, selecting the program content and settings to be the most meaningful and pragmatically useful. It is intended that individual objective sequence formats be copied out of this book as necessary to aid in that process.

Summary

Steps which must be taken in planning and implementing individualized speech and language intervention programs in accordance with P.L. 94–142, and in using these objective sequences, could be summarized as follows:

1. Obtain informed parental consent to evaluate (see Section 121a.504(b,1) of P.L. 94–142 Rules and Regulations).

2. Conduct a full and nondiscriminatory evaluation which can identify:

    a. whether a child is handicapped in that he/she needs a speech–language special education program; and if so,

    b. which areas of communicative disability should be addressed in the speech–language intervention program.

3. Select goal areas (probably three or less), enter appropriate diagnostic information into the headings of corresponding objective sequences, and make preliminary determination of target content and projected number of short–term objectives which can likely be accomplished in each sequence within the one–year (or shorter) time span during which the I.E.P. will be in effect.

4. Obtain written parental consent to place the child in a special program and, together with the parents, child (if appropriate) and other I.E.P. team members, determine actual long–range or intermediate instructional objectives which should be written on the child's coordinated I.E.P., along with the details of the appropriate delivery model.

5. Implement the child's intervention program and enter ongoing results on the recording sheet. Results are recorded as actual sample responses, numerical data, and dates when specific objective criteria are met. Minor programming revisions should also be added to the instructional objectives form. In many cases it will be helpful to select or design supplementary materials, charts, or recording forms to assist in meeting objectives, in determining when objectives have been met, and in providing more immediate feedback to the child, clinician, parents and teachers that the short–term objectives are being met.

6. Conduct and record results of other activities outlined in the evaluation plan of the I.E.P. for measuring progress (e.g., post–testing).

7. At least annually, come together with other I.E.P. meeting participants to review the appropriateness of the instructional plan(s) by using the evaluation plan to determine:

    a. the child's progress;

    b. whether the child needs continued speech and language programming; and if so,

    c. what revisions should be made in the I.E.P.

8. At least every three years, conduct a formal re-evaluation to determine whether the child continues to demonstrate a handicapping condition, as well as to obtain a broader estimate of the degree to which special programming has improved the child's overall abilities.

References and Other Resources

Dublinske, S. P.L. 94-142: Developing the Individualized Education Program (IEP). *Asha, 20,* 380-393, 1978.

Dublinske, S. and W. C. Healey. P. L. 94-142: Questions and Answers for the Speech-Language Pathologist and Audiologist. *Asha, 20,* 188-205, 1978.

Garrard, K. R. The Changing Role of Speech and Hearing Professionals in Public Education. *Asha, 21,* 91-98, 1979.

Nelson, N. W. and E. L. Lockwood. Steps in Implementing P.L. 94-142 with Speech and Language Impaired Children. *Monograph* based upon the short course presented at the annual conference of the American Speech and Hearing Association, Chicago, 1978. Evanston, Ill.: Institute for Continuing Professional Education, in press.

Rules and Regulations for P.L. 94-142. *Federal Register,* Tuesday, August 23, 1977.

INSTRUCTIONAL OBJECTIVES

This section includes the *Index of Goals*, with instructional objective formats numbered sequentially from 1 to 28 under the headings *Preverbal, Early Language, Articulation, Language, Auditory Processing, Voice* and *Fluency*. Each instructional objective chart is identified with a letter code and a number. The letters stand for the goal area heading, and the numbers for the position of the particular format within the entire set. Chapters explain each of the instructional objective sequences and are accompanied by a chart and a list of references and other resources.

Index of Goals

1. **Preverbal:** Oral–Motor Skill Acquisition

   Goal:
   The student will demonstrate sufficient oral–motor, voicing and respiratory skill in reflexive activities to support the development of speech. (See PV–1a through PV–1c.)

   Subobjectives:
   Straw Drinking: The student will be able to drink through a straw correctly and independently.

   Cup Drinking: The student will be able to drink from a cup independently.

   Chewing: The student will be able to bite, chew and swallow hard foods independently.

2. **Preverbal:** Early Functional Communication Acquisition

   Goal:
   The student will show interest in and early development of supralinguistic, intonation, and body language communication. (See PV–2a and PV–2b.)

3. **Early Language:** One–Word Utterance Acquisition

   Goal:
   The student will use one–word utterances to communicate sentence–like meanings (holophrases) to others in the environment. (See EL–3a and EL–3b.)

4. **Early Language:** Two–Word Utterance Acquisition

   Goal:
   The student will use two–word utterances to communicate sentence–like meanings (with semantic–grammatic rules) to others in the environment. (See EL–4a and EL–4b.)

5. **Early Language:** Syntactic Acquisition of the Basic Sentence

   Goal:
   The student will use basic subject–verb–object constructions to communicate a variety of meanings to others in the environment. (See EL–5a through EL–5c.)

6. **Articulation:** Early Phonological Acquisition

   Goal:
   The student will be able to produce sound and word approximations close enough to adult models to be intelligible to others in the environment. (See A–6a and A–6b.)

7. **Articulation:** Phoneme Acquisition

   Goal:
   The student will produce all phonemes correctly (for age and linguistic community). (See A–7a and A–7b.)

8. **Language:** Semantic Acquisition of Vocabulary

   Goal:
   The student will have a sufficient vocabulary store to be able to comprehend and produce most messages appropriate to his/her age and level. (See L–8a through L–8h.)

9. **Language:** Morphological and Syntactic Rule Acquisition

   Goal:
   The student will demonstrate competence for morphological and syntactic rules sufficient for comprehending and generating creative sentences appropriate to his/her age and level. (See L–9Aa through L–9Bb.)

10. **Language:** Early Semantic Acquisition of Yes/ No Question Answering

Goal:

> The student will be able to answer all yes/no questions within his/her semantic–cognitive ability appropriately. (See L–10.)

11. **Language:** Later Semantic Acquisition of Yes/No Question Answering

    Goal:

    > The student will be able to answer all yes/no questions within his/her semantic–cognitive ability appropriately. (See L–11a and L–11b.)

12. **Language:** Semantic Acquisition of WH-Question Answering

    Goal:

    > The student will be able to answer all Wh-questions within his/her semantic–cognitive ability appropriately. (See L–12a and L–12b.)

13. **Language:** Early Pragmatic–Functional Acquisition

    Goal:

    > The student will use developing language skills as the method of choice to communicate immediate needs/awareness/feelings with others in the environment. (See L–13a and L–13b.)

14. **Language:** Intermediate Pragmatic–Functional Acquisition

    Goal:

    > The student will use developing language skills to communicate about events and people not immediately present. (See L–14.)

15. **Language:** Later Pragmatic–Functional Acquisition

    Goal:

    > The student will use effective linguistic communication skills in personal, school and vocational activities of daily living. (See L–15a through L–15c.)

16. **Language:** Semantic Acquisition of Abstract and Categorical Uses

    Goal:

    > The student will be able to use language as a tool for thinking at a level corresponding to his/her cognitive development. (See L–16.)

17. **Auditory Processing:** Discrimination

    Goal:

    > The student will be able to discriminate sufficient intensity, frequency, and duration of sound patterns to enable accurate perception, production and self-monitoring of speech. (See AP–17a and AP–17b.)

Subobjectives:

> Sound/Symbol Association: The student will demonstrate sound–symbol associations at the syllable level.
>
> Phonological Analysis and Synthesis: The student will be able to articulate, read and write multisyllabic words and use them meaningfully in sentences. (See AP–17c through AP–17f.)

18. **Auditory Processing:** Short-Term Sequential Memory

    Goal:

    > The student will demonstrate ability to recall and reproduce, in sequence, speech information of a length appropriate to his/her age and level. (See AP–18a and AP–18b.)

19. **Auditory Processing:** Word Retrieval

    Goal:

    > The student will be able to recall words in his/her vocabulary without abnormal delay during spontaneous communication with others in the environment. (See AP–19a and AP–19b.)

20. **Auditory Processing:** Long-Term Memory

    Goal:

    > The student will be able to recall and communicate events which occurred a week or more in the past. (See AP–20a and AP–20b).

21. **Voice:** Awareness and Modification of Environmental Influences on Vocal Abuse

    Goal:

    > The student and his/her parents and siblings will work together to create an environment which will encourage normal use of voice. (See V–21a and V–21b.)

22. **Voice:** Establishment and Transfer of Increased Laryngeal Hypofunctioning to Replace Vocal Abuse

    Goal:

    > The student will use a clear voice, free from tension and with appropriate pitch and loudness in all settings. (See V–22.)

23. **Voice:** Establishment and Transfer of Increased Laryngeal Hyperfunctioning to Replace Breathy Voice

    Goal:

    > The student will use strong and clear voice production with appropriate pitch and loudness in all settings. (See V–23a and V–23b.)

24. **Voice:** Establishment and Transfer of Velopharyngeal Resonatory Functioning

Goal:
The student will use speech with normal nasal resonance in all settings. (See V–24a and V–24b.)

25. **Fluency:** Modification of Environmental Influences

Goal:
The student, parents and teacher will work together to create an environment which will encourage fluent speech. (See F–25.)

26. **Fluency:** Establishment Using Gradual Increase in Length and Complexity

Goal:
The student will speak in all situations with no more than normal dysfluencies. (See F–26a and F–26b.)

27. **Fluency:** Establishment and Transfer Using Control of Speaking Rate and Breath Flow

Goal:
The student will speak in all situations with no more than normal dysfluencies. (See F–27a and F–27b.)

28. **Fluency:** Establishment Using Traditional Approach

Goal:
The student will speak in all situations with no more than normal dysfluencies. (See F–28a and F–28b.)

29. **Fluency:** Transfer and Maintenance

Goal:
The student will permanently use normally fluent speech. (See F–29a and F–29b.)

PV–1 PREVERBAL:
ORAL—MOTOR SKILL ACQUISITION

This sequence is most likely to be of use with children who are very young or severely physically or mentally impaired. Since these are early occurring behaviors which usually unfold seemingly automatically, the criteria are quantified in terms of observational instances rather than as responses to specific stimuli. Parents and teachers need to be taught which critical elements to prompt and reinforce at each step. Ongoing diagnosis is an important part of identifying which components of the child's motor ability represent (a) normal function, (b) neuromotor dysfunction, or (c) abnormal compensatory function.

The subobjective sequences represent a further breakdown for facilitating the development of feeding behaviors and the preparation of the oral–motor mechanism for speech. This is a somewhat controversial area. Those at the Curative Workshop in Milwaukee (e.g., Morris 1977a, 1977b), where much of the current research in this area has been conducted, emphasize the implementation of a feeding program which centers around mealtime and works to normalize, as much as possible, the global processes of feeding itself — with facilitatory body positioning, bringing food to the mouth, and chewing and cup drinking with jaw stabilization. Straw drinking is generally discouraged because if not handled skillfully, it may lead to immature suckle patterns or abnormal compensatory behaviors, such as excessive lip pursing.

Others (Bosley 1965, 1966; Palmer 1947; Westlake and Rutherford 1961) suggest specialized techniques to supplement the overall feeding program. These may best be implemented separately from mealtimes in the early stages, using food materials chosen more for their physical characteristics, such as crunchiness or chewiness, than for their nutritional value. Such techniques are designed to encourage movements which will be directly applicable to speech production, including specificity of tongue movement, lip closure, and disassociation of abnormal reflexes — such as hyperextension of the mandible — from phonation and chewing. Although both approaches include the same general goals, this second approach is more likely to include such controlled compensatory techniques as straw drinking. For children with lip retraction, for example, the clinician must determine whether the benefits of a straw drinking program to lip closure,

speech sound production and independent drinking outweigh the possibility that additional abnormal muscular behavior (such as lip pursing) will be practiced inadvertently. With this more narrow focus, the clinician must make certain that the child and the parents obtain the occupational or physical therapy needed for total development. In either instance, multidisciplinary teamwork is essential. A good overall resource for parents is Finnie's (1975) *Helping the Young Cerebral Palsied Child at Home*.

The respiratory component of this objective sequence is especially important for cerebral palsied children and others who do not have adequate breath control for speaking. Westlake and Rutherford (1961) emphasize the development of appropriate rate, vital capacity and control for speech breathing by concentrating upon functioning of the muscles of respiration. Postural stabilization and head and neck control are important. Since many athetoid children are belly breathers, it may be desirable to shift the major locus of respiratory expansion from the abdominal region to a balance of upper and lower thoracic activity. Westlake and Rutherford also suggest methods for achieving passive control and enhancing sensory feedback for the purpose of normalizing the locus and degree of muscular activity and the duration of phonation.

References and Other Resources

Bosley, E. Development of sucking and swallowing. *The Cerebral Palsy Journal, 26,* 14-16, 1965.

Bosley, E. Teaching the cerebral palsied to chew. *The Cerebral Palsy Journal, 27,* 8-9, 1966.

Crickmay, M. Principles of speech therapy. In *Speech Therapy and the Bobath Approach to Cerebral Palsy.* Springfield: Charles C. Thomas, 91-117, 1966.

Di Carlo, L. M. Communication therapy for problems associated with cerebral palsy. In Dickson, S. (ed.), *Communication Disorders: Remedial Principles and Practices.* Glenview, Ill: Scott, Foresman and Company, 358-397, 1974.

Finnie, N. *Handling the Young Cerebral Palsied Child at Home.* New York: E. P. Dutton and Co., 1975.

Kline, J. *Children Move to Learn: A Guide to Planning Gross Motor Activities.* Tucson, Ariz.: Communication Skill Builders, 1978.

Morris, S. E. Body language at mealtimes. In Perske, R., *et al. Mealtimes for Severely and Profoundly Handicapped Persons: New Concepts and Attitudes.* Baltimore: University Park Press, 51-56, 1977a.

Morris, S. E. *Program Guidelines for Children with Feeding Problems.* Edison, N.J.: Childcraft Education Corp., 1977b.

Mueller, H. A. Facilitating feeding and prespeech. In Pearson, P. H. and C. E. Williams (eds.), *Physical Therapy Services in the Development Disabilities.* Springfield: Charles C. Thomas, 1972.

Palmer, M. F. Studies in clinicial techniques, II. Normalization of chewing, sucking and swallowing reflexes in cerebral palsy: A home program. *Journal of Speech and Hearing Disroders, 14,* 415-418, 1947.

Westlake, H. and D. Rutherford. *Speech Therapy for the Cerebral Palsied.* 2023 West Ogden Ave., Chicago, Ill. 60612: National Easter Seal Society for Crippled Children and Adults, 1961.

PV-1a

PREVERBAL: ORAL–MOTOR SKILL ACQUISITION

STUDENT: _____ AGE: _____ SCHOOL: _____ GRADE/LEVEL: _____ SPEECH–LANGUAGE CLINICIAN: _____

Date: _____

GOAL: The student will demonstrate sufficient oral–motor, voicing and respiratory skill in vegetative activities to support the development of speech.

DIAGNOSTIC: Motor _____
Cognitive _____
Affective _____

Communicative _____
Oral Structure and Function _____
Audiological Assessment _____
Other _____

LONG–RANGE OBJECTIVE: The child will demonstrate adequate tongue–jaw–lip movements during eating, and sound play and thoracic breathing during quiet and sound play, on three consecutive occasions with clinician, teacher and parent.

SHORT–TERM OBJECTIVES THE STUDENT WILL:	DATE IN.	DESCRIPTION OF MATERIALS AND CONTEXTS	DATE ACCOM.	COMMENTS TECHNIQUES EVALUATION
1. demonstrate normal tactile sensitivity and ability to provide oral stimulation by moving three to five play objects or finger foods placed in hand to mouth for exploration or eating as appropriate (three consecutive sessions).				
2. exhibit adequate coordination of sucking, swallowing and breathing as demonstrated by his ability to sequence three suck–swallows while drinking from a cup or straw without major pauses.*				
3. exhibit adequate tongue, jaw and lip movements during five consecutive feeding and sound play sessions with clinician.*				
4. exhibit adequate tongue, jaw and lip movements in feeding and sound play activities for five consecutive days as reported by parent or teacher.				
5. demonstrate coordinated thoracic and abdominal breathing during quiet activities and appropriately alter breathing rhythm for speech–like activities (i.e., can sustain phonation for 6 to 8 seconds on one breath during vocal play and 8 to 10 seconds during crying).				

*If objectives two or three are very difficult for the child (especially for cerebral palsied children), the following subobjective breakdowns would be appropriate.

This form may be reproduced as often as necessary. / Copyright © 1979 by Communication Skill Builders, Inc.

PV–1b

PREVERBAL: ORAL–MOTOR SKILL ACQUISITION

Date: _____

Student: _____

SUBOBJECTIVE ONE – CUP–DRINKING

SHORT-TERM OBJECTIVES THE STUDENT WILL:	DATE IN.	DESCRIPTION OF MATERIALS AND CONTEXTS	DATE ACCOM.	COMMENTS TECHNIQUES EVALUATION
1a. swallow when small amount of liquid is tilted into mouth by clinician using cup with cut–out upper lip (thickened liquids can be used in initial training stages).				
1b. maintain enough lower lip tonus to prevent dribbling from cup positioned against lip by clinician for one swallow.				
1c. use two coordinated suck–swallow sequences with no dribbling when cup is positioned and verbal prompts are provided by clinician.				

SUBOBJECTIVE TWO – STRAW–DRINKING*

SHORT-TERM OBJECTIVES THE STUDENT WILL:	DATE IN.	DESCRIPTION OF MATERIALS AND CONTEXTS	DATE ACCOM.	COMMENTS TECHNIQUES EVALUATION
2a. form lip seal around short, wide outer and small inner diameter straw (or tubing) and obtain liquid with aid of gravity (straw tilted down toward mouth, or by squeezing liquid up to the lips using a soft plastic bottle).				
2b. form lip seal around normal sized, but short straw (positioned between lips, but *in front* of teeth – *not between*) with horizontal angle.				
2c. form lip seal around normal sized, but short straw tilted up from cup by using actual suction, making sure that the child is using tongue action (*inside* the mouth) and not jaw depression to obtain suction.				
2d. form lip seal and use two coordinated suck–swallow sequences drawing liquid up through normal size and length straw with verbal prompting by clinician.				

*In teaching straw–drinking, it is essential to guard against the tendency of children to revert to a suckle pattern by correct positioning of the straw and stabilization of the mandible. Straw–drinking is particularly useful in establishing independent drinking ability and working for better lip closure. See Morris (1977) for further cautionary notes.

PV-1c

PREVERBAL: ORAL-MOTOR SKILL ACQUISITION

Date: _____

Student: _____

SUBOBJECTIVE THREE — CHEWING

SHORT-TERM OBJECTIVES THE STUDENT WILL:	DATE IN.	DESCRIPTION OF MATERIALS AND CONTEXTS	DATE ACCOM.	COMMENTS TECHNIQUES EVALUATION
3a. keep food placed between molars by clinician/teacher/parent in position for grinding by using lateral tongue action and cheek tonus and will grind food sufficiently before swallowing (four or five successes on each side for three consecutive sessions).				
3b. move food placed between molars on one side to the other side by using lateral tongue action; gravity can be used for prompting the skill by tilting the head, but not to reach criterion (four or five successful transfers for three consecutive sessions).				
3c. move food placed centrally on the tongue tip back under the molars on either side and transfer it to the other side, grinding sufficiently before swallowing (four or five successes for three consecutive sessions).				
3d. bite food with medial incisors, move it back under the molars on either side, and transfer it to the other side, grinding sufficiently before swallowing, with proper jaw alignment (four or five success for three consecutive sessions).				

PV-2 PREVERBAL:
EARLY FUNCTIONAL COMMUNICATION ACQUISITION

The richness of this stage of normal development is just beginning to be tapped by cognitive psychologists and psycholinguists, and the resources being developed for severely physically and/or mentally handicapped children and infant intervention programs are exciting.

It is particularly difficult to write objective criteria in quantifiable terms for this area of intervention. In normal development, early communicative events seem to occur more in response to internal states affected by external stimuli than directly to external stimuli in the relatively predictable stimulus-response time frame frequently used in formal intervention. Therefore, carefully developed powers of observation and sensitivity to even the most obscure communicative attempts of children are especially critical to the success of intervention efforts, and the criteria presented here should be viewed only as guidelines and varied as necessary. The column labeled *Description of Communicative Units and Contexts* will be useful for recording actual observational data which can be judged for their appropriateness in meeting the objective criteria for a particular child.

Since the observational process may extend over a long period for some children, and the desired behavior may occur most spontaneously in the context of daily care activities, it will be helpful for the speech-language pathologist to give a copy of the form to the child's parents and teacher (if the child is placed in a school program) so that they can record examples of desired behavior which occur in those contexts. Explanation, demonstration and further detail regarding the types of desired behavior will make parents and teachers better interactive observers.

For example, in *objective number one,* it could first be noted that the child is aware of sudden *loud* changes in the acoustic environment (via eye blink, change of sucking pattern, etc.) and that he or she attempts to localize the sound (via head turning, eye shifts, etc.). Then, demonstrations in which visual stimuli can occupy the child's attention prior to the presentation of a sudden noise — first close, then farther away; first loud, then softer; first with a familiar squeak toy, then with less familiar sounds — could be used to help others know how to control the stimulus environment and what to look for in responses from the child. The findings of McCall and Kagan (1967) should be of particular use to the clinician.

The later occurring discrimination task *(objective number four)* could be presented by having mother talk softly and continuously to the child, then adding father's voice speaking in a similar fashion and observing the child's response. If the behavior needs to be shaped, or developed to be more immediate and/or consistent, the discriminative stimuli could be presented as more obviously distinct, and any hint of appropriate response should be reinforced with a great deal of social attention using the toy or person which made the noise.

Babbling and other prespeech vocalizations are best encouraged by first imitating the child's spontaneous production of sounds which even remotely resemble the desired response. Van Riper (1978 and previous editions) has long advocated the use of interactive imitation techniques in early intervention. Such techniques may be used by parents, teachers or clinicians in carefully-timed communicative interchanges. For example, steps might include:

1. Child produces repetitive sound; adult imitates and waits; child reproduces sound.

2. Child produces repetitive sound; adult imitates with slight variation, heard previously from the child; child shifts sound production. (This step often involves many smaller steps.)

3. Adult presents sound child has previously vocalized; child imitates.

MacDonald's Environmental Language Intervention materials (especially *Ready, Set, Go: Talk to Me,* Horstmeier and MacDonald 1978), provide information designed to teach parents such techniques. Imitative interchanges should take place with facial closeness and warmth of expression, and the child will be most responsive when his or her physical needs (feeding, changing, etc.) have just been cared for and he or she is feeling comfortable.

Of course, these objectives are met most rapidly for children who are already interested in their environment, and particularly in human faces and voices, but a similar technique has recently been found successful in developing more normal attending skills in some autistic children as well (Tiegerman and Silverman 1977).

References and Other Resources

Bangs, T. E. and S. Garrett. *Birth-3 Scale: Handbook for Observing and Scoring Behaviors.* University of Houston, prepublication copy, undated.

Bayley, N. *Bayley Scales of Infant Development.* New York: The Psychological Corporation, 1969.

Bricker, W. A. and D. D. Bricker. An early language training strategy. In Schiefelbusch, R. and L. Lloyd (eds.), *Language Perspectives – Acquisition, Retardation and Intervention.* Baltimore: University Park Press, 429-468, 1974.

Bzoch, K. and R. League. *The Receptive Expressive Emergent Language Scale (REEL).* Gainesville, Fla.: Language Education Division, Computer Management Corporation, 1971.

DiLeo, J. *Exceptional Infant, I. The Normal Infant.* New York: Brunner/Mazel Publishers, 121-142, 1967.

Gesell, A. *The First Five Years of Life.* New York: Harper and Brothers, 1940.

Hanson, M. J. *Teaching Your Down's Syndrome Infant: A Guide for Parents.* Eugene: University of Oregon, 1977.

Horton, K. B. Infant intervention and language learning. In Schiefelbusch, R. and L. Lloyd (eds.), *Language Perspectives – Acquisition, Retardation and Intervention.* Baltimore: University Park Press, 469-492, 1974.

Horstmeier, D. S. and J. D. MacDonald. *Ready, Set, Go: Talk to Me.* Part of the Environmental Language Intervention Program Kit. Columbus, Ohio: Charles E. Merrill Publishing Company, 1978.

MacDonald, J. D. and D. S. Horstmeier. *The Environmental Language Intervention (ELI) Program Kit.* Columbus: Charles E. Merrill Publishing Company, 1978.

McCall, R. and J. Kagan. Attention in the infant: Effects of complexity, contour, perimeter and familiarity. *Child Development, 38,* 939-952, 1967.

Menyuk, P. *The Development of Speech.* Indianapolis: The Bobbs-Merrill Company, Inc., 1972.

Reichle, J. E., D. E. Yoder and M. Kruel-Starr. Communication behaviors in severely and profoundly developmentally delayed children: Assessment and intervention. Short course presented at the annual meeting of the American Speech and Hearing Association, Chicago, 1977.

Seitz, S. Language intervention – changing the language environment of the retarded child. Paper presented at the Annual Convention of the American Speech and Hearing Association, Detroit, 1973.

Striefel, S. *Behavior Modification: Teaching a Child to Imitate.* No. 7 in the Managing Behavior Series. Lawrence, Kansas: H & H Enterprises, Inc., 1974.

Tiegerman, E. and R. C. Silverman. Mirror-image interaction: The development of attending behaviors in nonverbal nonimitative autistic children. Paper presented at the Annual Conference of the American Speech and Hearing Association, Authors at Queens College Speech and Hearing Center, Flushing, New York, 1977.

Uzgiris, I. C. and J. Mc. V. Hunt. *Assessment in Infancy.* Urbana, Illinois: University of Illinois Press, 1975.

Van Riper, C. *Speech Correction: Principles and Methods* (sixth and previous editions), Englewood Cliffs, New Jersey: Prentice Hall, Inc., 1978.

PV-2a

PREVERBAL: EARLY FUNCTIONAL COMMUNICATION ACQUISITION

Date: _____

STUDENT: _____ AGE: _____ SCHOOL: _____ GRADE/LEVEL: _____ SPEECH–LANGUAGE CLINICIAN: _____

GOAL: The student will show interest in and early development of supralinguistic, intonation and body language communication.

DIAGNOSTIC: Motor _____
Cognitive _____
Affective _____

Communicative _____
Audiological Assessment _____
Other _____

LONG–RANGE OBJECTIVE: The student will use one or more gestures, signs or vocalizations meaningfully in 80 percent or more of expected contexts.

SHORT–TERM OBJECTIVES THE STUDENT WILL:	DATE IN.	DESCRIPTION OF COMMUNICATIVE UNITS AND CONTEXTS	DATE ACCOM.	COMMENTS TECHNIQUES EVALUATION
1. demonstrate sound awareness (via eye blink, changes in sucking pattern, etc.) and attempt to localize the sound (via head turning, eye shifts, etc.) as observed on five occasions.				
2. demonstrate ability to use at least five differentiated sounds (usually more vowels than consonants) during a five–minute play session.				
3. initiate pitch and loudness variations during sound play (as observed by clinician over two sessions).				
4. orient differently or momentarily cease activity as evidence of discrimination of male/female, friendly/angry, familiar/unfamiliar or intonation patterns (occurs between two and six months).*				
5. initiate variation in pitch, loudness, and rhythm patterns in three consecutive one–to–one vocal interplay sessions with clinician and parent (separately).				
6. produce similar repeated syllable utterances over three consecutive one–to–one vocal interplay sessions (e.g., ba ba ba; ma ma ma; ga ga ga).				
7. produce three or more different speech–like utterances with intonation over three consecutive one–to–one vocal interplay sessions (e.g., be ba ma bo).				

*See Manyuk (1972) for discussion of speech production and perception during the first year of life.

This form may be reproduced as often as necessary. / Copyright © 1979 by Communication Skill Builders, Inc.

PV–2b

PREVERBAL: EARLY FUNCTIONAL COMMUNICATION ACQUISITION

Date: _____

Student: _____

SHORT-TERM OBJECTIVES THE STUDENT WILL:	DATE IN.	DESCRIPTION OF COMMUNICATIVE UNITS AND CONTEXTS	DATE ACCOM.	COMMENTS TECHNIQUES EVALUATION
8. spontaneously vocalize to express recognition or desire to continue an activity with parent, teacher or clinician on five separate occasions.				
9. initiate attempts to get attention of parent, teacher or clinician on five separate occasions by making random speech sounds with declarative, exclamatory or questioning (rather than crying or whining) intonation.				
10. intelligibly imitate most sounds, gestures or motor activities during a two-minute one-to-one interplay situation over three consecutive sessions.				
11. LONG-RANGE: use one or more gestures, signs, or vocalizations meaningfully in 80 percent or more of expected contexts.				

EL–3 EARLY LANGUAGE: ONE-WORD UTTERANCES

Efforts to teach communicatively–impaired children first words have traditionally involved presentation of common objects and attempts to develop comprehension before production — usually with some type of object selection task. *Objectives one* and *two* of this sequence can be used for such a purpose, with the added element of gestural expression. This addition will help adults in the child's environment become aware of and encourage communicative content which is intrinsically motivating to the child.

Objective number six is presented in recognition of the fact that early words in normal development are much more than just words. They generally communicate a sentence–like meaning (holophrase) for the child. Objective six lists the most common functions of first words and the first lexicon content and form suggested by Lahey and Bloom (1977). All normal children, and most communicatively-impaired children, do a great deal of meaningful nonverbal communicating prior to speaking their first words. If adults are tuned in to the contexts, forms, and functions of such expression (such as pushing away an unwanted bowl of food), they can supply the appropriate one– or two–word phrase whenever the opportunity presents itself (e.g, *No more?* Scott wants *no more*. Scott tells me "no," but Mommy says one more bite — good. Okay, *No more, no more.*) Holland (1975) and MacDonald and Horstmeier (1978) present additional suggestions for taking advantage of natural communication opportunities.

Some children who are severely communicatively impaired, particularly mentally retarded and autistic children, need to be taught first words in a manner which relies more heavily upon behavior modification principles, and perhaps using nonverbal signs. For such children, this sequence can still be used to outline short–term objectives, and a more detailed language program, such as that presented by Bricker (1972), Kent (1974), Miller and Yoder (1974) or Guess, Sailor and Baer (1976) may be implemented.

References and Other Resources

Bloom, L. *Language Development: Form and Function in Emerging Grammars.* Research Monograph No. 59. Cambridge, Mass.: The M.I.T. Press, 1970.

Bricker, W. A. A systematic approach to language training. In Schiefelbusch, R. L. (ed.), *Language of the Mentally Retarded.* Baltimore: University Park Press, 95-92, 1972.

Guess, D., W. Sailor and D. M. Baer. *Functional Speech and Language Training for the Severely Handicapped, Part I: Persons and Things, Part II: Actions with Persons and Things.* Lawrence, Kansas: H & H Enterprises, 1976.

Guess, D., W. Sailor and D. M. Baer. Children with limited language. In Schiefelbusch, R. L. (ed.), *Language Intervention Strategies.* Baltimore: University Park Press, 101-144, 1978.

Hebald, B. and V. McCready. *A Book About Talking: Principles of Language Stimulation for Parents, Teachers, Clinicians.* 147 N. Dellrose, Wichita, Kansas 67208: Rhino Press, 1976.

Holland, A. Language therapy for children: Some thoughts on context and content. *Journal of Speech and Hearing Disorders, 40,* 514-523, 1975.

Kent, L. *Language Acquisition Program for the Retarded or Multiply Impaired.* Champaign, Illinois: Research Press, 1974.

Lahey, M. and L. Bloom. Planning a first Lexicon: Which words to teach first. *Journal of Speech and Hearing Disorders, 42,* 340-350, 1977.

MacDonald, J. D. and D. S. Horstmeier. *The Environmental Language Intervention (ELI) Program Kit.* Columbus: Charles E. Merrill Publishing Company, Inc., 1978.

Miller, J. and D. Yoder. An ontogenetic language teaching strategy for retarded children. In Schiefelbusch, R. L. and L. Lloyd (eds.), *Language Perspectives — Acquisition, Retardation and Intervention.* Baltimore: University Park Press, 1974.

EARLY LANGUAGE: ONE-WORD UTTERANCES

STUDENT: _____ AGE: _____ SCHOOL: _____ GRADE/LEVEL: _____ SPEECH–LANGUAGE CLINICIAN: _____ Date: _____

GOAL: The student will use one–word utterances to communicate sentence–like meanings (holophrases) to others in the environment.

DIAGNOSTIC: Motor _____
Cognitive _____   Communicative _____
Affective _____   Audiological Assessment _____
Other _____

LONG–RANGE OBJECTIVE: The student will spontaneously verbalize five different one–word phrases to communicate with others in the environment over a period of one week.

SHORT–TERM OBJECTIVES THE STUDENT WILL:	DATE IN.	EXAMPLE STRUCTURES AND CONTEXTS	DATE ACCOM.	COMMENTS TECHNIQUES EVALUATION
1. ask for or identify objects/people/animals in a structured situation by using gestures (four of five correct for three consecutive sessions).				
2. ask for or identify objects/people/animals in a spontaneous situation by using gestures in five different spontaneous situations over a period of one week (as observed and counted by parent/teacher/clinician).				
3. produce word approximations prompted by the clinician to correspond with at least five different objects and/or activities in an imitative situation (four of five correct for three consecutive sessions).				
4. produce word approximations to correspond with at least five different objects and/or activities in response to requests by clinician/teacher/parent with prompting (four of five correct for three consecutive sessions).				
5. initiate one true word to communicate with clinician/teacher/parent in un–trained context with no prompting.				

*6. initiate a one–word phrase expressing the following functions in a structured communication setting (at least two occurrences of six of the ten functions).
  a. rejection – (no)
  b. nonexistence or disappearance – (no, all gone, away)
  c. cessation of action – (stop, no)				

*Lahey and Bloom (1977) have suggested first lexicon content and form (in parentheses) to correspond with types found in normal development.

EL-3b

EARLY LANGUAGE: ONE-WORD UTTERANCES

Date: _____

Student: _____

SHORT-TERM OBJECTIVE THE STUDENT WILL:	DATE IN.	EXAMPLE STRUCTURES AND CONTEXTS	DATE ACCOM.	COMMENTS TECHNIQUES EVALUATION
6. Continued d. prohibition of action – (no) e. recurrence of objects and actions on objects – (more, again, another) f. noting the existence of or identifying objects, people or animals – (this, that, there, Mama, Daddy, doggie, baby, sock, etc.) g. actions on objects – (give, do, make, get, throw, eat, wash, kiss) h. actions involved in locating objects or self – (put, up, down, sit, fall, go) i. attributes or descriptions of objects – (big, hot, dirty, heavy) j. persons associated with objects (as in possession) – (person names)				
7. LONG-RANGE: The student will spontaneously verbalize five different one-word phrases to communicate with others in the environment over a period of one week.				

EL-4 EARLY LANGUAGE:
TWO-WORD UTTERANCES

Following the acquisition of single words — a process which seems to be largely regulated by functional meaning in normal children — two-word combinations begin to appear. Although the initial relationship of the words is best described as topic-comment, semantic-grammatic combinations soon emerge, representing some of the first uses of structural rules to generate utterances (Bloom 1970; Morehead and Ingram 1973).

The rules which are outlined in Part A of this sequence are represented universally and fairly predictably in the normal language acquisition process. They are not presented here in an order of development. The semantic-grammatic rules which appear to be most functional for a particular child are those which should be selected first for direct attention. Any of the others should be kept in mind and shaped and reinforced as the opportunity arises. The content phrases (in parentheses) are examples of possible utterances, and content for each child should be determined individually.

The four intervention formats, *Comprehension, Direct Request, Structured Conversation,* and *Structured Play,* are included in Part A. Although comprehension is traditionally thought to precede production in normal development, and is generally taught first in language intervention programs, it is not always possible to directly measure comprehension of phrases which have been chosen for their functional value to the child. Measurement of comprehension is also confounded by pragmatic and cognitive constraints at this level, and in many language-impaired children, production intervention in meaningful contexts provides the necessary vehicle for the development of comprehension rather than vice versa.

Likewise, language intervention programs generally start with highly structured training sessions and move to reinforcement of similar language content after some consistency of production has been established in the structured setting. The four intervention formats of this sequence can be implemented in the traditional vertical fashion by completing a comprehension phase prior to initiating imitation and production practice and activities in settings with increasingly less structure. However, the four formats are presented horizontally on this recording form because an effective method for encouraging development in this early stage of language acquisition is to implement activities of all four types concurrently. This is the approach found to be so successful by MacDonald and Blott (1974) and MacDonald and Horstmeier (1978) in which parents are enlisted as active language trainers. Fokes (1977) has also described the uses of "therapeutic conversational turns" by teachers for natural language training.

When the objectives are implemented in the four formats concurrently, the same day might include a number of both formal and informal language intervention exchanges. Parents and teachers may be made aware of informal natural opportunities to develop language comprehension and production using these steps:

1. Present a question which includes the type of utterance being encouraged; e.g., "Where's Mommy's purse?" (when mother's and grandmother's purses are both in evidence); "Want to go bye-bye?"; "Where's the kitty?" (kitty on bed); "Show Mommy the *big* truck" (when both a big and little truck are present); etc.

2. If necessary, prompt an appropriate nonverbal response to the question which would demonstrate comprehension.

3. While prompting the nonverbal response to the question (e.g., while putting the child through the activity of finding Mommy's purse), or while the child performs the nonverbal response spontaneously, present the two-word utterance which accompanies the activity. If the response occurs spontaneously, record the results in the *Comprehension* column.

4. Hesitate for a moment to give the child an opportunity to imitate. If a production does occur, record the results in the *Structured Play* column.

5. Reinforce any attempts at production socially and with an additional production of the utterance.

6. Expand the verbal and nonverbal aspects of the interchange by producing additional short, but adult, complete sentences about the topic, making the activity interesting to the child (e.g., "Mommy's purse; You found Mommy's purse; Let's see what's in it . . .").

A more structured formal session — about 15 minutes in length — may be included during the same day, using the same, or similar, content. Sessions of this type should be kept interesting and fun; however, children with communicative impairments often require more intense procedures with many repetitions to acquire new forms and tangible reinforcers (such as pieces of pretzel, etc.) may help to maintain the child's active participation. Steps for these more formal sessions might include:

1. Present a comprehension task similar to that described above, but using assembled materials so that the child may remain seated, perhaps on the table in front of the adult, or on a chair high enough so that the faces of the adult and the child are level. In this way, the adult may gently remind the child that this short session is a time to stay put.

2. Present a direct question designed to elicit one of the types of two-word responses listed. If the child responds verbally as well as nonverbally, record the results in the *Structured Conversation* column.

3. If the child does not produce a spontaneous verbal (or signed) response, make a direct request for imitation (e.g., "Bobby say 'Kitty box.'" The speech–language pathologist should assist parents and teachers in selecting utterances which can be produced, and in knowing how much accuracy to require for reinforcement at each step. If the child responds with a successful imitation, record the results in the *Direct Request* column. If not, additional shaping procedures should be implemented by the speech–language pathologist.

4. If the child produces the desired imitation, follow with social and tangible reinforcement, and a re-presentation of the original comprehension question, hoping for a second, delayed-imitation response.

5. Production of the desired utterance in the delayed-imitation format is an intermediate part of developing *Structured Conversation* answers to questions. If the child is successful in answering the repeated question immediately following an imitative interchange, the chances of success are much greater in the *Structured Conversa-*tion and *Structured Play* formats later during the same and subsequent sessions.

6. To be considered successful in the *Structured Conversation* format, the child must answer a direct question correctly without prompting.

7. The *Structured Play* format, described previously, should be used all along and to double-check a child's creative use of semantic–grammatic rules before leaving this level of language intervention.

References and Other Resources

Bloom, L. *Language Development: Form and Function in Emerging Grammars.* Research Monograph No. 59. Cambridge, Mass.: The M.I.T. Press, 1970.

Bloom, L. and M. Lahey. *Language Development and Language Disorders.* New York: John Wiley & Sons, 1978.

Fokes, J. Language (Therapy) in Context. Unpublished paper, Athens, Ohio: Ohio University, 1977.

Hatten, J. and P. Hatten. *Natural Language.* Tucson, Ariz.: Communication Skill Builders, 1975.

Holland, A. Language therapy for children: Some thoughts on context and content. *Journal of Speech and Hearing Disorders, 40,* 514-523, 1975.

Lahey, M. and L. Bloom. Planning a first lexicon: Which words to teach first. *Journal of Speech and Hearing Disorders, 42,* 340-350, 1977.

Lee, L. L. *Developmental Sentence Analysis.* Evanston, Ill.: The Northwestern University Press, 1974.

MacDonald, J. D. and D. S. Horstmeier. *The Environmental Language Intervention (ELI) Program Kit.* Columbus: Charles E. Merrill Publishing Company, Inc., 1978.

MacDonald, J. D. and J. P. Blott. Environmental language intervention: The rationale for a diagnostic and training strategy through rules, context, and generalization. *Journal of Speech and Hearing Disorders, 39,* 244-257, 1974.

Morehead, D. and D. Ingram. The development of base syntax in normal and linguistically deviant children. *Journal of Speech and Hearing Research, 16,* 330-352, 1974.

Tyack, D. and R. Gottsleben. *Language Sampling, Analysis and Training: A Handbook for Teachers and Clinicians.* Palo Alto, Calif.: Consulting Psychological Press, 1974.

Wilmot, K. B., S. B. Bober and B. L. Askew. *Structured Environmental Activities for the Rehabilitation of the Communicatively Handicapped* (SEARCH). Austin, Tex.: Learning Concepts.

EARLY LANGUAGE: TWO-WORD UTTERANCES*

STUDENT: _____ AGE: _____ SCHOOL: _____ GRADE/LEVEL: _____ SPEECH-LANGUAGE CLINICIAN: _____

Date: _____

GOAL: The student will use two-word utterances to communicate sentence-like meanings (with semantic-grammatic rules*) to others in the environment.

DIAGNOSTIC:

Motor _____
 Cognitive _____
 Affective _____
 Speech _____
 Communicative _____
 Early Structures Showing Restriction _____
 Structures Showing Consistent Control _____
 Late Structures Showing Partial Control _____
 Semantics _____

Audiological _____
Other _____
Formal Assessment _____
Spontaneous Sample _____
MLU _____

LONG-RANGE OBJECTIVE: The student will spontaneously use two-word utterances to communicate 10 of the 12 semantic-grammatic rules listed below in unstructured play with parents/teachers/peers with and without the clinician (two separate occasions).

SHORT-TERM OBJECTIVE THE STUDENT WILL:	COMPREHENSION		DIRECT REQUEST (Stim.-Response)		STRUCTURED CONVERSATION		STRUCTURED PLAY		COMMENTS TECHNIQUES EVALUATION
	Date Accom.	How Demo.	Date In.	Date Accom.	Date In.	Date Accom.	Date In.	Date Accom.	
1. use more than one example of 10 of the 12 semantic-grammatic rules listed below with the clinician on three separate occasions with minimal or no prompting in each of the four formats: comprehension/direct request (including imitation)/structured conversation/structured play.									
a. Nomination (that book)									
b. Notice (Hi doggie)									
c. Demands (go bye-bye)									
d. Recurrence (more milk)									
e. Nonexistence (all gone juice)									
f. Attribute (big potty)									
g. Possession (mommy purse)									

This form may be reproduced as often as necessary. / Copyright ©1979 by Communication Skill Builders, Inc.

EL-4b

Date: _____

Student: _____

EARLY LANGUAGE: TWO-WORD UTTERANCES*

SHORT-TERM OBJECTIVE THE STUDENT WILL:	COMPREHENSION		DIRECT REQUEST (Stim.–Response)		STRUCTURED CONVERSATION		STRUCTURED PLAY		COMMENTS TECHNIQUES EVALUATION
	Date Accom.	How Demo.	Date In.	Date Accom.	Date In.	Date Accom.	Date In.	Date Accom.	
1. Continued									
h. Location (mommy hospital)									
i. Agent and action (Eve read)									
j. Action and object (put book)									
k. Agent and object (mommy sock)									
l. Conjunction (umbrella boot)									
2. use more than one example of 8 of the 12 semantic–grammatic rules listed above in unstructured play (two separate occasions):	UTTERANCES OBSERVED TO DEMONSTRATE USE OF SEMANTIC–GRAMMATIC RULES							Date In.	Date Accom.
a. with the clinician both inside and outside the speech room.									
b. with parents/teachers/peers outside the speech room with and without the clinician.									

*The arrangement of objectives in this sequence is based upon work by MacDonald and Blott (1974). Prior to implementation, spontaneous language can be analyzed with the Developmental Sentence Types procedure described by Lee (1974) or the technique described by Tyack and Gottsleben (1974). Although comprehension is listed first among the types of formats designed to elicit examples of rule acquisition, comprehension should not be required as a prerequisite to implementation of production formats, and any or all of the production formats may be in process concurrently. Direct measurement of comprehension is strongly confounded by pragmatic and cognitive constraints at this level, and in many clinical children, production intervention in meaningful contexts provides the necessary vehicle for the development of comprehension rather than vice versa.

EL–5 EARLY LANGUAGE:
SYNTACTIC ACQUISITION OF THE BASIC SENTENCE

As a normal child acquires language skills, the controlling emphasis — which appears to be almost exclusively semantic and pragmatic in the early stages — gradually shifts through the combined use of semantic–grammatic rules to generate utterances, and later leads to a stage in which structural rules appear to become more important as the child needs them to code increasingly complex ideas into communicative units.

This normal evolution of the two–word stage into elaborated components — which later become the Noun Phrase and Verb Phrase branches of basic sentence structure — can also serve as an intervention model for speech– and language–impaired students. Semantic features and cases, or the functional roles of words in sentences, still play an important part in determining what kinds of combinations children produce (and continue to do so through adulthood), but the basic elements of syntactic structure are beginning to emerge.

One of the most striking features of language-impaired students at this, and later stages, is the sensitive interaction of length and complexity. Something which Lee (1974) terms "grammatical overload" seems to make it difficult for clinical children to produce sentences which are both lengthy and grammatically complex. As length increases, the application of syntactic rules becomes more and more restricted. Similarly, Leonard (1975) has found that reduction of either length or developmental level of utterances presented as intervention models seems to assist in the acquisition process — with a slight advantage for developmentally less complex models.

This sequence of instructional objectives is designed to capitalize on the normal developmental process as it was applied to speech– and language-impaired children by Morehead and Ingram (1973) and Tyack and Gottsleben (1974). Each of the basic sentence components is alternatively focused upon until both Noun Phrase and Verb Phrase elements are developed at an increasingly higher level and can be combined.

A variety of clinical techniques are available to be used in developing a greater richness of sentence structure rules for creative use by language disordered students. The ASHA Monograph (Number 18) edited by McReynolds (1974) offers some suggestions, and the Waryas and Stremel–Campbell approach, which appears both in the McReynold's monograph and Schiefelbusch's (1978) *Language Intervention Strategies,* is particularly applicable. Numerous other commercially available materials are also appropriate, including Hatten, Goman and Lent's *Emerging Language 2* (1976), *Syntax One,* the *Fokes Sentence Builder, Developmental Language Lessons,* and *Language Structure Simplified,* but real experiences (see, for example, Weigel and Morningstar 1978) and situation pictures from magazines often provide some of the best stimulus material. Lee, Koenigsknecht and Mulhern's (1975) *Interactive Language Development Teaching* technique has been found to be effective with several types of children.

Again, the recording format for this sequence of objectives is designed to encourage an experience-based approach to language intervention. Emphasis upon the value of creativity, or spontaneity and variety, over adult accuracy in the objective criteria, highlights the clinical question of whether adults should present models to children which are incomplete or inaccurate according to adult standards. Although Leonard (1975) does present some evidence in favor of following normal developmental stages in the modeling process, the evidence is limited and far from conclusive. There is a great deal of room for individualization of teaching and learning styles in this area. One possible solution to the problem is to produce a number of models in each communicative interchange so that the child will hear both adult– and child–like possibilities associated with the event. It is also possible to produce complete adult (though short) utterances as models, but reinforce developmental responses as long as they include the critical elements.

As in the previous sequence, comprehension is an important, but difficult to measure, part of the developmental process. Basic cognitive awarenes of semantic role possibilities appears to be a critical prerequisite for entry into this stage of linguistic development (see, for example, Bloom and Lahey 1978). The introduction of a limited set of possible combinations illustrated with concrete objects and/ or real people, with systematic substitutions of one element while holding the others constant, will help develop such semantic concepts as agent, action and object of action. Wetherby and Striefel (1978) have even demonstrated how a "matrix approach" can be used successfully with severely and profoundly impaired students to help develop similar semantic role concepts, although those authors' strictly behavioristic orientations lead them to a different interpretation of their results.

References and Other Resources

Ausberger, C. *Syntax One: Syntactic Skills Development.* Tucson, Ariz.: Communication Skill Builders, Inc. 1976.

Bangs, T. E. *Language and Learning Disorders of the Pre-Academic Child: With Curriculum Guide.* Englewood Cliffs, N.J.: Prentice-Hall, Inc., 1968.

Bloom, L. and M. Lahey. *Language Development and Language Disorders.* New York: John Wiley & Sons, 1978.

Fokes, J. *Fokes Sentence Builder.* Boston, Mass.: Teaching Resources.

Hatten, J., T. Goman, and C. Lent. *Emerging Language 2.* Tucson, Ariz.: Communication Skill Builders, Inc., 1976.

Hebald, B. and V. McCready. *A Book About Talking: Principles of Language Stimulation for Parents, Teachers, Clinicians.* 147 N. Dellrose, Wichita, Kansas 67208: Rhino Press, 1976.

Karnes, M. B. *Learning Language at Home.* Arlington, Va.: The Council for Exceptional Children, 1977.

Lee, L. L. *Developmental Sentence Analysis.* Evanston, Ill.: The Northwestern University Press, 1974.

Lee, L. L., R. A. Koenigsknecht, and S. T. Mulhern. *Interactive Language Development Teaching.* Evanston, Ill.: The Northwestern University Press, 1975.

Leonard, L. B. Modeling as a clinical procedure in language training. *Language, Speech, and Hearing Services in Schools, VI,* 72-85, 1975.

McReynolds, L. V. (ed.). Developing systematic procedures for training children's language. *ASHA Monograph Number 18.* Washington, D.C.: American Speech and Hearing Association, 1974.

Millstein, B. *Language Structure Simplified.* Freeport, NY: Educational Activities, Inc., 1978.

Morehead, D. and D. Ingram. The development of base syntax in normal and language deviant children. *Journal of Speech and Hearing Research, 16,* 330-352, 1973.

Mowery, C. W. and A. Replogle. *Developmental Language Lessons.* Boston, Mass.: Teaching Resources.

Muma, J. R. *Language Handbook: Concepts, Assessment, Intervention.* Englewood Cliffs, N.J.: Prentice-Hall, Inc., 1978.

Murdock, J. Y. and B. Hartmann. *Imitative Gestures to Basic Syntactic Structures.* Salt Lake City, Utah: Word Making Productions.

Schiefelbusch, R. L. (ed.). *Language Intervention Strategies.* Baltimore: University Park Press, 1978.

Stremel, K. and C. Waryas. A behavioral-psycholinguistic approach to language training. In McReynolds, L. V. (ed.,), Developing systematic procedures for training children's language. *ASHA Monograph Number 18.* Washington, D.C.: American Speech and Hearing Association, 96-130, 1974.

Tyack, D. and R. Gottsleben. *Language Sampling, Analysis and Training: A Handbook for Teachers and Clinicians.* Palo Alto, Calif.: Consulting Psychological Press, 1974.

Waryas, C. L. and K. Stremel-Campbell. Grammatical training for the language-delayed child: A new perspective. In Schiefelbusch, R. L. (ed.), *Language Intervention Strategies.* Baltimore: University Park Press, 145-192, 1978.

Weigel, R. S. and J. S. Morningstar. *Learning Language Through Experience: A Manual for Therapists, Teachers and Parents.* 36 Annie Lou, Hamilton, Ohio 45013, 1978.

Wetherby, B. and S. Striefel. Application of miniature linguistic system or matrix-training procedures. In Schiefelbusch, R. L. (ed.), *Language Intervention Strategies.* Baltimore: University Park Press, 317-356, 1978.

EL-5a

EARLY LANGUAGE: SYNTACTIC ACQUISITION OF THE BASIC SENTENCE

Date: _____

STUDENT: _____ AGE: _____ SCHOOL: _____ GRADE/LEVEL: _____ SPEECH–LANGUAGE CLINICIAN: _____

GOAL: The student will use basic subject–verb–object constructions to communicate a variety of meanings to others in the environment.

DIAGNOSTIC: Motor _____
- Cognitive _____
- Affective _____
- Speech _____
- Communicative _____
- Early Structures Showing Restriction _____
- Structures Showing Consistent Control _____
- Late Structures Showing Partial Control _____
- Semantics _____

Audiological _____
Other _____
Formal Assessment _____
Spontaneous Sample _____
MLU _____

LONG–RANGE OBJECTIVE: The student will spontaneously use at least five creative, three–word (or more) utterances of the type NP + VP (+NP) in unstructured play with parents/teachers/peers with and without the clinician (three separate occasions).

SHORT–TERM OBJECTIVES THE STUDENT WILL:	DIRECT REQUEST (Stim.–Response)		STRUCTURED CONVERSATION		STRUCTURED PLAY		COMMENTS TECHNIQUES EVALUATION
	Date In.	Date Accom.	Date In.	Date Accom.	Date In.	Date Accom.	
*1. demonstrate comprehension of the semantic functions, agent, action, object/location in subject + verb + (object/prepositional phrase) type constructions spoken by the clinician by pointing to objects/pictures or performing an action (four of five trials correct on each for two consecutive sessions).							
2. use at least two different noun phrases (NPs) illustrating three of the four early developing types listed below with the clinician on two separate occasions with minimal prompting:							
a. Dem. + N (That car.)							
b. Quantity + N (Some apple.)							
c. Possession + N (John wagon.)							
d. Adjective + N (Red house).							

*See note on page 41.

This form may be reproduced as often as necessary. / Copyright © 1979 by Communication Skill Builders, Inc.

37

EARLY LANGUAGE: SYNTACTIC ACQUISITION OF THE BASIC SENTENCE

Date: _____
Student: _____

SHORT-TERM OBJECTIVES THE STUDENT WILL:	DIRECT REQUEST (Stim.-Response)		STRUCTURED CONVERSATION		STRUCTURED PLAY		COMMENTS TECHNIQUES EVALUATION
	Date In.	Date Accom.	Date In.	Date Accom.	Date In.	Date Accom.	
3. use at least two different verb phrases (VPs) illustrating each of the two early developing types listed below with the clinician on two separate occasions with minimal prompting:							
a. V + N (Play ball.)							
b. V + N (Go in house.)							
4. use at least two different NP + VP (+NP) structures illustrating each of the early developing types listed below with the clinician on two separate occasions with minimal prompting:							
a. N + V (Them sleeping. Baby lay down.)							
b. N + omitted copula + N/Adj. (That big. Him there. What that?)							
5. use at least two different later occurring VP + NP structures illustrating two of the three types listed below with the clinician on two separate occasions with minimal prompting:							
a. V + modifier + N (Throw that ball. Want some milk?)							
b. V + N + N (Give it to me. Throw ball in big box.)							
c. Modal + V + N (Hafta go home. Gonna go in the house.)							
6. use at least two different later occurring NP + VP + (NP) structures illustrating three of the four types listed below with the clinician on two separate occasions with minimal prompting:							
a. N + V + N (Them eat cake. That boy go in here.)							
b. N + V + N + N (I give dog a bone. He sleep in bed upstairs.)							
c. N + modal + V (I wanna come. I can't go.)							
d. N + modal + V + N (I hafta go home.)							

EL-5c

EARLY LANGUAGE: SYNTACTIC ACQUISITION OF THE BASIC SENTENCE

Date: _____

Student: _____

USE IN UNSTRUCTURED SITUATIONS THE STUDENT WILL:	Date In.	SENTENCES OBSERVED TO DEMONSTRATE USE OF NP + VP + (NP) SYN. RULES	Date Accom.	COMMENTS TECHNIQUES EVALUATION
7. use basic sentences of the type NP + VP + (NP) in all required contexts in unstructured communication situations with the clinician (three separate occasions with at least five spontaneous creative sentences).				
8. use basic sentences of the type NP + VP + (NP) in all required contexts in unstructured communications with teacher/parents/peers with and without the clinician (three separate occasions with at least five spontaneous creative sentences).				

*The measurement of comprehension of basic sentence structure depends, first, on informal observation of the child's cognitive awareness of semantic role possibilities for people/objects/places/actions, etc. and next on quasi-formal assessment of comprehension of sentences composed of vocabulary the child has been observed to use in a variety of semantic role combinations within the basic syntactic structure. The ordering of development as presented here is based upon that presented by Morehead and Ingram (1973) and used in the analysis procedures suggested by Tyack and Gottlesben (1974).

A–6 ARTICULATION:
EARLY PHONOLOGICAL RULE ACQUISITION

Many young language–delayed children exhibit multiple restrictions of psycholinguistic ability. Not only do they have limited words to express ideas but, in many cases, articulatory ability is equally limited, and utterances are so unintelligible that they frequently go unreinforced. This leads to the clinical dilemma of whether to emphasize the acquisition of new whole words or clearer production of component speech sounds in preexisting words. Acquisition of new words carries the clear advantage of greater communicative power, and many children can model whole words readily enough without direct attention to sound production. However, other children seem to be unable to shape their phonological productions into intelligible approximations without direct help.

Recent advances in understanding the expansion of distinctive feature categories in normal development (see, e.g., Menyuk 1972) have been applied to articulation intervention with speech– and language–impaired children (Costello 1975; McReynolds and Engmann 1975; Weiner and Bankson 1978). Such approaches usually involve selection of stimulus content for training which illustrates a phonological feature distinction not previously apparent in the child's speech.

Another approach found particularly useful with young children is to select training content entirely on the basis of word meaning, paying little or no attention to phoneme content. The "semantically potent word" approach, as developed by Hillard, Goepfert and Farber (1976), forms the basis for the sequence of objectives presented here. It provides an option to more traditional articulation training sequences.

In using this variation of the semantically potent word approach, one selects a core of three to five training words which are communicatively powerful for an individual child. Rather than selecting words on the basis of developmental order of phonemes and avoiding highly practiced immature words, words are selected which are already occurring frequently, although unintelligibly, in the child's repertoire. Occasionally, however, words are selected to match a child's apparent communicative intent, even when no word approximation is currently being used — thus supplying the child with a word to replace a preexisting form of nonverbal

communication. For example, one three–year–old who frequently stood and screamed when an older brother tried to take a toy was taught "don't" and "mine" as more acceptable, but still powerful, ways to affect his environment. Some examples of categories which were provided by Hillard, Goepfert and Farber (1976) are attached to this sequence. Each child's words should be chosen individually with his or her parents based upon their semantic potency for the child.

After a child's beginning core of semantically potent words has been selected, it is useful to take a baseline count using other words which have similar phonological content so that generalization of new speech sound production ability can be tested later. The small core of words which are directly trained are expected to serve as "key words" for the development of many new feature and phoneme distinctions. If a number of words with similar phonological errors have been identified during pretesting, post–testing with the same set of words can be used to establish whether generalization is already taking place or whether a few sessions with direct attention to generalization training are needed. Both the creators of this approach (Hillard, *et al.* 1976) and speech–language pathologists in Berrien County, Michigan, preprimary programs for Learning and Language Impaired Children (Kerrigan 1979) have found evidence of rapid generalization of new sound production skills to previously untrained words and situations. With older students who have multiple phoneme problems, the use of this approach, followed by the "Paired Stimuli Technique" (Irwin, *et al.* 1976) can result in much more rapid progress than the phoneme–by–phoneme approach used traditionally.

The use of the first two objectives of this sequence varies with the individual child and his or her core of words. A picture is drawn or glued to a card to represent each of the semantically potent words, and the appropriate occasions of use are either explained or demonstrated until the child associates the picture with the word. The word is also printed on each stimulus card and target phonemes are underlined as they come under focus. The intervention steps involve the following:

1. Focus on one phoneme at a time in each word; provide whatever prompting is necessary, and

elicit productions of the word in blocks of five. Hillard and Goepfert suggest the cue, "I am listening for the /d/ sound; say 'don't.'" Further breakdown may be necessary at this stage, but the whole word level should be used eventually.

2. Once the child produces the target phoneme in the word to the clinician's satisfaction (not necessarily perfect, but perhaps with an additional distinctive feature), *objective two* is implemented until the child can produce the target phoneme in the word in response only to the picture and a question such as, "What's this one?"

3. If the word includes other error phonemes which require shaping, the clinician can move back and forth between objectives one and two several times, until the whole word is ready to be practiced in the fill-in-the-blank task of *objective three*, mixed with other possible words which have also reached that stage.

4. Meeting criterion for a word at step three is a big event for children in the preschool programs in Berrien County, because then they get to take the pictured words into the classroom and tack them on the bulletin board, or hang them from a clothesline, under their own symbols.

5. Following *objectives four* and *five*, pictures are taken home to become "refrigerator words," where they are reinforced by parents and siblings.

6. *Objectives four, five* and *six* might have to be collapsed for children not enrolled in classroom programs.

7. Generalization probing, and possibly training, could then be used to assess the broader usefulness of this approach for a particular child.

Semantically Potent Words — Examples of Categories
(Hillard, Goepfert and Farber 1976; with additions by Kerrigan 1979)

Protection Words	Attention Words	Refusal/Acceptance Words	Bathroom Words
don't	look	no	bathroom
stop	watch	yes	wash
quit	hey	want	brush
	help	more	

Personal Words	Body Parts	Social Words	Location Words
child's name	eye	please	there
me/I	mouth	thank you	this
age	teeth	okay	that
boy/girl	nose	fine (as in "How are you?")	here
friend's name	ear	Hi	
	face	Bye	
	hair		
	hand		
	tummy		
	leg		
	foot		

Action Words	Family Words	Emotion Words	Preschool Words
push/pull	siblings' names	love	play
hit	pets' names	mad	cup/spoon
go	favorite food	like	juice/milk/cookie
run/walk/fall	sister/brother	sleepy	truck/book/ball
climb	mama	happy	doll/block/bike
open	daddy	hungry	scissors
throw/roll	baby	sad	teacher's name
eat		kiss	paint
drink			outside
			names of colors
			numbers
			shoes/socks
			pants/shirt
			coat/hat

Some Words which Parents Request be Taught

refrigerator	7-11
crying	pretend
cereal	zipper
school	very
salami	potato chip
flush	McDonald's
excuse me	thing
Saturday	ice cream
bed	meat
hot	hamburger
cold	french fries

References and Other Resources

Costello, J. Articulation instruction based on distinctive features theory. *Language, Speech and Hearing Services in Schools, VI,* 61-71, 1975.

Hillard, S. W., L. P. Goepfert and B. G. Farber. A preschool for communicatively impaired children: An Innovative Approach. Miniseminar presented at the annual conference of the American Speech and Hearing Association, Houston, 1976.

Irwin, J. V., A. J. Weston, F. A. Griffith and C. Rocconi. Phoneme acquisition using the paired-stimuli technique in the public school setting. *Language, Speech and Hearing Services in Schools, VII,* 220-229, 1976.

Kerrigan, A. A semantically potent word approach to early phonological development. Poster session presented at the annual meeting of the Michigan Speech and Hearing Association, Kalamazoo, 1979.

McReynolds, L. V. and D. L. Engmann. *Distinctive Feature Analysis of Misarticulations.* Baltimore: University Park Press, 1975.

Menyuk, P. *The Development of Speech.* Indianapolis: The Bobbs-Merrill Company, Inc., 1972.

Weiner, F. F. and N. Bankson. Teaching features. *Language, Speech and Hearing Services in Schools, IX,* 29-34, 1978.

Winitz, H. *From Syllable to Conversation.* Baltimore: University Park Press, 1975.

A-6a

ARTICULATION: EARLY PHONOLOGICAL ACQUISITION*

Date: _____

STUDENT: _____ AGE: _____ SCHOOL: _____ GRADE/LEVEL: _____ SPEECH–LANGUAGE CLINICIAN: _____

GOAL: The student will be able to produce sound and word approximations close enough to adult models to be intelligible to others in the environment.

DIAGNOSTIC: Phonetic Analysis _____
Oral Structure and Function _____
Audiological Assessment _____

MLU _____
Core Vocabulary _____
Other _____

LONG-RANGE OBJECTIVE: The student will produce target phoneme(s) in five previously untrained words spontaneously or following clinician model with no prompting.

SHORT-TERM OBJECTIVE THE STUDENT WILL:	Wd. _____ TARGET PHONEME(S)		Wd. _____ TARGET PHONEME(S)		Wd. _____ TARGET PHONEME(S)		Wd. _____ TARGET PHONEME(S)		Wd. _____ TARGET PHONEME(S)		COMMENTS TECHNIQUES EVALUATION
	Date In.	Date Accom.	Date In.	Date Accom.	Date In.	Date Accom.	Date In.	Date Accom.	Date In.	Date Accom.	
1. produce an intelligible approximation of each target phoneme in a "semantically potent word" in response to a representative picture and verbal prompting by clinician (100% tangible and social reinforcement with 10 consecutive correct).											
2. produce each target phoneme (one trained at a time) in its "semantically potent word" in response to pictures with no prompting (100% tangible and social reinforcement with 10 consecutive correct).											
3. produce all target phonemes in the "semantically potent word" in response to fill-in-the-blank statements such as "when Stewart pushes you, you say 'don't'" when mixed with two other possible "semantically potent words" and pictures (50% tangible/100% social reinforcement with 10 consecutive correct over two sessions).											
4. produce the "semantically potent word" (with all target phonemes) in a fill-in task outside the speech room with the clinician (100% social reinforcement with five consecutive correct).											

*See note on page 49.

This form may be reproduced as often as necessary. / Copyright © 1979 by Communication Skill Builders, Inc.

ARTICULATION: EARLY PHONOLOGICAL ACQUISITION*

A-6b

Date: _____

Student: _____

SHORT-TERM OBJECTIVE	Wd. _____ TARGET PHONEME(S)		Wd. _____ TARGET PHONEME(S)		Wd. _____ TARGET PHONEME(S)		Wd. _____ TARGET PHONEME(S)		Wd. _____ TARGET PHONEME(S)		COMMENTS TECHNIQUES EVALUATION
	Date In.	Date Accom.	Date In.	Date Accom.	Date In.	Date Accom.	Date In.	Date Accom.	Date In.	Date Accom.	
THE STUDENT WILL:											
5. produce the "semantically potent word" (with all target phonemes) in a fill-in task outside the speech room with someone other than the clinician (100% social reinforcement with five consecutive correct).											
6. produce the "semantically potent word" (with all target phonemes) spontaneously in appropriate communication at least three times as observed by parent, teacher, or clinician.											
7. LONG-RANGE: produce target phoneme(s) from "semantically potent words" in five previously untrained words spontaneously or following clinician model with no prompting.											

*This approach has been developed for use with phonologically impaired children at an early stage of language acquisition. It is based on the "Semantically Potent Word Approach" as presented by Hillard and Goepfert at the 1976 Annual Convention of the American Speech and Hearing Association in Houston.

A-7 ARTICULATION:
PHONEME ACQUISITION

This sequence of objectives provides the basic outline of "traditional" articulation intervention (see, e.g., Van Riper 1978). It can be used traditionally, with one phoneme in active process, another in discrimination training, and a third in carryover activities, or it can be used in many creative ways, with alterations for a particular child or approach. Specific short-term objectives can be used or not, as the clinician so desires, and they can be renumbered or dated to indicate a change in the sequence of implementation.

For example, a discrimination objective is provided first in the sequence, but it may be omitted or implemented later in the training process in some instances. Winitz (1976) offers some creative suggestions regarding the role of speech discrimination in articulation intervention, particularly with young children; however, the value of spending many sessions on "ear training" activities with school-age children is coming under increasing scrutiny (McReynolds, Kohn and Williams 1975). Many children seem to acquire the ability to discriminate the distinctive features of a phoneme as their own productions of the sound are shaped. The clinician's comments of the sort, "Good, I like the way your tongue went up; That's great!", often lead the child to be critically aware of the discriminative features of a sound with a great savings of therapy time.

Many professionals also question the appropriateness of ever working with a phoneme in isolation, and it is certainly possible to omit objective number two entirely. However, it often appears that the same coarticulatory variations that shape a sound in differing phonetic contexts during normal production make it difficult for some articulation-impaired children to develop a firm concept of the cardinal features which identify the phoneme and make it unique. Only by isolating the sound, and extending its duration if it is a continuant, or by simplifying the syllabic content which occurs with it if it is not, can some children begin to include previously omitted features in their own productions.

Other more radical variations of approach might also be accommodated within this sequence of objectives by grouping target phonemes based upon a distinctive feature analysis of the child's existing phonological system (Costello 1975; McReynolds and Engmann 1975). Although Weiner and Bankson (1978) suggest a program structured to teach features rather directly, many of the other distinctive feature approaches follow a traditional sequence, but with a cluster of phonemes which all exemplify a common distinctive feature. In such approaches, objective number eight, which uses minimal pairs, can be especially valuable in assigning meaning to phonemes or features. For example, the contrast in meaning between speaking the words "pan" and "ban" is made by the inclusion or absence of one feature (±voicing), and it becomes critical for the child to include the distinction in his or her production if the desired meaning is to be clear.

Another major variation, although still based on the general progression presented in this objective sequence, is the "systematic multiple phonemic approach" suggested by McCabe and Bradley (1975). Such an approach can involve simultaneous work on as many error phonemes as necessary for a child. A unique feature is to alternate focus on individual sounds at each level with focus on multiple target sounds in whole words, phrases and sentences by underlining them in written stimulus materials. A multiple phonemic approach can be particularly useful with older students who have normal intelligence and some reading skills, but severe misarticulations. In varying this sequence of objectives to use a multiple phonemic approach, the clinician could add explanatory notes and additional columns or copies of the recording format to keep track of progress on many phonemes at once.

The question of when to dismiss an articulation-impaired child from therapy is also an important one. Diedrich (1976) has recommended periodic Talk Samples with counting and charting of target phonemes to aid both in the intervention process and in deciding when the process can be safely discontinued with only intermittent rechecks. In his extensive research with children enrolled in public school articulation intervention programs, Diedrich found that once a child could produce the target phoneme at a 75 percent correct rate spontaneously in a three-minute Talk Sample, the remainder of carryover seemed to proceed without direct intervention, and much time was frequently spent unnecessarily in prolonging the final stages of intervention.

References and Other Resources

Ausberger, C. *Here's How to Handle /r/.* Tucson, Ariz.: Communication Skill Builders, 1976.

Brown, K. O., K. L. Timm and E. L. Evans. *Universal Articulation Program.* Boston: Teaching Resources.

Collins, P. J. and G. W. Cunningham. *Articulation Modification Programs.* Tigard, Ore.: C. C. Publications, Inc.

Costello, J. Articulation instruction based on distinctive features theory. *Language, Speech and Hearing Services in Schools, VI,* 61-71, 1975.

Costello, J. and J. M. Onstine. The modification of multiple articulation errors based on distinctive feature theory. *Journal of Speech and Hearing Disorders, 41,* 199-215, 1976.

Diedrich, W. M. Training speech clinicians in the recording and analysis of articulatory behavior: Final Performance Report. No. OEG-0-71-1689 (603); Special Projects, U.S. Office of Education, October 1976.

Jackson, M. *Programmed Articulation Therapy for Modification of /r/.* Salt Lake City, Utah: Word Making Productions.

McCabe, R. B. and D. P. Bradley. Systematic multiple phonemic approach to articulation therapy. *Acta Symbolica, VI* (No. 1), 1975.

McReynolds, L. V. and D. L. Engmann. *Distinctive Feature Analysis of Misarticulations.* Baltimore: University Park Press, 1975.

McReynolds, L. V., J. Kohn and G. C. Williams. Articulatory defective children's discrimination of their production errors. *Journal of Speech and Hearing Disorders, 40,* 327-338, 1975.

Rosenbek, J., R. Hansen, C. H. Baughman and M. Lemme. Treatment of developmental apraxia of speech: A case study. *Language, Speech and Hearing Services in Schools, V,* 13-22, 1974.

Sonderman, J. C. and D. H. Zwitman. *Programmed Articulation Skills Carryover Stories.* Tucson, Ariz.: Communication Skill Builders, 1976.

Usdan, V. L. Utilization of the "straw technique" for correction of the lateral lisp. *Language, Speech and Hearing Services in Schools, IX,* 5-7, 1978.

Van Riper, C. *Speech Correction: Principles and Methods* (sixth and previous editions). Englewood Cliffs, N.J.: Prentice-Hall, Inc., 1978.

Weiner, F. F. and N. Bankson. Teaching features. *Language, Speech and Hearing Services in Schools, IX,* 29-34, 1978.

Winitz, H. *From Syllable to Conversation.* Baltimore: University Park Press, 1975.

Yoss, K. A. and F. L. Darley. Therapy in developmental apraxia of speech. *Language, Speech and Hearing Services in Schools, V,* 23-31, 1974.

A-7a

ARTICULATION: PHONEME ACQUISITION

STUDENT: _____ AGE: _____ SCHOOL: _____ GRADE/LEVEL: _____ SPEECH–LANGUAGE CLINICIAN: _____ Date: _____

GOAL: The student will produce all phonemes correctly (for age and linguistic community).

DIAGNOSTIC: Phonetic Analysis _____

              Examination of Oral Structure and Function _____

              Audiological Assessment _____

              Assessment of Auditory Discrimination _____

              Other: _____

Talk sample: duration _____ phoneme _____ corr./inc. _____

_____ _____

_____ _____

LONG-RANGE OBJECTIVE: Produce target phoneme 90 to 100 percent correctly in a five-minute conversation with parent, teacher, or peer, outside the speech room.

SHORT-TERM OBJECTIVES **THE STUDENT WILL:**	TARGET PHONEME		TARGET PHONEME		TARGET PHONEME		COMMENTS TECHNIQUES EVALUATION
	Date In.	Date Accom.	Date In.	Date Accom.	Date In.	Date Accom.	
1. demonstrate discrimination of clinician's correct/incorrect production of target phoneme by pointing to one finger out of three raised to correspond to clinician's error production of target phoneme in cluster with two correct productions (18 of 20 trials in one session).							
2. produce target phoneme in isolation in speech room (35 of 40 trials over two sessions).							
3. produce target phoneme in nonsense syllables, multiple positions (35 of 40 trials over two sessions).							
4. produce target phoneme in the initial position in words (18 of 20 trials over two sessions).							
5. produce target phoneme in mixed medial and final positions in words (9 of 10 trials over two sessions).							

ARTICULATION: PHONEME ACQUISITION

Date: _____

Student: _____

SHORT-TERM OBJECTIVES THE STUDENT WILL:	TARGET PHONEME		TARGET PHONEME		TARGET PHONEME		COMMENTS TECHNIQUES EVALUATION
	Date In.	Date Accom.	Date In.	Date Accom.	Date In.	Date Accom.	
6. produce target phoneme in all positions in 10 carrier phrases such as "I see a _____; This is a _____; I like _____." (9 of 10 correct over two sessions).							
7. produce target phoneme in blends in words (18 of 20 over two sessions).							
8. demonstrate ability to discriminate occasion of use of the target phoneme by including it or not in minimally paired words, as appropriate (18 of 20 trials over two sessions).							
9. produce target phoneme in structured sentences (9 of 10 trials over two sessions).							
10. demonstrate ability to monitor own speech by self-correcting 80 percent of errors on target phoneme during structured conversation (e.g., spontaneous sentences, reading, concentration game) in speech room over two sessions.							
11. produce target phonemes in structured speaking situations (spontaneous sentences, reading, story-telling) with no more than five errors in each of two consecutive sessions.							
12. produce target phoneme 85 percent correctly in spontaneous speaking situations during a three-minute talk sample with a friend in the speech room.*							
13. LONG-RANGE OBJECTIVE: produce target phoneme 90 to 100 percent correctly in a five-minute conversation with parent, teacher, or peer, outside the speech room.							

*Research (Diedrich, 1976) indicates that once a child can produce the target phoneme at a 75 percent correct rate spontaneously in a three-minute talk sample, the remainder of carryover proceeds without direct intervention. Therefore, reduction of scheduling to monthly rechecks would be appropriate at this point.

This form may be reproduced as often as necessary. / Copyright © 1979 by Communication Skill Builders, Inc.

L–8 LANGUAGE:
SEMANTIC ACQUISITION OF CONCEPTUAL VOCABULARY

The vocabulary acquisition sequence is designed open–ended enough to be used at a variety of levels, from acquisition of first words by toddlers, through development of advanced categories by adolescents.

Recent psycholinguistic contributions (e.g., Clark 1973 and Bowerman 1973) to our understanding of semantic development have stressed that word meanings are developed gradually, from general to specific cases. Application of the cognitive processes, discrimination, association and classification, seems to make it possible for the child to attach increasingly abstract binary feature distinctions to words stored in the lexicon (internalized word classification system). Thus, in the process of normal development, children move rapidly from a brief stage of overextension, in which a cow might be labeled a "dog," because both share the (+animal) and (+four–legged) features, to the far more sophisticated, and yet very early, discrimination between dogs and cats as general categories — in spite of all of the individual differences of the exemplary items (Great Danes and Chihuahuas; Calicos and Angoras).

Children also learn to combine words into sentences so that appropriate rules of feature matching are satisfied and the desired meaning is communicated. This complex categorization process makes it possible for a child to know that one does not say, "Mama fixed a rice for supper," since "rice" is a (-count) noun and "a" is a (+count) determiner. Similarly, the normal child appears to learn easily such idiosyncratic rules as the one which allows us to recognize that, although it is not permissible to say, "The book ran off the table," since "book" is a (-animate) noun and "ran" is a (+animate) verb, it is okay to say, "The spilled milk ran off the table," because liquids can "run" in another sense of the word. Children also eventually learn that all carrots are vegetables, but that all vegetables are not necessarily carrots.

It is important to recognize the cognitive nature of such a process and build in the elements which will facilitate similar development in communicatively–impaired children. As the clinician or teacher plans an intervention program for vocabulary development, the process should be viewed as the acquisition of concepts, with multiple features attached, not just unitary words. Bloom and Lahey (1978)

also emphasize the overall interactions of content, form and function. The intervention planning process should include consideration of such factors as:

1. *Categorization.* Words are best learned, remembered and recalled based upon their similarities with, and differences from, each other.

2. *Perceptual saliency.* Especially in early stages of development, words are learned fastest when their perceptual features are most noticeable. Normal babies learn to recognize body part labels as they become aware of their own body parts. Conversely, assigning labels to a baby's body parts during nursery games probably helps the baby notice them.

   The perceptual saliency principle also leads to the suggestion that conceptual vocabulary items which can be expressed as opposites be presented in contrasting pairs — since materrials which can be used to illustrate gross differences along a dimension provide an effective method for teaching the concept (Blank 1973). However, it is important to note that one member of a pair of word opposites (usually the one which occurs most frequently in the question, "How _____ is it? ") is generally acquired significantly ahead of the other in normal development, and is used for a time to refer to both poles of the dimension (Clark 1974). Therefore, the clinician may wish to employ both members of an opposite word–pair concept only in making the distinction along the dimension apparent, and prompt the child with the first learned member of the pair, waiting until the concept is more firmly established before expecting the child to produce the opposite member.

3. *Repetition.* Language–impaired children generally need many models, followed immediately by requests for repetition, before they acquire a new word. Repetitions should take place within sessions, across sessions, and across a variety of environments. Classroom activities, including snack time, art time and gross motor activities, can all be designed to emphasize three or four conceptual dimensions over the period of a week. Parents can also be urged to pay particular attention to target words and concepts for that week.

4. *Concreteness.* New words should be introduced with concrete illustrations, but the child should be carefully led to recognize and use the words in broader appropriate contexts. Blank (1973) offers suggestions for a dialogue approach to accomplish the transition from more concrete to more abstract applications of new concepts.

Many programs are available for assisting vocabulary development. A few are listed below. Some of the more frequently taught categories of word types are listed with this sequence in a format which could be used for pre- and post-testing for children or classes. The *One to One* program (Palmer 1978) provides an especially good recording and training format for working with conceptual vocabulary. Other formal evaluation tools which can be used to assess vocabulary ability and assist in the selection of areas for remediation are those by Bangs (1975), Carrow (1973), Boehm (1969), and Hedrick, Prather and Tobin (1975). Sequence L-16 with these objectives, *Language: Semantic Acquisition of Abstract/Categorical Uses,* is designed for developing semantic processing skills at a more abstract cognitive level.

References and Other Resources

Andrews, M. and Brabson, C. Preparing the language-impaired child for classroom mathematics: Suggestions for the speech pathologist. *Language, Speech and Hearing Services in Schools, VIII,* 46-53, 1977.

Bangs, T. E. *Language and Learning Disorders of the Pre-Academic Child: With Curriculum Guide.* Englewood Cliffs, N.J.: Prentice-Hall, Inc., 1968.

Bangs, T. E. *Vocabulary Comprehension Scale.* Austin, Texas: Learning Concepts, 1975.

Blank, M. *Teaching Learning in the Preschool: A Dialogue Approach.* Columbus: Charles E. Merrill Publishing Company, 1973.

Bloom, L. and M. Lahey. *Language Development and Language Disorders.* New York: John Wiley & Sons, 1978.

Boehm, A. *Boehm Test of Basic Concepts.* New York: Psychological Corporation, 1969.

Bowerman, M. Structural relationships in children's utterances: Syntactic or semantic? In Moore, T. (ed.), *Cognitive Development and the Acquisition of Language.* New York: Academic Press, 1973.

Bright, H. M. *Some Suggestions for Remediation of Concepts of Boehm Test of Basic Concepts: Book 1, Form A or B.* 1020 Peach, San Luis Obispo, CA 93401, 1972.

Broad, L. P. and N. T. Butterworth. *The Playgroup Handbook.* New York: St. Martin's Press, 1974.

Brown, E. *Parts of Speech* (five units of picture cards). Boston, Mass.: Teaching Resources.

Carrow, E. *Test for Auditory Comprehension of Language.* Austin, Tex.: Learning Concepts, 1973.

Clark, E. What's in a word? On the child's acquisition of semantics in this first language. In Moore, T. (ed.), *Cognitive Development and the Acquisition of Language.* New York: Academic Press, 1973.

Clark, E. Some aspects of the conceptual basis for first language acquisition. In Schiefelbusch, R. L. and L. L. Lloyd (eds.), *Language Perspectives — Acquisition, Retardation and Intervention.* Baltimore: University Park Press, 1974.

Clark, H. H. On the use and meaning of prepositions. *Journal of Verbal Learning and Verbal Behavior, 7,* 421-431, 1968.

Collins, P. J. and G. W. Cunningham. *Plurals, STEP: A Basic Concepts Development Program, Vocabulary Instructional Program.* Tigard, Oregon: C. C. Publications, Inc.

Communication Skill Builders (publ.). *Peel & Put, Language Visuals,* and other support materials. Tucson, Ariz.: Communication Skill Builders.

Croft, D. J. and R. D. Hess. *An Activities Handbook for Teachers of Young Children.* Boston: Houghton Mifflin Co., 1975.

Developmental Learning Materials (publ). *Preposition Cards, Language Big Box, Backpack, Action Verb Boards,* etc. Niles, Illinois: Developmental Learning Materials.

Doran, S. and D. Campbell. *A Beginning Program of Independent Reading and Writing Activities.* Woburn, Mass.: Curriculum Associates, Inc.

Dunn, L. M., L. T. Chun, D. C. Crowell, L. G. Halevi and E. R. Yackel. *Peabody Early Experiences Kit* (PEEK). Circle Pines, Minn.: American Guidance Service, 1976.

Dunn, L. M., K. B. Horton and J. O. Smith. *Peabody Language Development Kit (Level P).* Circle Pines, Minn.: American Guidance Service, 1965.

Dunn, L. M. and J. O. Smith. *Peabody Language Development Kits, (Levels 1, 2, and 3).* Circle Pines, Minn.: American Guidance Service, 1966, 1967, 1968.

Emjay Corporation (publ.). *School-Readiness Story Cards.* 2747 Mary Street, Omaha, Neb., 68112: The Emjay Corporation.

Evans, B. *Communacad Multimedia Vocabulary Programs for All Levels.* Wilton, Conn.: The Communications Academy.

Flemming, B. M. and D. S. Hamilton. *Resources for Creative Teaching in Early Childhood Education.* New York: Harcourt Brace, 1972.

Frank, M. *I Can Make a Rainbow.* Nashville, Tenn.: Incentive Publications, Inc.

Hedrick, D., E. Prather and A. Tobin. *Sequential Inventory of Communication Development.* Seattle: University of Washington Press, 1975.

Holt, B. G. *Science with Young Children.* 1834 Connecticut Ave., N.W., Washington, D. C. 20009: National Association for Educators of Young Children, 1977.

Incentives for Learning, Inc. (publ.). *Money Counts,* etc. Chicago: Incentives for Learning, Inc.

Karnes, M. B. *Helping Young Children Develop Language Skills: A Book of Activities.* Arlington, Va.: The Council for Exceptional Children, 1968.

Karnes, M. B. *GOAL I* and *GOAL II: Language Development Programs.* Tucson, Ariz.: Communication Skill Builders, Inc.

Lugares, C. Y. *Places & Things.* (In English and in Spanish). Tulsa, Oklahoma: Modern Education Corporation.

Modern Education Corporation (publ.). *Language Stimulation Workbooks* (Verbs, Adjectives and Prepositions). Tulsa, Oklahoma: Modern Education Corporation.

Moran, J. M. and L. H. Kulalian. *Movement Experiences for the Mentally Retarded or Emotionally Disturbed Child.* Minneapolis, Minn.: Burgess Publishing Company, 1977.

Marzollo, J. and J. Lloyd. *Learning Through Play.* Harper Colophon Books, 1972.

Morehead, D. and D. Ingram. The development of base syntax in normal and language deviant children. *Journal of Speech and Hearing Research, 16,* 330-352, 1973.

Newby Visualanguage, Inc. (publ.). *Newby Visualanguage* (Verbs, Adjectives, Pronouns, Prepositions, Idioms). Eagleville, Pa.: Newby Visualanguage, Inc.

Palmer, F. H. *One to One: A Concept Training Curriculum for Children Ages Three to Five Years.* Stony Brook, N.Y.: Early Intellectual Development, Inc., 1978.

Proff, J. *Take Time.* Tigard, Oregon: C. C. Publications, Inc.

Rush, M. L. *The Language of Classifications: Animals.* Washington, D.C.: Alexander Graham Bell Association for the Deaf, 1977.

Teaching Resources (publ.). *People, Places and Things (Occupations, Stores, Recreation, Sports), TR Large Picture Cards: Sets 1 and 2,* etc. Boston: Teaching Resources.

Wilt, J., G. Hurn and J. Hurn. *More Puppets with Pizazz.* Waco, Tex.: Creative Resources, 1977.

Wilt, J. and T. Watson. *Touch.* Waco, Tex.: Creative Resources, 1977.

Wirth, M. J. *Teacher's Handbook of Children's Games: A Guide to Developing Perceptual-Motor Skills.* New York: Parker Publishing Co., Inc., 1976.

L-8a

LANGUAGE: SEMANTIC ACQUISITION OF CONCEPTUAL VOCABULARY

Date: _____

STUDENT: _____ AGE: _____ SCHOOL: _____ GRADE/LEVEL: _____ SPEECH–LANGUAGE CLINICIAN: _____

GOAL: The student will spontaneously and appropriately use the vocabulary being formally taught and will begin to acquire new vocabulary from the natural environment more rapidly.

DIAGNOSTIC: Cognitive _____   MLU _____   PPVT _____   TACL _____

Affective _____   Other Language Measures _____

Speech _____   Other: _____

Audiological _____

LONG-RANGE OBJECTIVE: The student will verbally label (older student will define) at least five previously untrained stimuli (objects/object relationships/pictures/actions/verbal descriptions) representing the category indicated (two consecutive sessions with no prompting).

SHORT-TERM OBJECTIVES	Category: _____ Vocabulary: _____		Category: _____ Vocabulary: _____		Category: _____ Vocabulary: _____		COMMENTS TECHNIQUES EVALUATION
THE STUDENT WILL:	Date In.	Date Accom.	Date In.	Date Accom.	Date In.	Date Accom.	
1. point to objects/pictures or perform an action, following concrete demonstration earlier in session, to represent target vocabulary items named by clinician (two consecutive sessions; 4 of 5 trials correct each item; minimal prompting).							
2. point to previously untrained objects/pictures or perform an action to represent concrete and obvious demonstration target vocabulary items named by clinician (two consecutive sessions; 4 of 5 trials correct each item; no prompting).							
3. label objects/object relationships/pictures/actions representing the target vocabulary, following demonstration earlier in session, in response to clinician's verbal question or fill-in task (two consecutive sessions; 4 of 5 trials correct each item; mixed presentation; minimal prompting).							
4. demonstrate ability to discriminate less obvious examples representing the target vocabulary by pointing or performing an action (two consecutive sessions; two trials correct each item; mixed presentation; no prompting).							

This form may be reproduced as often as necessary. / Copyright © 1979 Communication Skill Builders, Inc.

L-8b

LANGUAGE: SEMANTIC ACQUISITION OF CONCEPTUAL VOCABULARY

Date: _____

Student: _____

SHORT-TERM OBJECTIVES	Category: _____ Vocabulary: _____		Category: _____ Vocabulary: _____		Category: _____ Vocabulary: _____		COMMENTS TECHNIQUES EVALUATION
THE STUDENT WILL:	Date In.	Date Accom.	Date In.	Date Accom.	Date In.	Date Accom.	
*5. label previously untrained objects/object relationships/pictures/actions, representing the vocabulary, in response to clinician's verbal question or fill-in task (two consecutive sessions; two trials correct each item; mixed presentation; no prompting).							
6. label clinician's verbal description of target vocabulary items with no concrete stimuli present (two consecutive sessions; two trials correct each item; mixed presentation; no prompting).							
7. verbally define target vocabulary items, or use them in a unique sentence, in response to clinician's label/picture/written word (two consecutive sessions; two trials correct each item; mixed presentation; no prompting).							
8. **LONG-RANGE:** The student will verbally label (older student will define) at least five previously untrained stimuli (objects/object relationships/pictures/actions/verbal descriptions) representing the category indicated (two consecutive sessions with no prompting).							

*For younger or severely retarded students, objective number 5 may be the most appropriate terminal objective for most vocabulary items. However, Hedrick, Tobin, and Prather (1975) reported that their standardization sample children could "Show me what Mom cooks on," and "Show me what you wear on your feet," at 32 months.

L-8c

LANGUAGE: VOCABULARY ACQUISITION CATEGORY LISTINGS*

Student: _____

Speech–Language Clinician: _____   Date: _____

The student's ability to pass (+) or fail (−) a comprehension or production task for selected vocabulary items may be periodically assessed, and the results may be entered on this chart, or a chart may be constructed for an entire class.

BODY PARTS	Date: Comp.	Prod.	ACTIONS	Date: Comp.	Prod.	ACTIONS	Date: Comp.	Prod.	CLOTHING	Date: Comp.	Prod.	FOOD	Date: Comp.	Prod.
eyes (2–0)			drink			laugh			socks			milk		
hair (2–0)			sleep			yell			shoes			cookie		
mouth (2–0)			eat			talk			hat			juice		
nose (2–0)			kiss			whisper			pants			apple		
ears (2–0)			hug			blow			shirt			orange		
tummy			cry			brush			sneakers			banana		
feet			come			pat			dress			hot dog		
arms			go			point			button			french fries		
legs			see			show			zipper			coke		
hands			go potty (or			cut			coat			pop		
knees			other potty			paste			jacket			peas		
fingers			word)			other:			boots			peanut butter		
toes			put on						sandals			ice cream		
back			put away						pajamas			cracker		
elbows			hit						night gown			meat		
eyebrows			lie down						underpants			soup		
teeth			sit (down)						undershirt			ice		
other:			stand (up)						skirt			water		
			throw						jeans			kool-aid		
			catch						bib			jello		
			walk						apron			pudding		
			run						sleeve			beans		
			pull						collar			corn		
			push						belt			eggs		
			touch						waist			pancakes		
			wash						tie			waffles		
			get						other:			bacon		
			make									sandwich		
			hide									bread		
			scare									potato chips		
			tickle									butter		
			swim									carrots		
			fly									potatoes		
			tip-toe									pears		
			hop									grapes		
			skip									salt		
			wave									pepper		
			smile									other:		

*See note on page 71.

This form may be reproduced as often as necessary. / Copyright © 1979 by Communication Skill Builders, Inc.

LANGUAGE: VOCABULARY ACQUISITION CATEGORY LISTINGS*

L-8d

Student: _____

Speech–Language Clinician: _____   Date: _____

FOOD	Date:		ANIMALS	Date:		HOUSEHOLD ITEMS	Date:		TOYS & PLAY EQUIPMENT	Date:	
	Comp.	Prod.		Comp.	Prod.		Comp.	Prod.		Comp.	Prod.
For older students: Fruits and vebetables may be taught as part of a categorization activity			dog (doggie)			spoon			ball		
			cat (kitty)			bottle			baby		
			cow			key			doll		
			horse			cup			teddy bear		
			pig			bowl			car		
			bird			blanket			truck		
			fish			pillow			squeak toy		
			duck			plate			book		
			chicken			knife			tricycle		
			goat			fork			baby buggy		
			elephant			napkin			airplane		
			lion			placemat			puzzle		
			tiger			coffee pot			stack up toy		
			zebra			pan			swings		
			seal			can opener			slippery slide		
			snake			toaster			teeter-totter		
			bug			mixer			jungle gym		
			spider			other:			scooter board		
			butterfly						skateboard		
			mouse						other:		
			other:								

PLACES	Date:		ANIMALS FOR OLDER STUDENTS	Date:		TRANSPORTATION	Date:		COMMUNICATION MODES	Date:	
	Comp.	Prod.		Comp.	Prod.		Comp.	Prod.		Comp.	Prod.
bye-bye			Animals may be taught in the categories farm, zoo, flying, swimming, mammals, etc.			car			telephone		
home						truck			t.v./television		
church						van			radio		
school						airplane			movie		
grocery store						train			letters		
shoe store						boat			telegrams		
hardware store						submarine			walkie-talkie		
dime (variety) store						ship			other:		
drugstore						bicycle					
toy (department) store						vehicle					
ice cream (candy) store						jet					
doctor's (dentist's) office						ticket					
downtown/uptown						other:					
fire station											
hospital											
restaurant											
other:											

*See note on page 71.

L-8e

LANGUAGE: VOCABULARY ACQUISITION CATEGORY LISTINGS*

Student: _____   Speech–Language Clinician: _____   Date: _____

FURNITURE	Date: Comp.	Prod.	ROOMS/PARTS/ OUTSIDE	Date: Comp.	Prod.	TOOLS	Date: Comp.	Prod.	CLASSROOM EQUIPMENT	Date: Comp.	Prod.
bed			*Home:*			hammer			paper		
baby bed			kitchen			nails			scissors		
chair			bathroom			pliers			paste		
high chair			bedroom			wrench			crayon		
table			living room			saw			pencil		
lamp			dining room			screwdriver			paint		
sofa/divan/couch			closet			screws			tape		
desk			basement			drill			mat		
dresser			porch			tape measure			desk		
shelves			family room			paint brush			blackboard		
cupboard/cabinet			upstairs			roller			chalk		
stove			downstairs			ladder			bulletin board		
refrigerator/ice box			outside			scraper			ruler		
toilet			front door						other:		
bathtub			back door			sewing machine					
sink			window			pins					
picture			door knob			scissors					
rocking chair			steps			pattern					
end table			ceiling								
dirty clothes hamper			floor			broom					
foot stool			rug			sweeper (vacuum)					
other:			carpet			sponge/mop					
			curtains/drapes			pail					
			other:								
						film					
			Outside:			camera					
			roof			flashcube (bulb)					
			screen								
			shutters			rake					
			chimney			shovel					
			driveway			hoe					
			garage			clippers					
			fence			lawnmower					
			tree								
			bush			tractor					
			flowers			plow					
			swimming pool								
			mud								
			grass								
			other:								

SCHOOL ROOMS	Date: Comp.	Prod.
classroom		
music room		
speech room		
gym		
bus area		
bathroom		
girls		
boys		
coat hook		
cubby		
circle		
quiet table		
playground		
other:		

*See note on page 71.

L-8f

LANGUAGE: VOCABULARY ACQUISITION CATEGORY LISTINGS*

Student: _____   Speech–Language Clinician: _____   Date: _____

| HEALTH & SELF-CARE | Date: | | VOCABULARY OF SCHOOL SUBJECTS | Date: | | | Date: | |
	Comp.	Prod.		Comp.	Prod.		Comp.	Prod.
brush								
toothbrush								
comb								
towel								
washcloth								
soap								
shampoo								
toothpaste								
kleenex								
cold								
stomach ache								
headache								
other:								

| HEALTH & SELF-CARE for Older Students | Date: | | CAREERS | Date: | | CAREERS (continued) | Date: | |
	Comp.	Prod.		Comp.	Prod.		Comp.	Prod.
Brand names:			baker			mail carrier		
			beautician			mechanic		
			bus driver			newspaper carrier		
aspirin			carpenter			nurse		
temperature/thermometer			cashier			pilot		
prescription			dentist			plumber		
deoderant			farmer			repair person		
hair dryer			fire fighter			salesperson		
razor			garbage collector			secretary		
shaving cream			gas station attendant			taxi driver		
perfume			jeweler			truck driver		
makeup			librarian			waiter		
other:			magician			other:		

FAMILY ROLES

mother/mom/mama/mommy
father/dad/papa/daddy
brother
sister
grandmother/grandma
grandfather/grandpa
aunt
uncle
cousin
other:

*Concept labels are organized roughly by order of acquisition. In the few instances for which research evidence is available (Bangs, 1975; Carrow, 1973; Hedrick, Prather and Tobin, 1975), ages in parentheses are the youngest reported at which 80 to 90 percent of the standardization subjects passed the item on a comprehension task. Location concepts are also grouped into the five stages of acquisition reported by Morehead and Ingram (1975). In some categories, words are listed in contrasting pairs because presentation of pairs of objects, pictures, or actions illustrating gross differences along a dimension provide an effective method of teaching concept (see, for example, Blank, 1973). However, it is *important to note* that one member of a pair of word opposites (the one which occurs most frequently in the question "How ____ is it?" is generally acquired significantly ahead of the other in normal development (Clark, 1974). For most children, it is suggested that three or four categories with approximately five representative items each be under training at any one time. (Continued on p. 73.)

L-8g

LANGUAGE: VOCABULARY ACQUISITION CATEGORY LISTINGS

Student: _____   Speech–Language Clinician: _____   Date: _____

POSITION CONCEPTS	Date: Comp.	Prod.	POSITION CONCEPTS (continued)	Date: Comp.	Prod.	QUALITY CONCEPTS	Date: Comp.	Prod.
Stage I:			*Stage IV:*			hot		
in (2–0 to 2–6)			behind (5–0 to 5–6)			cold		
off (2–0 to 2–6)			ahead of (5–0 to 5–6)			dirty		
on (2–6 to 3–0)			first (5–0 to 5–6)			clean		
under (2–6 to 3–0)			last (5–0 to 5–6)			happy		
out of (2–6 to 3–0)						sad		
together (2–6 to 3–0)			*Other:*			soft (2–6 to 3–0)		
away from (2–6 to 3–0)			above			hard (3–0 to 3–6)		
			over			heavy (2–6 to 3–0)		
Stage II:			between (4–0 to 5–6)			light (3–6 to 4–0)		
up (3–0 to 3–6)			below			fast (3–0 to 3–6)		
top (3–0 to 3–6)			inside (4–0 to 5–6)			slow (3–6 to 4–0)		
apart (3–0 to 3–6)			middle			same (3–0 to 3–6)		
toward (3–0 to 3–6)			outside			different (3–6 to 4–0)		
around (3–6 to 4–0)			through			pretty		
in front of (3–6 to 4–0)			near			ugly		
high (3–6 to 4–0)			far			noisy		
in back of (3–6 to 4–0)			center			quiet		
next to (3–6 to 4–0)			corner			rough (4–0+)		
			right			smooth (4–0+)		
Stage III:			left			dark		
beside (4–0 to 4–6)			separated			light		
bottom (4–0 to 4–6)			after			warm		
backward (4–0 to 4–6)			in order			cool		
forward (4–0 to 4–6)			first			other:		
down (4–6 to 5–0)			second (6–0 to 6–6)					
low (4–6 to 5–0)			third					
			last					

*Position concepts are grouped into five stages of acquisition, according to Morehead and Ingram (1973), with ages (in parentheses) at which 80 percent of Bangs' (1975) subjects comprehended the word meaning. Since comprehension frequently precedes production by quite a bit for such concepts, one would not necessarily wait until reaching criterion on objective number 5 for a particular set of words before initiating comprehension training on new vocabulary under objectives number 1 and 2.

LANGUAGE: VOCABULARY ACQUISITION CATEGORY LISTINGS

Student: _____

Speech–Language Clinician: _____   Date: _____

QUALITY CONCEPTS	Date:	
	Comp.	Prod.
Colors:		
orange		
purple		
red		
yellow		
green		
blue		
black		
white		
brown		
other:		
Shapes:		
line		
circle		
square		
triangle		
rectangle		
diamond		
cross		
Other:		

QUANTITY CONCEPTS		Date:	
		Comp.	Prod.
big	(2–6 to 3–0)		
little	(3–6 to 4–0)		
tall	(2–6 to 3–0)		
short	(4–0 to 4–6)		
all	(2–6 to 3–0)		
none			
empty	(3–0 to 3–6)		
full	(3–6 to 4–0)		
more	(3–6 to 4–0)		
less	(3–6 to 4–0)		
fat	(4–0 to 4–6)		
thin			
skinny			
long	(4–0 to 4–6)		
short			
wide			
narrow			
most			
least			
many	(5–0 to 5–6)		
few	(5–6 to 7–0)		
whole			
half			
every			
each			
several			
almost			
as many			
a couple			
a pair			
zero			
same size			
equal			
a lot			

QUANTITY CONCEPTS (continued)		Date:	
		Comp.	Prod.
Number Words:			
one	(2–4)		
two	(3–6 to 4–0)		
three	(3–8)		
four	(4–0)		
five	(5–0 to 5–6)		

TIME & SEQUENCE CONCEPTS	Date:	
	Comp.	Prod.
today		
tomorrow		
yesterday		
morning		
afternoon		
now		
later		
soon		
before		
after		
beginning		
end		
early		
late		
always		
never		
day		
noon		
night		
week		
month		
year		
this		
next		
last		
minute		
hour		
first		
other:		

L-9 LANGUAGE:
MORPHOLOGICAL AND SYNTACTICAL RULE ACQUISITION

The short-term objectives for planning syntactic and morphological intervention programs are particularly open to individualization for students' specific needs. Children who exhibit problems in this area — even though they have been exposed to the same type of linguistic evidence as others who have learned language normally — seem to need the regularities of linguistic rules highlighted for them.

The most powerful tool we possess for assisting children to learn the "rules" (without being required to spout the rules) is to structure situations which will elicit many examples of a selected syntactic or morphological rule, but with varying content which at first places few semantic, cognitive and pragmatic demands upon the child. As the clinician leads the child to produce many sentences which are generated with the target rule, the structural similarities of the sentences become apparent in contrast to the differences, and the child is able to internalize both the target rule and new strategies for acquiring other rules.

One of the most frustrating aspects of working with children having difficulty acquiring rules of language is variability. Just when the clinician thinks the child has acquired creative use of a new rule for generating sentences, the child fails to apply the rule in a required context. Or, in analyzing a spontaneous language sample, the clinician discovers that a rule is used inconsistently. When these situations occur, the clinician must determine what factors within the child's language learning system are affecting the variability, and how they can be employed to increase the efficiency of the language intervention process.

In planning effective language intervention programs, it is helpful to consider three related concepts. One is from the normal acquisition literature, one addresses both normal and language-disordered children, and one is applied rather specifically to clinical (i.e., language-disordered) children.

1. *Form and function.* A general process of normal development, described in the unfolding of cognitive stages by Piaget (1955), and of psycholinguistic stages by Slobin (1971), is that of the dovetailing interaction of *form* and *function,* in which new forms are first used for old functions, and new functions are first expressed by old forms. That is, either newly acquired structural forms are generally used to accomplish well practiced communicative functions, or when the child has something new to communicate, the novel information or pragmatic intent is generally expressed using an old structural form. Bloom and Lahey (1978) have developed the concept further to describe language development within the dimensions of content, form and use, and have devised an integrated theory of language disorders, based upon those dimensions, which holds great clinical promise.

2. *Co-occurring restricted structures* (CORS). Muma (1973) has applied the term *co-occurring restricted structures* to describe a process observed in the language of both normal and language-disordered children when they attempt to use a sentence requiring the combined use of elements of more than one actively developing rule system. That is, when a sentence requires the application of two or more rules, which are both at the child's developing edge of competence, the increased complexity of the task may lead to the restricted use of at least one of the developing rules. Therefore, what looks like variability, when rules are analyzed individually, is discovered to have a pattern if one attempts a multidimensional analysis. For example, the child who appears to be using the auxiliary "is" inconsistently in the sentences:

> The dog gonna bite the boy,
> Man is running a help,
> Mommy gonna hit dog,
> The boy is crying,

may actually be using the adult auxiliary consistently in simple "is + Ving" contexts, and omitting it consistently when it co-occurs with the early future tense form "is + gonna + V." Further analysis of a larger corpus from this child might also yield some valuable information about restrictions upon use of determiners, such as "the" in co-occurrence with other developing structures.

3. *Grammatical overload.* The concept of *grammatical overload* was developed by Lee (1974) to emphasize the excessive sensitivity of the utterances of language-disordered children to interactions of length and complexity, and the difficulty such children experience when

attempting to handle multiple psycholinguistic tasks simultaneously. This concept was described previously, with the early language sequence, *Syntactic Acquisition of the Basic Sentence* (EL-5).

While we tend to apply the concepts of grammatical overload and co-occurring restricted structures primarily to children's uses of syntactic and morphological rules, the concepts are also applicable to other dimensions of a communicative event. When high attentional, cognitive, semantic or pragmatic demands are placed upon a language-disordered child's psycholinguistic system, restrictions tend to occur. The dovetailing of form and function, which naturally controls the multidimensional complexity of communicative events for normal children, can also be used by clinicians in planning effective language intervention programs. By managing communicative contexts carefully, we can reduce the functional demands placed upon our special clients so that they can concentrate on practicing the new forms which have been selected for training.

One of the first things the clinician must do in individualizing this sequence of short-term objectives for a particular child is to examine the child's existing communicative system carefully and select a target structure (perhaps with a number of variations) for direct attention, and some others for less direct attention. By far the best method for identifying potential target structures for syntactic and morphological development is to gather a spontaneous language sample. The clinician may then use such analysis procedures as those described by Lee (1974) or Tyack and Gottsleben (1974) along with error analysis (Edwards and Nelson 1975) and co-occurring restricted structure technique (Muma 1973) to select at least one target structure characterized by some of the following:

1. The occasion for occurrence of the structure already appears frequently in the spontaneous communication of the child and is functionally powerful for him or her. (We want to develop new forms to serve old functions first.)

2. A number of blatant errors of omission or substitution of the structure are currently in evidence.

3. Development of the structure is less mature than the overall mean length of utterance would suggest (see listing on page 81 for help in making this determination).

4. Inconsistent use of the structure can be viewed as a sign of its readiness for development and can provide material for further analysis of features which affect use of the structure by the child.

Once a target structure is selected for a child, and further analyzed, the clinician must make some decisions about which instructional objectives are necessary for the child to acquire better creative control of the structure. The three elements we must keep under control are *form* (the target structure and its variations, which are held constant or carefully varied in multiple examples), *content* (the semantic information, which usually changes from example to example), and *function* (the pragmatic purpose, which is gradually shifted from activities making few communicative demands on the child, through a desensitization process, to activities in which the target structure can be used to accomplish new functions).

The variation of functional demands can be planned to occur both in a vertical and horizontal fashion. The objectives for syntactic and morphological rule acquisition are divided vertically into two parts so that the child may be led from an establishment phase, where new forms can serve such old functions as imitation of the clinician or answering individual questions over repeated trials, to expansion and transfer phases, where the target form is combined with other developing forms which have been identified using the CORS procedure. In the later phases the newly taught form is used, sometimes in combination with other formerly difficult forms, to serve such new functions as story-telling, game-playing and conversational interaction.

While most language-disordered children seem to need such a gradual, vertical progression to achieve "carryover" (i.e., spontaneous appropriate use of the target structure), another type of functional variation is built into this objective sequence horizontally. The "structured conversation" and "structured play" columns are designed to be used by parents and teachers, as well as clinicians, for the purpose of noticing, modeling and reinforcing occasions for use of the target structure which occur naturally. The explanatory notes with sequence EL-4, *Two-Word Utterance Acquisition*, provide some suggestions for using those columns. In addition to using multiple formats for one target structure, the multiple formats can provide a way to keep track of more than one syntactic-morphological goal area at a time. The speech-language pathologist may have one target structure in direct training for a child, and she or he may be working with the classroom teacher to structure other language experiences to elicit both the target form and some additional structures which have been identified as useful for the entire class. In this way, the children are given opportunities to use their new rules when the situation is so structured that the probability of successful practice is high, and also to notice the advantages of using the rule in meaningful combination.

Specific suggestions for using the short-term objectives of this sequence follow.

L-9a Objectives

1. In normal development, comprehension generally precedes production slightly at each developmental step. However, attempts to measure comprehension of some nonpicturable, or difficult to act out, morphological and syntactic structures often lead to cognitive demands at a level beyond the stage of a child who would be using the structure normally. In such cases, it is often better to work directly on production, and to teach and measure the student's ability to discriminate appropriate semantic, syntactic and pragmatic contexts for use of the new structure as part of the ongoing program. Appropriate meaning should always be part of success criteria if one is to avoid reinforcing semantic errors inadvertently. However, if a particularly difficult concept or vocabulary item seems to be interfering with a child's use of the target structure, it should be avoided in future examples, and perhaps trained separately in a different component of the child's total program before an attempt is made to recombine that particular form and content.

2. It is likely that *objective two* could be skipped for many children since sequence EL-5, *Acquisition of the Basic Sentence,* is more specifically designed to assist children into a stage of readiness to acquire adult forms. However, the second objective might be necessary as a review step or to provide initial success which will encourage a hesitant child. For example, for the target structure, "is + Ving," the clinician could specify the following format for the modeling process, including the entire adult stimulus, the developmental imitative model, and the child's name, as a signal of the intent for the child to reproduce the model (after suggestions of Gray and Ryan 1973). Writing the model in syntactic code (explained in the glossary) facilitates presentation of varying content in the consistent form of the target structure.

   a. Clin: *"The N is Ving . . . Kim, N Ving."*
      Child: *"N Ving."*
   b. Clin: *"The N is Ving the N . . . Kim, N Ving."*
      Child: *"N Ving N."*
   c. Clin: *"The N is Ving Prep the N . . . Kim, N Ving Prep N."*
      Child: *"N Ving Prep N."*

3. An imitation step is helpful in providing the most undemanding function possible for a child who needs extra reduction of task complexity to concentrate on the phonological and other structural features of the target form. Control of utterance length is another way to assist children who have special difficulty producing the new rule. (See Bloom and Lahey 1978 for much of the research on uses of imitation, comprehension and production in language intervention; also, several chapters in Schiefelbusch 1978). For the child in the example from objective two, *objective three* could be written as an alternative approach to the development of the "is + Ving" structure, using pictures and the following stimulus and response forms. Parentheses signify that use of the article is optional for judging correctness of response.

   a. Clin: *"The N is Ving . . . Kim, is Ving."*
      Child: *"is Ving."*
   b. Clin: *"The N is Ving . . . Kim, The N is Ving."*
      Child: *"(The) N is Ving."*
   c. Clin: *"The N is Ving the N/Prep the N . . . Kim."*
      Child: *"(The) N is Ving (the) N/Prep (the) N."*

   Some children need further breakdown of the imitative modeling process, and Gray and Ryan (1973) suggest detailed steps for this procedure.

4. Although all children do not need the direct imitation provided in using objective three, it is generally helpful for the clinician to produce an indirect model of the target structure in some of the early intervention stages. Leonard (1975) suggests a way to use puppets or peers to provide the models. For a child learning the target structure "he/she," *objective four* might involve use of action pictures and such stimulus-response exchanges as:

   a. Clin: *"What is SHE doing?"*
      Child: *"She is Ving (the N/Prep the N)."*
   b. Clin: *"What is HE doing?"*
      Child: *"He is Ving (the N/Prep the N)."*
   c. Clin: *"What is SHE/HE doing?"*
      Child: *"She/He is Ving (etc.)."*

5. Gradually the child should be given more responsibility for self-generation of the target rule. For example, with the child from the illustration in objective four, *objective five* could be written:

   a. Clin: *"What is the girl/woman/lady doing?"*
      Child: *"She is Ving (etc.)."*
   b. Clin: *"What is the boy/man/father doing?"*
      Child: *"He is Ving (etc.)."*
   c. Clin: *"What is (mixed types) doing?"*
      Child: *"He/She is Ving (etc.)."*

6. As the new rule becomes stronger, mildly increased functional demands can be placed upon the child for making decisions, such as (still with the target structure "he/she"):

   a. Clin: *"Is the girl/woman/lady PN/PAdj or PN/PAdj?"*
      Child: *"She is PN/PAdj."* (e.g., Clin: "Is the woman a mother or a grandmother?" Child: "She is a grandmother.")

   b. Clin: *"Is the boy/man/father PN/PAdj or PN/PAdj?"*
      Child: *"He is PN/PAdj."* (e.g., Clin: "Is the man happy or sad?" Child: "He is happy.")

   c. Mixed types

7. In *objective seven,* the child moves from individual trials, with each response following a direct stimulus, to clustered responses. For example, if the child has been learning to form yes/no questions using "do," the clinician might set up a situation to elicit clustered examples of the target structure by saying, "I am thinking of something I want to do. Let's see how many questions before you guess it," whereupon the child must ask, "Do you want to V?" until the answer is discovered.

L–9b Objectives

1. In order to expand consistent use of a target structure, the new rule may have to be practiced directly in co–occurrence with other forms which have previously been associated with its restricted use. *Objective one* of sequence L–9b can also be used to sort out overextension problems which do not diminish quickly on their own (as many do). For example, if the child from some of the previous illustrations begins to say things such as, "Give the book to she," the clinician may set up situations with toy dolls or pictures to elicit multiple sentences of the types, "She/He gave the N to her/him."

2. *Objective two* of this subsequence can be used to provide the child with opportunities for practicing the target rule to perform a variety of new functions. The child's focus should now be led to shift from the structure of her or his responses to the semantic and cognitive demands of a task, such as story–telling (e.g., Lee, Koenigsknecht and Mulhern 1975), or conversation. This is a good time to combine elements from more than one component of the child's total program. For example, if a child has been learning such concepts as "big/little" and color words using sequence L–8, *Semantic Acquisition of Vocabulary,* and has been using sequence L–9 for learning to include the copula "is" in increasingly longer sentences, the clinician might

structure an activity to encourage such distinctions as: "This is a big *yellow* ball. This is a big *green* ball." and: "This is a *big* yellow ball. This is a *little* yellow ball."

Clinicians will find that awareness of the use of contrasting word stress is an important tool in planning language intervention strategies, especially when sentences are grouped around a single topic. Contrastive word stress then serves to signify the functional importance of key words in sentences.

Some of the elements which are most frequently omitted from the language of clinical children (e.g., verb agreement morphemes, articles, auxiliary "is," etc.) are those which carry little communicative load and are generally unstressed. The uncontractible forms of the copula and auxiliary are also acquired prior to their contractible counterparts in normal development. Awareness of such factors can help the creative speech–language pathologist or teacher restructure prepared lessons from a commercially available kit to be more meaningful by making the target structure the distinctive feature between two otherwise similar sentences. For example, in using some of the materials from the Peabody Kits (Dunn *et al.* 1966–1976), the puppet Ohno (who habitually makes mistakes) might tell the children, "This is a banana," but Mr. Pazoo or P. Mooney might counter with a model for the children, "Oh no, Ohno! That *is not* a banana. This *is* a banana." Then the children might be led to tutor Ohno with a series of examples, such as: "This *is* a banana. That *is not* a banana." "This *is* a girl. That *is not* a girl."

3–7. *Objectives three* through *seven* of sequence L–9b are designed primarily to extend use of the new target structure to perform new functions in settings beyond the speech room or classroom, and with people other than the speech–language pathologist. For most children, the only reinforcement required is social, and the best reinforcement is an adult's response to the child's communicative intent. Occasionally, however, an intermediate step may be required in which direct stimulation and a token reinforcement system are implemented by the classroom teacher or parents in a manner similar to the clinician's.

Throughout the process of language intervention, the clinician may wonder about the desirability of correcting a child's error responses. The decision of whether to do so generally depends upon the stage in which the child is engaged. In the earlier stages, when many rapid responses are elicited and 100 percent reinforced, it is usually advisable to ignore errors, fail to reinforce, and move ahead quickly. If prior steps have been sufficient, the child will notice the lack of reinforcement and get him– or herself back on track. Later in the intervention process, the clinician may have to request a repetition to signal occurrence of an error, or may even correct it overtly. Correction strategies have been found to be largely ineffectual in speeding up the process of normal development, but may save time in the remediation process if sufficient practice opportunities have been previously provided.

Potential Morphological Syntactic Target Structures Related to Student's M.L.U. (Mean Length of Utterance)

Early Development of the Basic Sentence
(Brown's Stage II – M.L.U. 2.26 to 2.75)

1. Prepositions "in" and "on" in isolated prepositional phrases.
2. Some demonstrative pronouns (this, that, these, those).
3. Some personal pronouns (me, mine, you, your, yours).
4. Some articles (a, the).
5. Some plurals (/s/ cats, /z/ bugs, /ɨz/ buses).
6. Negative terms used, but not necessarily in adult form (no, not, can't, don't).
7. Some WH-Q forms (what + doing, where).
8. Present progressive –ing on verbs (usually without auxiliary).
9. Some catenative verb forms (gonna, wanna, hafta) as semi-auxiliaries
10. Yes/no questions with appropriate inflection (but usually no subject/verb inversion).

Early Intermediate Development of the Basic Sentence
(Brown's Stage III – M.L.U. 2.76 to 3.50)

1. Adjectives after articles and other modifiers (some, other, more, one, the + Adj + N).
2. Additional prepositions (with, of, to, for) to signify semantic case.
3. Consistent use of plural and possessive morphemes (/s/, /z/, /ɨz/).
4. Irregular past verb forms (e.g., came, went).
5. Personal pronoun "I" at the beginning of sentences.
6. Additional personal pronouns (he, him, his, she, her, hers, we, us, ours, they, them, their).

Late Intermediate Development of the Basic Sentence
(Brown's Stage IV – M.L.U. 3.51 to 4.00)

1. Auxiliaries with the Main Verb (MV) in affirmative, declarative sentences.
2. Subject/verb inversion in yes/no questions.
3. Auxiliary verb form in WH-Qs (but usually not inverted, "Where the truck is?").
4. Later developing pronouns (another, something, somebody, someone, nothing, nobody, none, no one).
5. Inflections of the verb *to be* (am, was, are, were).

Late Development of the Basic Sentence
(Brown's Stage V – M.L.U. 4.01 to 5.25)

1. Regular past tense, –ed form.
2. Inflected forms of copula "be."
3. Third person singular –s on Vs.
4. Present tense modals (can, may, will).
5. Forms of "do."

6. Inflected forms of the auxiliary "be" in contractible and uncontractible forms.
7. Contractions (e.g., It's a, there's a).
8. Verb separated from adverb or participle (He took it off, He pushed her hard).
9. Auxiliary/subject inversion and the verb "do" used in forming yes/no questions.
10. Negatives formed with modals, auxiliary, or copular "be."

Later Morphological and Syntactic Development

1. Derivational endings for Nouns (e.g., –er, –ist).
2. Comparative forms of adjectives (big/bigger/biggest).
3. Past tense modal forms (could, would, should, might, must).
4. Reflexive pronouns (myself, yourself, himself, herself, itself, themselves).
5. Subject/verb inversion in WH-Qs.
6. Differentiates future/present/past semantic tenses syntactically (e.g., will jump/jumps/jumped).
7. Passive rule (The N was Ved by the N).
8. Correct forms in "ask/tell" constructions.
9. Complex verb forms using the auxiliary construction rule tense + (modal) + (have + en) + (be + ing) + Verb.

Combining Sentences

1. "And/but/or" separating two independent clauses (I fell down and I bumped my head).
2. "And" in a list or series (shoes and hat and mittens).
3. "And" to conjoin sentences with delections (He came and played with me; The boy and his brother are nice).
4. Infinitives incorporated into sentence (I want to eat a cookie).
5. "So" as a conjunction.
6. "If" as a conjunction.
7. "Because" as a conjunction.
8. Adverbial clauses (He was eating when I came).
9. Adjectival clauses (The girl with the puppy is my sister).
10. Embeddings with relative pronouns (I know *what's* going on).
11. Nominals (Hitting kids is bad).
12. Participles (She got hurt playing baseball).
13. Infinitival complements with differing subjects (I want you to come).
14. Reversible and non-reversible indirect/direct object relationships (Show the teacher the girl).
15. Semantically complex conjunction uses (except for, although, however, etc.).

References and Other Resources

Blackwell, P. M., E. Engen, J. E. Fischgrund and C. Zarca-doolas. *Sentences and Other Systems: A Language Learning Curriculum for Hearing Impaired Children.* Washington, D.C.: Alexander Graham Bell Association for the Deaf, 1978.

Blank, M. *Teaching Learning in the Preschool: A Dialogue Approach.* Columbus: Charles E. Merrill Publishing Company, 1973.

Bloom, L. and M. Lahey. *Language Development and Language Disorders.* New York: John Wiley & Sons, 1978.

Brown, R. *A First Language, The Early Stages.* Cambridge, Mass.: Harvard University Press, 1973.

Coughran, L. and B. Z. Liles. *Developmental Syntax Program.* Austin, Tex.: Learning Concepts.

Dunn, L. M., L. T. Chun, D. C. Crowell, L. G. Halevi and E. R. Yackel. *Peabody Early Experiences Kit (PEEK).* Circle Pines, Minnesota: American Guidance Service, 1976.

Dunn, L. M., K. B. Horton and J. O. Smith. *Peabody Language Development Kit (Level P).* Circle Pines, Minn.: American Guidance Service, 1965.

Dunn, L. M. and J. O. Smith. *Peabody Language Development Kits (Levels 1, 2, and 3).* Circle Pines, Minn.: American Guidance Service, 1966, 1967, 1968.

Edwards, H. T. and N. W. Nelson. Individualized language intervention programming. Paper presented at the spring conference of the Kansas Speech and Hearing Association, Hayes, Kansas, 1975.

Fokes, J. *Fokes Sentence Builder* and *Fokes Sentence Builder Expansion.* Boston, Mass.: Teaching Resources.

Gray, B. B. and B. Ryan. *A Language Training Program for the Non-Language Child.* Champaign, Ill.: Research Press, 1973.

Hallum, R. and E. H. Newhart. *Oral Language Expansion.* Freeport, N.Y.: Educational Activities, Inc.

Lee, L. L. *Developmental Sentence Analysis.* Evanston, Ill.: The Northwestern University Press, 1974.

Lee, L. L., R. A. Koenigsknecht and S. Mulhern. *Interactive Language Development Teaching.* Evanston, Ill.: The Northwestern University Press, 1975.

Leonard, L. B. Modeling as a clinical procedure in language training. *Language, Speech and Hearing Services in Schools, VI,* 72-85, 1975.

Millstein, B. *Language Structure Simplified.* Freeport, N.Y.: Educational Activities, Inc., 1978.

Morehead, D. and D. Ingram. The development of base syntax in normal and language deviant children. *Journal of Speech and Hearing Research, 16,* 330-352, 1973.

Mowery, C. W. and A. Replogle. *Developmental Language Lessons.* Boston: Teaching Resources.

Muma, J. Language intervention: Ten techniques. *Language, Speech and Hearing Services in Schools, V,* 7-17, 1971.

Muma, J. Language assessment: The co-occurring and restricted structure procedure. *Acta Symbolica, 4,* 12-29, 1973.

Muma, J. *Language Handbook: Concepts, Assessment, Intervention.* Englewood Cliffs, N.J.: Prentice-Hall, Inc., 1978.

Muma, J. *Make-Change: A Game of Sentence Sense.* Boston: Teaching Resources.

Piaget, J. *The Language and Thought of the Child.* Cleveland, Ohio: The World Publishing Company, 1955.

Schiefelbusch, R. L. (ed.). *Language Intervention Strategies.* Baltimore: University Park Press, 1978.

Semel, E. *Semel Auditory Processing Program* (SAPP). Chicago: Follett Publishing Corp., 1976.

Slobin, D. I. *Psycholinguistics.* Glenview, Ill.: Scott, Foresman and Company, 1971.

Tyack, D. and R. Gottsleben. *Language Sampling, Analysis and Training: A Handbook for Teachers and Clinicians.* Palo Alto, Calif.: Consulting Psychological Press, 1974.

Wiig, E. H. and E. M. Semel. *Language Disabilities in Children and Adolescents.* Columbus, Ohio: Charles E. Merrill Publishing Company, 1976.

L-9Aa

LANGUAGE: MORPHOLOGICAL AND SYNTACTIC RULE ACQUISITION

STUDENT: _____ AGE: _____ SCHOOL: _____ GRADE/LEVEL: _____ SPEECH–LANGUAGE CLINICIAN: _____

Date: _____

GOAL: The student will demonstrate competence for morphological and syntactic rules sufficient for comprehending and generating creative sentences appropriate to his/her age and level.

DIAGNOSTIC:
Motor _____
Cognitive _____
Affective _____
Speech _____
Communicative _____
Early Structures Showing Restriction _____
Structures Showing Consistent Control _____
Late Structures Showing Partial Control _____
Semantics _____

Audiological _____
Other _____
Formal Assessment _____
Spontaneous Sample _____
MLU _____

LONG-RANGE OBJECTIVE: The student will use the target structure(s) _____ in at least five creative utterances with the clinician in three consecutive structured play situations.

SHORT-TERM OBJECTIVES FOR THE TARGET STRUCTURE(S) _____ THE STUDENT WILL:	DIRECT REQUEST (Stim.-Response)		STRUCTURED CONVERSATION		STRUCTURED PLAY		COMMENTS TECHNIQUES EVALUATION
	Date In.	Date Accom.	Date In.	Date Accom.	Date In.	Date Accom.	
*1. demonstrate comprehension of the target structures (TS) in simple contexts spoken by the clinician by pointing to objects/pictures or performing an action unprompted (4 of 5 trials correct on each for two consecutive sessions).							
2. produce early developmental forms of the TS in the types listed below following an immediately preceding full model by clinician or peer (4 of 5 trials each for two sessions with no additional prompting).							
a.							
b.							
c.							
3. produce shortened adult forms of the TS in the types listed below following an immediately preceding full model by clinician or peer (4 of 5 trials each for two sessions with no additional prompting).							
a.							

*See note on page 85.

This form may be reproduced as often as necessary. / Copyright © 1979 by Communication Skill Builders, Inc.

L-9Ab

Date: _____
Student: _____

LANGUAGE: MORPHOLOGICAL AND SYNTACTIC RULE ACQUISITION

SHORT-TERM OBJECTIVES FOR THE TARGET STRUCTURE(S) THE STUDENT WILL:	DIRECT REQUEST (Stim.-Response)		STRUCTURED CONVERSATION		STRUCTURED PLAY		COMMENTS TECHNIQUES EVALUATION
	Date In.	Date Accom.	Date In.	Date Accom.	Date In.	Date Accom.	
3. Continued							
b.							
c.							
4. produce the TS in complete utterances of the types listed below in combination with other structures already under control, following the clinician's immediately preceding question containing an indirect model of the TS (4 of 5 trials each for two sessions, no prompting).							
a.							
b.							
c.							
5. produce the TS in complete utterances of mixed types following each question by the clinician containing no model of the target structure (4 of 5 trials each for two sessions, no prompting).							
a.							
b.							
c.							
6. produce the TS in complete utterances following "or" or "Wh" questions by the clinician which require a simple semantic decision (9 of 10 trials for two sessions).							
7. produce the TS in groups of three or more complete utterances following intermittent questions by the clinician or in story-telling type activity (4 of 5 sets for two sessions).							

MOVE TO MORPHOLOGICAL AND SYNTACTIC EXPANSION AND TRANSFER SEQUENCE

*In normal development, comprehension generally precedes production slightly at each developmental step, but attempts to measure comprehension of some nonpicturable, or difficult to act out, morphological or syntactic structures often lead to cognitive demands at a level beyond the stage of a child who would already be using the target structure normally. In such cases, it is often better to work directly on production, and to teach and measure the student's ability to discriminate appropriate semantic, syntactic and pragmatic contexts for use of the new structure as part of the ongoing program. Appropriate meaning should always be part of success criteria. The number of target structures in training at one time should be determined by the severity of the disorder.

Determination of appropriate target structures should be made through analysis of the child's communicative needs and existing language-using; for example, Lee (1974) or Tyack and Gottsleben (1974). Selection of training contexts can be made through an analysis of *CoOccurring Restricted Structures* (CORS procedure – Muma, 1973; Edwards and Nelson, 1975). Information on developmental sequences can also be found in Brown (1973) and Morehead and Ingram (1973). Suggestions for using peers as models are found in Leonard (1975). The dialogue approach is explained by Blank (1973).

This form may be reproduced as often as necessary. / Copyright © 1979 by Communication Skill Builders, Inc.

LANGUAGE: MORPHOLOGICAL AND SYNTACTIC RULE EXPANSION AND TRANSFER

Date: _____

STUDENT: _____ AGE: _____ SCHOOL: _____ GRADE/LEVEL: _____ SPEECH–LANGUAGE CLINICIAN: _____

GOAL: The student will demonstrate competence for morphological and syntactic rules sufficient for comprehending and generating creative sentences appropriate to his/her age and level in all situations.

DIAGNOSTIC:

Motor _____
Cognitive _____
Affective _____
Speech _____
Communication _____
Early Structures Showing Restriction _____
Structures Showing Consistent Control _____
Late Structures Showing Partial Control _____

Audiological _____
Other _____
Formal Assessment _____
Spontaneous Sample _____
MLU _____

LONG-RANGE OBJECTIVE: The student will use the target structure(s) _____ in at least five creative utterances with parents/teachers/peers in three different unstructured play situations with and without the clinician present.

SHORT–TERM OBJECTIVES FOR THE TARGET STRUCTURE(S) _____ THE STUDENT WILL:	DIRECT REQUEST (Stim.–Response)		STRUCTURED CONVERSATION		STRUCTURED PLAY		COMMENTS TECHNIQUES EVALUATIONS
	Date In.	Date Accom.	Date In.	Date Accom.	Date In.	Date Accom.	
1. produce the target structure (TS) in contexts with increasingly complex co-occurring syntactic structures with the clinician (4 of 5 trials each; two sessions – old function, new forms).							
a.							
b.							
c.							
2. produce the TS form in contexts requiring new functions with increasing semantic demands (4 of 5 trials each; no prompting; two sessions).							
a.							
b.							
c.							

L-9Bb

LANGUAGE: MORPHOLOGICAL AND SYNTACTIC RULE EXPANSION AND TRANSFER

Date: _____

Student: _____

SHORT-TERM OBJECTIVES FOR THE TARGET STRUCTURE(S) _____ THE STUDENT WILL:	DIRECT REQUEST (Stim.-Response)		STRUCTURED CONVERSATION		STRUCTURED PLAY		COMMENTS TECHNIQUES EVALUATION
	Date In.	Date Accom.	Date In.	Date Accom.	Date In.	Date Accom.	
3. produce the TS in complete utterances following intermittent questions by parents/teachers/others with the clinician present at a distance (4 of 5 correct on two occasions with social reinforcement but no prompting).							
4. produce the TS in complete utterances following intermittent questions by parents/teachers/others without clinician present (report of two occasions with no errors and social reinforcement only).							

USE IN UNSTRUCTURED CONTEXTS THE STUDENT WILL:	DESCRIPTION OF UNSTRUCTURED ACTIVITY	Date In.	Date Accom.	COMMENTS TECHNIQUES EVALUATION
5. demonstrate comprehension of TS in unstructured settings with the clinician by pointing/acting out/using it correctly (five trials with no errors).				
6. use TS spontaneously and correctly in all required contexts in an unstructured communication situation or spontaneous language sample with the clinician (two sessions).				
7. use TS spontaneously and correctly in all required contexts in an unstructured communication situation with parents/teacher/others (reported correct for one week).				

L-10 LANGUAGE:
EARLY SEMANTIC ACQUISITION OF YES/NO QUESTION ANSWERING

Parents ask their very young children a good many questions without expecting answers, but one of the earliest answers a child learns to give is an affirmation of desire in response to a question such as, "Wanta go bye–bye?" Answering these and later forms of yes/no questions appropriately requires a number of interrelated skills. One of the first appears when the child begins to recognize the pragmatic aspects of question asking, and to direct special attention when a sentence is heard to end with a rising intonation.

Early questions usually center around the here and now. A little one is asked if she wants to go bye-bye as her snowsuit is being pulled on, or another is asked if he has Mommy's keys while they are put in his hand. Questions of this sort are useful in checking a young, or severely handicapped, child's comprehension of linguistic and contextual clues and in drawing his or her attention to critical features of an experience (e.g., "Does Jason see the kitty?") thus providing an indirect model for something the child might say (e.g., "See kitty!").

Later, children learn to identify the accuracy of basic information about themselves ("Are you a girl?") and others ("Is Jack a girl?"). By the time such copular forms of yes/no questions are asked, the child is likely to be engaged in learning other pragmatic conventions, such as the special intonation pattern used in teasing, by which an adult signals to the child, "What I am asking you is really silly, and you should tell me 'no.'" This device can be used to help children learn new semantic rules. For example, object labeling and categorization may be taught indirectly by presenting multiple foils which are similar to an object's real label, but different in some significant manner, so that the child has an early experience with comparing and contrasting objects. A sample teaching sequence, with a picture of a whale, might include the following:

> Is this a horse? (with teasing intonation)
> No, It's too big.
> Is it an elephant? (still teasing)
> No, it hasn't got a long nose.
> Is it a puppy? (teasing again)
> No, that's really silly, isn't it?
> Is it a whale? (now seriously)
> Yes, Erin, you're so smart!
> It *is* a whale.

This objective sequence for *answering* questions is intentionally presented separately from the question *asking* objectives, which can be written into sequence L-9, *Syntactic and Morphological Rule Acquisition*. In their summary of the research related to questioning in adult–child discourse, Bloom and Lahey (1978) point out that children do not learn to ask and answer questions in general, but rather, "It appears that children learn to ask particular kinds of questions only after they learn to respond to questions of the same kind" (p. 188).

References and Other Resources

Bloom, L. and M. Lahey. *Language Development and Language Disorders*. New York: John Wiley & Sons, 1978.

Broen, P. The verbal environment of the language learning child. *ASHA Monographs, Number 17*. Washington, D.C.: American Speech and Hearing Association, 1972.

Nelson, K. Structure and strategy in learning to talk. *Monographs of the Society for Research in Child Development, 38* (Serial No. 149), 1973.

Wiig, E. H. and E. M. Semel. *Language Disabilities in Children and Adolescents*. Columbus, Ohio: Charles E. Merrill Publishing Company, 1976.

L-10

LANGUAGE: EARLY SEMANTIC ACQUISITION OF YES/NO QUESTION ANSWERING

Date: _____

STUDENT: _____ AGE: _____ SCHOOL: _____ GRADE/LEVEL: _____ SPEECH–LANGUAGE CLINICIAN: _____

GOAL: The student will be able to answer all yes/no questions within his/her semantic–cognitive ability appropriately.

DIAGNOSTIC:
Speech Characteristics _____
Audiological _____
Cognitive: Psych. Assess. _____
Piagetian Level _____
Other _____

Language: General Characteristics _____
Formal Testing _____
(ITPA subtests/Basic Concept Inv./etc.) _____
Other _____

LONG–RANGE OBJECTIVE: The student will verbally answer simple yes/no questions of mixed (reversed copula and "do") types (4 of 5 correct for two sessions).

SHORT–TERM OBJECTIVES THE STUDENT WILL:	Date In.	DESCRIPTION OF MATERIALS, COGNITIVE DEMANDS, ETC.	Date Accom.	COMMENTS TECHNIQUES EVALUATION
1. indicate affirmative/negative discrimination by gesturing rejection or desire (observed spontaneously on three separate occasions).				
2. answer "Do you want _____?" with a head shake or nod as appropriate (4 of 5 immediately following question with no prompting for two sessions).				
3. answer "Do you want _____?" with a verbal and gestural appropriate response (4 of 5 immediate responses with no prompting).				
4. verbally answer mixed "do" questions of the types "Do you want/have/see/ _____?" etc. (4 of 5 immediate, correct responses with no prompting).				
5. verbally answer reversed copula questions of the types "Is (name) here? Are you a boy/girl?" etc. (4 of 5 immediate, correct responses, no prompting).				
6. LONG–RANGE: verbally answer simple yes/no questions of mixed (reversed copula and "do") types (4 of 5 correct for two sessions).				

L-11 LANGUAGE:
LATER SEMANTIC ACQUISITION OF YES/NO QUESTION ANSWERING

It is important for the clinician to realize that it is cognitively more difficult to affirm or deny the accuracy of an identity question such as "Is this _____?" than to point out a response to a request of the sort, "Show me _____." In addition, the complexity of the task of yes/no question answering is determined much more by the difficulty of the cognitive operation required to arrive at an answer than by the form of the question itself. Questions of identical syntactic form can vary widely in the difficulty children have in answering them, and the clinician may wish to select single objectives from this sequence at different points in a child's total program to match his or her cognitive processing abilities at those times.

One way of doing so is to use the yes/no questions of formalized tests to assess not only the child's basic knowledge of word meaning, but also his or her awareness of semantic feature-matching constraints. The latter function can be accomplished using the subtest labeled "Auditory Reception" from the *Illinois Test of Psycholinguistic Ability* (Kirk, McCarthy and Kirk 1968), in which the child must decode only one syntactic structure, "Do Ns V?", but must make increasingly more difficult semantic judgments about the correctness of coupling the test noun with the given verb. Such a task may be used clinically to encourage children who have restrictions of semantic usage to practice thinking about and matching the multiple semantic features of individual nouns and verbs in a relatively abstract fashion. It can also be used to challenge the intelligence of children who are severely physically, but not mentally, impaired. For example:

> Do pianos fly?
> Do dogs fly?
> Do 727s fly?

The difficulty of answering questions of the type in *objective three* is also determined primarily by the cognitive operation required, since the syntactic decoding aspects of the task are relatively straightforward. In order to answer questions such as, "Can the boy see _____?", a student must have left the egocentricity of the sensorimotor and preoperational stages and have reached the stage of concrete operations, which allows her or him to assume another person's point of view.

Attempts to teach children to answer questions of this type before they reach the mental age of seven will often end in failure.

Another cognitive function difficult for a child is to process and retain *multiple* bits of information and to draw upon both long-term and more immediate memory to answer a series of questions. For example, *objective four* could be used to test a child's comprehension, retention and recall of facts about a story just heard. It could also be used to encourage a child to think more abstractly about nonfactual information in a situation requiring judgment. Workbook pages with regular reading series often use yes/no question-answering tasks to assess a child's reading comprehension. For example, some couplets from Level 7 (second grade) of the Ginn and Company (Clymer and Martin 1976) story, "The Bradleys Come Home," are:

1. A puppy is a little dog.
   Can a puppy cook a meal?

2. Dick was the only one home.
   Were there lots of people at home?

3. Beth's answer was exactly right.
   Did Beth know the answer?

4. Sam was leaning against the tree.
   Was Sam beside the tree?

5. Kirk doesn't have any pets.
   Does Kirk have a dog?

Yes/no questions of the type in *objective five* are included in Englemann's (1967) *Basic Concept Inventory,* a nonstandardized assessment tool that taps many of the abilities highlighted in this sequence of short-term objectives. The *Wechsler Intelligence Scale for Children — Revised* (1974) and the *McCarthy Scales of Children's Abilities* (1974) also involve verbal tasks of related types, which should not be used directly in intervention, but which can provide information as to the child's general developmental level and readiness to handle similar remediation activities.

When a student is requested to form a judgment regarding a hypothesized situation, he or she must be able to make a pragmatic decision whether sufficient shared information is available to answer the question which has been asked. An additional element of complexity occurs when the real question is presented in a syntactically more difficult context. When a cognitively immature child, or one with a linguistic processing problem, is shown a picture of the feet of children whose upper torsos are hidden behind a truck (an item on the *Basic Concept Inventory*), and is asked, "Do you *know* which child is tallest?", the answer will likely be "This one" — in answer to the embedded Wh-question — rather than "No" — in response to the yes/no question which was actually asked. Demonstrations with concrete objects and role-taking activities may help the child who is at the developing edge of competence internalize such operations. Combining tasks from this sequence with some from sequence L-12, *Semantic Acquisition of Wh-Question Answering,* may also help a child sort out the differences.

References and Other Resources

Bereiter, C. and S. Englemann. *Teaching Disadvantaged Children in the Preschool.* Englewood Cliffs, N.J.: Prentice-Hall, Inc., 1966.

Clymer, T. and P. M. Martin. The Bradleys come home. In *The Dog Next Door and Other Stories: Skill Pack.* Lexington, Mass.: Ginn and Company, 1976.

Englemann, S. *The Basic Concept Inventory: Pupil's Test and Scoring Booklet* (Field Research Edition). Chicago: Follett Educational Corporation, 1967.

Inhelder, B., H. Sinclair and M. Bovet. *Learning and the Development of Cognition.* Cambridge, Mass.: Harvard University Press, 1974.

Johnson, D. J. and H. R. Myklebust. *Learning Disabilities: Educational Principles and Practices.* New York: Grune & Stratton, Inc., 1967.

Kirk, S., J. McCarthy and W. Kirk. *The Illinois Test of Psycholinguistic Abilities* (Revised Edition). Urbana, Ill.: University of Illinois Press,1968.

McCarthy, D. *McCarthy's Scales of Children's Abilities.* New York: Psychological Corporation, 1974.

Semel, E. M. *Semel Auditory Processing Program* (SAPP). Chicago: Follett Publishing Corporation, 1976.

Wechsler, D. *Wechsler Intelligence Scale for Children — Revised* (Manual). New York: The Psychological Corporation, 1974.

Wiig, E. H. and E. M. Semel. *Language Disabilities in Children and Adolescents.* Columbus, Ohio: Charles E. Merrill Publishing Company, 1976.

L-11a

LANGUAGE: LATER SEMANTIC ACQUISITION OF YES/NO QUESTION ANSWERING

Date: _____

STUDENT: _____ AGE: _____ SCHOOL: _____ GRADE/LEVEL: _____ SPEECH–LANGUAGE CLINICIAN: _____

GOAL: The student will be able to answer all yes/no questions within his/her semantic–cognitive ability appropriately.*

DIAGNOSTIC: Speech Characteristics _____   Language: Genrl. Char. _____
Audiological _____   Formal Testing _____
Cognitive: Psych. Assess. _____   (ITPA subtests/Basic Concept Inv./etc.)
Piagetian Level _____
Other _____   Other _____

LONG-RANGE OBJECTIVE: The student will appropriately answer yes/no questions of mixed types requiring semantic and social judgments of a complexity commensurate with his/her mental age (4 of 5 untrained questions answered appropriately for two sessions).

SHORT-TERM OBJECTIVES THE STUDENT WILL:	Date In.	DESCRIPTION OF QUESTION TYPES AND REQUIREMENTS	Date Accom.	COMMENTS TECHNIQUES EVALUATION
1. verify the accuracy of "Is this _____?" questions by answering yes or no appropriately (4 of 5 correct for two sessions).				
2. verify the accuracy of "Do *Ns Verb*?" type questions using vocabulary at the child's developmental level (4 of 5 correct for two sessions; note – this type of question requires accurate semantic feature matching by the child).				
3. answer questions asked by the clinician using complex present tense forms of the auxiliary construction rule; e.g., "Can the boy see _____?" "Will you be able to _____?" etc. (4 of 5 correct for two sessions).				
4. answer questions asked by the clinician using simple or complex past tense (subjunctive) forms of the auxiliary construction rule; e.g., "Did the boy _____?" "Could the man _____?" "Would it be okay to _____?" "Should you _____?" etc., and explain qualifications of the answer (4 of 5 appropriate, two sessions).				

*Objectives in this sequence should be cross-referenced with those regarding vocabulary acquisition and cognitive development.

This form may be reproduced as often as necessary. / Copyright © 1979 by Communication Skill Builders, Inc.

L-11b

LANGUAGE: LATER SEMANTIC ACQUISITION OF YES/NO QUESTION ANSWERING

Date: _____

Student: _____

SHORT-TERM OBJECTIVES THE STUDENT WILL:	Date In.	DESCRIPTION OF QUESTION TYPES AND REQUIREMENTS	Date Accom.	COMMENTS TECHNIQUES EVALUATION
5. answer complex questions with conjoined or embedded sentences; e.g., "In this situation would it be better to ____ or ____?" "Look at this picture. Do you *know* how many ____? etc. and explain qualifications of the answer (4 of 5 appropriate for two sessions).				
6. LONG–RANGE: The student will appropriately answer yes/no questions of mixed types requiring semantic and social judgments of a complexity commensurate with his/her mental age (4 of 5 untrained questions answered appropriately for two sessions).				

L–12 LANGUAGE:
SEMANTIC ACQUISITION OF WH–QUESTION ANSWERING

As in answering yes/no questions, comprehension required to answer Wh-questions seems to rely as heavily on pre-existing cognitive skills as upon the immediate decoding of the question itself. We know that children who simply echo a Wh-question are critically impaired in comprehension and communicative interaction skills, and that there is a major difference between the type of error which occurs when a child answers a question with an out-of-category error as opposed to an in-category one. For example, a child who answers the question "Where is California?" by saying "summertime" has made a much more serious error than the child who responds "East Coast." The first child is also more likely to need the assistance of a speech-language pathologist in learning to comprehend questions.

Developmental research indicates that there are differences in the level of difficulty of the various Wh-question types. Ervin-Tripp (1970) reported the following sequence in which five children (from the age 21 months) learned to respond to questions "where," "what," "whose," and "who" and later, "why," "how," and "when." Chapman (1976) found a similar developmental ordering of Wh-question comprehension, and her results are provided with this sequence of objectives. Chapman's study involved 40 children of parents with professional occupations (i.e., an *un*representative normative group), who ranged in age from 2-0 to 5-6, including five children at each half-year age level. The task was to answer a brief question immediately following a sentence in a story. The preceding sentence gave the answer, as well as other information, and the conceptual content varied from one instance to another Therefore, the "norms" reported in the table are dependent upon the complexity of the missing information. Children's answers were scored appropriate if they included information in the conceptual category sought by the question (e.g., number or person), regardless of the form or truthfulness of the answer. Adults do not appropriately answer Wh-questions with whole sentences, but just provide the missing information (location, quantity, etc.), and responses of children should be judged by the same criteria.

The objectives of sequence L-12 are often useful with emotionally impaired or cognitively involved children who exhibit echolalia and/or semantic categorization confusions. Before asking questions of such children, it is important to give them many opportunities to establish an understanding of the associations required to answer the questions. For example, one effective way to teach children in a preprimary classroom for language-impaired children to answer "whose" and "who" questions is to assign each child in the classroom a symbol (such as cookie, star, ball, tree, etc.), which is of a specific color. Every take-home project that each child makes is identified with his or her colored symbol. The symbol also appears on the child's placemat, coat hook, job chart nametag, and notebook and carrying pouch which go back and forth between home and school. Each child sits on his or her own carpet square "mat" during relatively structured floor activities, and eventually this intensity of association leads to natural learning opportunities, not only for color recognition and appreciation of the value of symbols, but also for answering Wh-questions, such as "Whose pouch is this?" and "Who is not here today?" (when an empty carpet square is apparent in the learning circle).

Children who have difficulty developing the semantic categories necessary for appropriately answering Wh-questions may also benefit from the concrete representation of the categorical columns of the *Fitgerald Key* (Fitzgerald 1949; Pugh 1955), or the boxes of the *Fokes Sentence Builder* (1975) and *Fokes Sentence Builder Expansion* (1977). Wiig and Semel (1976) and the *Semel Auditory Processing Program* (SAPP, Semel 1976) contain a number of related activities which are applicable to this area of intervention as well.

The following table displays the developmental ordering of Wh-question comprehension reported by Chapman (1976) according to the number of children out of 40 answering appropriately (all children passed yes/no questions).

Question Type	Concept	Number of Children Answering at Least 7 out of 10 Questions Appropriately (N = 40)	Approximate Age* (In Years)	
WHAT	Object	36	2–2½	
WHAT-DO	Action	35		
WHERE	Location (Place)	34		Early Preoperational
WHERE-TO and –FROM	Location (Direction)	33		
WHOSE	Possessor	30	3	
WHO	Person	30		
WHY	Cause or Reason	30		
HOW MANY	Number	30		
WHICH				
HOW	Manner or Instrument (action) (with what)	23	3½	
HOW MUCH	Amount	18	4	
HOW LONG	Duration	18		Late Preoperational
HOW FAR	Distance	16		
HOW OFTEN	Frequency	8	4½–5	
WHEN	Time	7		

*All "norms" reported are dependent upon the complexity of the missing information (Chapman 1976). See explanatory notes with this sequence for further information.

References and Other Resources

Boning, R. A. *Specific Skill Series* (2nd edition). New York: Barnell Loft, Ltd., 1976.

Brown, R. The development of Wh-questions in child speech. *Journal of Verbal Learning and Verbal Behavior, 7,* 279-290, 1978.

Chapman, R. S. Developmental ordering of WH-question comprehension. Unpublished paper, University of Wisconsin-Madison, 1976.

Ervin-Tripp, S. Discourse agreement: How children answer questions. In Hayes, J. R. (ed.), *Cognition and the Development of Language.* New York: John Wiley & Sons, 1970.

Fitzgerald, E. *Straight Language for the Deaf.* Washington, D.C.: Alexander Graham Bell Association for the Deaf, 1949.

Fokes, J. *Fokes Sentence Builder* and *Fokes Sentence Builder Expansion.* Boston: Mass: Teaching Resources.

Moore, G. N., G. W. Woodruff and L. Ferguson. *Story Starters – Primary and Intermediate.* Woburn, Mass.: Curriculum Associates.

Pugh, B. *Steps in Language Development for the Deaf.* Washington, D.C.: Alexander Graham Bell Association for the Deaf, 1955.

Semel, E. M. *Semel Auditory Processing Program (SAPP).* Chicago: Follett Publishing Corp., 1976.

LANGUAGE: SEMANTIC ACQUISITION OF WH–QUESTION ANSWERING

STUDENT: _____ AGE: _____ SCHOOL: _____ GRADE/LEVEL: _____ SPEECH–LANGUAGE CLINICIAN: _____

Date: _____

GOAL: The student will be able to answer all WH–questions within his/her semantic–cognitive ability appropriately.

DIAGNOSTIC:
Speech Characteristics _____
Audiological _____
Cognitive: Psych. Assess. _____
Piagetian Level _____
Other _____

Language: General Characteristics _____
Formal Testing _____
(ITPA subtests/Basic Concept Inv./etc.) _____
Other _____

LONG–RANGE OBJECTIVE: The student will answer mixed WH–questions of the types _____ about short paragraphs spoken by the teacher/clinician (at least three correct questions each about five different paragraphs).

SHORT-TERM OBJECTIVES THE STUDENT WILL:	WH–QUESTION TYPE:		WH–QUESTION TYPE:		WH–QUESTION TYPE:		WH–QUESTION TYPE:		COMMENTS TECHNIQUES EVALUATION
	Date In.	Date Accom.	Date In.	Date Accom.	Date In.	Date Accom.	Date In.	Date Accom.	
1. answer WH–questions of one type asked by the clinician about immediately observable objects/pictures/actions (4 of 5 responses in correct category, but not necessarily correct information).									
2. answer WH–questions of one type asked by the clinician about immediately observable objects/pictures/actions (4 of 5 responses in correct category and with correct information).									
3. answer WH–questions of mixed types asked by the clinician about immediately observable objects/pictures/actions (4 of 5 responses in correct category).									
4. answer WH–questions of mixed types when the question word is embedded in a sentence; e.g., "Tell me who _____?" "Will you tell us where _____?" etc. (4 of 5 correct category responses about immediately observable stimuli).									
5. answer mixed WH–questions asked by someone other than the clinician about immediately observable stimuli (4 of 5 correct responses).									

L-12b

LANGUAGE: SEMANTIC ACQUISITION OF WH-QUESTION ANSWERING

Date: _____

Student: _____

SHORT-TERM OBJECTIVES THE STUDENT WILL:	WH-QUESTION TYPE:		WH-QUESTION TYPE:		WH-QUESTION TYPE:		COMMENTS TECHNIQUES EVALUATION
	Date In.	Date Accom.	Date In.	Date Accom.	Date In.	Date Accom.	
6. answer mixed WH-questions asked by the clinician about two-line "stories" (2 of 3 correct for four different stories).							
7. answer mixed questions about short paragraphs or events/people/places not present (4 of 5 correct about at least three contexts).							
8. LONG–RANGE: The student will answer mixed WH-questions of the types _____ about short paragraphs spoken by the teacher/clinician (at least three correct questions each about about five different paragraphs).							

L–13 LANGUAGE:
EARLY PRAGMATIC—FUNCTIONAL USES

Children who are able to apply pragmatic rules (both verbal and nonverbal) for communicating with others in the environment have a tremendous advantage in the language learning process. From their early use of discriminative crying and appropriate eye–to–face contact, to their later appreciation of the rules of social discourse and turn-taking, such children are more likely to be provided with, and capable of taking advantage of, communicative experiences. Our understanding of the pragmatic rules of communication is still in the early stages of evolution, but Bloom and Lahey (1978) provide a clinically useful summary of taxonomical categories and developmental stages, and emphasize the pervasive nature of pragmatic concerns with their *content, form* and *function* model of language acquisition and intervention.

The objectives of sequence L–13 are designed to isolate a few of the component skills which might be selected as appropriate for children who have cognitive and attentional deficits making it difficult for them to use contextual and conversational cues to acquire language. This sequence could also be of use with children who have been so often frustrated in previous communicative attempts that they have ceased trying. Hart and Rogers–Warren (1978) provide suggestions which are particularly suited to implementation of *objectives four* and *five* with such children in a classroom environment.

When a selectively nonverbal child requires help in learning to talk in a variety of environments, the objectives of sequence L–13 may provide a hierarchy of experiences for demonstrating progress. Once the factors in the environment that reinforce nontalking have been identified and removed, communicative expectations can be placed upon the child following the objectives of this sequence or adaptations. References for application of communicative intervention techniques with selectively mute children who can talk but will not in certain situations are Reid *et al.* (1967) and Dmitriev and Hawkins (1974).

References and Other Resources

Bates, E. *Language and Context: The Acquisition of Pragmatics.* New York: Academic Press, 1976.

Bates, E. Pragmatics and sociolinguistics in child language. In Morehead, D. and A. Morehead (eds.), *Normal and Deficient Child Language.* Baltimore: University Park Press, 1976.

Bates, E. and J. R. Johnson. Pragmatics in normal and deficient child language. A short course presented at the annual conference of the American Speech and Hearing Association, Chicago, 1977.

Bloom, L. and M. Lahey. *Language Development and Language Disorders.* New York: John Wiley & Sons, 1978.

Cole, P. and J. Morgan. *Syntax and Semantics: Vol. 3 — Speech Acts.* New York: Academic Press, 1975.

Dmitriev, V. and J. Hawkins. Susie never used to say a word. *Teaching Exceptional Children, 6,* 68-77, 1974.

Dore, J. Children's illocutionary acts. In Freedle, R. O. (ed.). *Discourse Processes: Advances in Research and Theory. Vol. I: Discourse Production and Comprehension.* Norwood: N.J.: Ablex Publishing Co., 1977.

Ervin-Tripp, S. and C. Mitchell-Kernan. *Child Discourse.* New York: Academic Press, 1977.

Hart, B. and A. Rogers-Warren. A milieu approach to teaching language. In Schiefelbusch, R. L. (ed.). *Language Intervention Strategies,* 193-236. Baltimore: University Park Press, 1978.

Li, C. *Subject and Topic.* New York: Academic Press, 1976.

Maratsos, M. Preschool children's use of definite and indefinite articles. *Child Development, 45,* 446-455, 1974.

Prutting, C. and N. Rees. Pragmatics in language. A short course presented at the annual conference of the American Speech and Hearing Association, Chicago, 1977.

Reid, J. B., N. Hawkins, C. Keutzer, S. McNeal, R. E. Phelps, K. M. Reid and H. L. Mees. A marathon behavior modification of a selectively mute child. *Journal of Child Psychology and Psychiatry, 8,* 27-30, 1967.

Searle, J. *Speech Acts: An Essay in the Philosophy of Language.* London: Cambridge University Press, 1969.

Weiman, L. Stress patterns of early child language. *Journal of Child Language, 3,* 283-286, 1976.

LANGUAGE: EARLY PRAGMATIC-FUNCTIONAL USES

STUDENT: _____ AGE: _____ SCHOOL: _____ GRADE/LEVEL: _____ SPEECH–LANGUAGE CLINICIAN: _____

Date: _____

GOAL: The student will use developing language skills as the method of choice to communicate needs/awareness/feelings with others in the environment.

DIAGNOSTIC: Motor _____

                    Cognitive _____

                    Affective _____

                    Communicative _____

MLU _____

Recept. Lang. Age/Test _____

Audiological Assessment _____

Other _____

LONG-RANGE OBJECTIVE: The child will express affirmative wants and negative wants (at least three of each) in appropriate adult structure (perfect articulation *not* required) in at least two separate contexts (speech room, classroom, home) on 9 of 10 consecutive occasions with no prompting (e.g., "I need more paint; I don't like spinach."

SHORT–TERM OBJECTIVES — THE STUDENT WILL:	Date In.	EXAMPLE STRUCTURES & CONTEXTS	Date Accom.	COMMENTS TECHNIQUES EVALUATION
1. look at speaker within two seconds when name is called from across a room which includes other people (4 of 5 times, three consecutive sessions).				
2. volunteer social greetings such as "hi" and "bye" without prompting when approaching or leaving at least two different settings/people on 4 of 5 consecutive occasions.				
3. tell own first and last name (last name optional, depending upon child's age and level) and age on five consecutive occasions when introduced by teacher, parent or clinician to a "stranger" who asks, "What's your name?" and "How old are you?"				
4. express want verbally and completely for level (perfect syntax and articulation *not* required) *in speech room* with clinician in appropriate context on 9 of 10 consecutive occasions with no prompting (e.g., "Me need more paint.")				
5. express want verbally and completely for level (perfect syntax and articulation *not* required) *in classroom* with teacher or *at home* with parent in appropriate contexts on 9 of 10 consecutive occasions with no prompting (e.g., "Me want ice cream.").				

L-13b

LANGUAGE: EARLY PRAGMATIC–FUNCTIONAL USES

Date: _____

Student: _____

SHORT-TERM OBJECTIVES THE STUDENT WILL:	Date In.	EXAMPLE STRUCTURES & CONTEXTS	Date Accom.	COMMENTS TECHNIQUES EVALUATION
6. express negative want verbally (rather than through gesturing, whining or crying) and completely for level (perfect syntax and articulation *not* required) in at least two separate contexts (speech room, classroom, home) on 9 of 10 consecutive occasions with no prompting (e.g., "Me no want spinach.")				
7. use polite forms "please" and "thank you" appropriately in at least two separate contexts (speech room, classroom, home) on 9 of 10 consecutive occasions with no prompting.				
*8. LONG–RANGE: The student will express affirmative and negative wants (at least three of each) in appropriate adult structure (perfect articulation *not* required) in at least two separate contexts (speech room, classroom, home) on 9 of 10 consecutive occasions with no prompting (e.g., "I need more paint; I don't like spinach.")				

*For some children and structures it would not necessarily be appropriate to require adult syntax as part of the criteria for correctness in the long–range objective.

L–14 LANGUAGE:
INTERMEDIATE PRAGMATIC—FUNCTIONAL ACQUISITION

A major part of learning to engage in connected discourse is the ability to sort out that information related to the topic which is "old," or shared with the listener, from that which is "new," or intended to be focused upon (Bates 1976; Li 1976). Children who have emotional and/or attentional deficits often have difficulty with the subtle rules of communication, and tend to engage in excessive topic switching without preparing their listeners. Such children also frequently exhibit unusual intonational and prosodic speaking patterns, and may sound as though they are learning English as a second language.

Bates and Johnson (1977) have pointed out that many rules previously viewed as primarily syntactic actually serve specifically pragmatic functions, and are based upon awareness of shared, versus new, information. Among these are rules for knowing:

1. when and how to use pronouns (once the referent is clear, a pronoun can, and should be substituted).

2. when "incomplete" (i.e., elliptical) sentences with deleted elements are appropriate (e.g., in answer to Wh–questions).

3. when definite and indefinite pronouns can be used (e.g., "a," "the," "this," "these," "those").

4. where to place contrastive stress to focus on new information (e.g., "Not the red hat, the *green* one.").

5. how to use adjectives and relative clauses to identify referents (e.g., "The boy in the back row is my friend.").

6. how to use conjunctions, adverbials and other elements to serve as connectors to previous discourse (e.g., "since," "and," "still," "yet," "therefore").

If a language–impaired child seems to be having specific difficulty acquiring one or more of the above rule conventions, the clinician may wish to select one of the other related sequences of objectives to be used in conjunction with this one. Comments on using contrastive stress appear in the notes with sequence L–9, *Syntactic and Morphological Rule Acquisition,* and additional suggestions for helping a child acquire relational terms appear with sequence L–16, *Semantic Acquisition of Abstract–Categorical Uses.*

Although formal evaluation is difficult in the pragmatic area, an analysis strategy suggested by Bates and Johnson (1977) could be used to count such baseline behaviors as the number of:

1. topics in a specified time period (to measure the child's adherence to the relevance postulate).

2. inaccurate pieces of information — unless spoken with sarcastic intonation (to measure the child's adherence to the belief postulate).

3. violations of the rule to supply only and all the needed information (to measure the child's adherence to the amount of information postulate).

4. misuses or omissions of any of the syntactic–pragmatic devices listed earlier in this set of explanatory notes.

5. speech act signifiers, such as acknowledgements ("mmhmm," "uh–huh," "uh–uh," "O.K.," etc.) or placeholders ("well," "uhhh," "ummm," etc.).

Stimulus materials for the pragmatic area of intervention are abundantly available in the form of sequenced story cards, language pictures, and portions of language kits (the *GOAL* Kits, and *Concepts for Communication,* for example), but the best material is usually that which is of intrinsic interest to the child. The clinician and/or classroom teacher can plan walks, art activities, cooking, science or movement experiences to provide meaningful communicative opportunities (see, e.g., Lee *et al.* 1975, and Weigel and Morningstar 1978). These activities can then be represented with sentences and simple drawings as a story chart or booklet. Experience stories written into notebooks to be taken home can be shared with parents who can reinforce the child's communicative attempts and report back to the teachers on the accuracy and appropriateness of the child's retelling of the day's events.

Notebooks which go back and forth between home and school are also a good way of obtaining reliable information about real life events which take place outside of school. Parents can be asked to draw stick pictures and write one or two sentence "stories" about something which happens at home each evening. Some examples, such as "Anne watched T.V.," or "We went to McDonalds," with very primitive drawings help parents get over their shyness as artists. The pictures can then be redrawn by the teacher at school on larger paper while he or she converses with the child about the event. The children can color portions of the picture and add details such as facial features, and they can practice telling about their events with sentences which are appropriate to their levels of development. Then each child can proudly share his or her language picture with the rest of the group during a representational activity, using at least the sentence model which has been written underneath the picture. Children love this activity, and for many it helps bridge the gap between communicating just about the "here and now," and communicating about more remote events. Parents also learn to pay attention to their own language models, to provide models which are closer to their child's developing edge of competence, and especially to spend more time enjoying their child. This language experience technique is used extensively in the Berrien County Day Program for Hearing Impaired Children, and has been developed further by Liz Garey with her preprimary aged learning- and language–impaired students in Berrien Springs, Michigan.

References and Other Resources

Bates, E. *Language and Context: The Acquisition of Pragmatics.* New York: Academic Press, 1976.

Bates, E. and J. R. Johnson. Pragmatics in normal and deficient child language. A short course presented at the annual conference of the American Speech and Hearing Association, Chicago, 1977.

Boning, R. A. *Specific Skill Series* (2nd edition). New York: Barnell Loft, Ltd., 1976.

Davis, D. E. *My Friends & Me.* Circle Pines, Minn.: American Guidance Service, 1977.

Developmental Learning Materials (publ.). *Concepts for Communication, Language Big Box* and other sequence cards and materials. Niles, Ill.: Developmental Learning Materials.

Evans, J. *Developmental Storybooks.* Niles, Ill.: Developmental Learning Materials.

Karnes, M. B. *GOAL I* and *GOAL II: Language Development Programs.* Tucson, Ariz.: Communication Skill Builders.

Lee, L. L., R. A. Koenigsknecht and S. Mulhern. *Interactive Language Development Teaching.* Evanston, Ill.: The Northwestern University Press, 1975.

Li, C. *Subject and Topic.* New York: Academic Press, 1976.

McCann, E. *Fairy Tale Plays for Oral Reading.* Woburn, Mass.: Curriculum Associates, Inc.

Modern Education Corporation (publ.). *Picture Sequence Cards, Photo Sequence Cards,* etc. Tulsa, Okla.: Modern Education Corporation.

Pirie, J. and A. Pirie. *Following Directions – Primary and Intermediate.* Woburn, Mass.: Curriculum Associates, Inc.

Teaching Resources (publ.). *Open-Ended Sequence Cards, Science Sequence Cards,* etc. Boston, Mass.: Teaching Resources.

Weigel, R. S. and J. S. Morningstar. *Learning Language Through Experience: A Manual for Therapists, Teachers and Parents.* 36 Annie Lou, Hamilton, Ohio 45013, 1978.

Worthley, W. J. *Sourcebook of Language Learning Activities.* Boston, Mass.: Little, Brown and Company, 1978.

L-14

LANGUAGE: INTERMEDIATE PRAGMATIC–FUNCTIONAL ACQUISITION

Date: _____

STUDENT: _____ AGE: _____ SCHOOL: _____ GRADE/LEVEL: _____ SPEECH–LANGUAGE CLINICIAN: _____

GOAL: The student will use developing language skills to communicate about events and people not immediately present.

DIAGNOSTIC: Motor _____
Cognitive _____
Affective _____
Communicative _____

MLU _____
Recept. Lang. Age/Test _____
Audiological Assessment _____
Other _____

LONG-RANGE OBJECTIVE: The student will tell parent an experience which took place earlier the same day, away from parent and home, with appropriate listing of main events in actual temporal order to correspond with experience story sent home by teacher or clinician (correct listing of 3 of 4 main events over three consecutive occasions).

SHORT–TERM OBJECTIVES THE STUDENT WILL:	Date In.	EXAMPLE STRUCTURES AND CONTEXTS	Date Accom.	COMMENTS TECHNIQUES EVALUATION
1. use polite forms "please" and "thank you" and polite tense forms to make in-direct requests in at least two different appropriate contexts (speech room, classroom, home) on 9 of 10 consecutive occasions with no prompting (e.g., "I would like _____; May I have _____; Do you have any more _____?"**				
2. describe pictures or objects (at least two of each) in an organized fashion, by first providing label or topic sentence and then adding less obvious details, in speech room with clinician (4 of 5 correct over three consecutive sessions).				
3. describe actual object or picture of object (at least two of each), without labeling it, in a manner which will enable a listener (clinician or normal peer, as appropriate) to label the object without seeing it (4 of 5 correct over three consecutive sessions).				
4. with the aid of pictures, retell to clinician or teacher an experience immediately after completing it (correct listing of 3 of 4 main events in correct sequence on three consecutive occasions).				
5. LONG-RANGE: The student will tell parent an experience which took place earlier the same day, away from parent and home, with appropriate listing of main events in actual temporal order to correspond with experience story sent home by teacher or clinician (correct listing of 3 of 4 main events over three consecutive occasions).				

*Children with language disorders involving syntactic rule acquisition should not be required to use such advanced forms of the auxiliary construction rule during intermediate phases of training.

L–15 LANGUAGE:
LATER PRAGMATIC—FUNCTIONAL USES

One of the most difficult tasks facing older students to whom the pragmatic rules of communication do not come easily is that of carrying on a conversation. Cognitive limitations on the ability to take the other person's point of view seem to reduce the ability of such students to adhere to the "amount of information" postulate. They either provide too much or too little information, and have difficulty determining the "all and only" necessary bits of comment. Objective sequence L–15 is designed to assist older children in developing some skill in conversational interaction and applying it for a variety of personal and vocational functions.

With this sequence, it may be appropriate to implement several of the objectives simultaneously, in a horizontal fashion. The telephone company has special equipment which can be used for the activities of *objective five*. The Roll-a-Role game (Zakich, no date) and *Let's Talk* (Sathre, Olson and Whitney 1973) offer clever suggestions for developing role–playing situations. Simple one–frame cartoon books provide stimulus material for *objective eight*, and students may be assigned to keep a diary or watch a particular T.V. program to provide material for the retelling of personal experiences or other events in *objective ten*.

References and Other Resources

Developmental Learning Materials (publ.). *Concept Town, Consumer Sequential Cards, Independent-Living Sequential Cards, People Puppets and Scripts*, etc. Niles, Ill.: Developmental Learning Materials.

Dinkmeyer, D. *Developing Understanding of Self and Others.* Circle Pines, Minn.: American Guidance Service, 1973.

Dupont, H., O. S. Gardner and D. S. Brody. *Toward Affective Development.* Circle Pines, Minn.: American Guidance Service, 1974.

Hill, H. D. and M. J. McKenna. *Outline-Building.* Woburn, Mass.: Curriculum Associates, Inc.

Incentives for Learning, Inc. (publ.). *Money Counts,* etc. Chicago: Incentives for Learning, Inc.

Kessler, R. and J. Friedland. *Following Directions – Advanced.* Woburn, Mass.: Curriculum Associates, Inc.

Laird, S. *Reading Skills Practice Kit* (especially, Main Idea, Story Analysis, Comprehension). Woburn, Mass.: Curriculum Associates, Inc.

Longhurst, T. and J. Reichle. The applied communication game: A comment on Muma's "Communication game: Dump and play." *Journal of Speech and Hearing Disorders, 40,* 315-319, 1975.

Modern Education Corporation (publ.). *Touch Type – Set 2: Common Signs.* Tulsa, Okla.: Modern Education Corporation.

Muma, J. The communication game: Dump and Play. *Journal of Speech and Hearing Disorders, 40,* 296-309, 1975.

Sathre, F. S., R. W. Olson and C. I. Whitney. *Let's Talk: An Introduction to Interpersonal Communication.* Glenview, Ill.: Scott, Foresman & Co., 1973.

Wiig, E. H. and E. M. Semel. Social perception: A component language skill. In Wiig, E. H. and E. M. Semel, *Language Disabilities in Children and Adolescents.* Columbus, Ohio: Charles E. Merrill Publishing Company, 297-319, 1976.

Zakich, R. *Roll-a-Role.* Anaheim, Calif.: Ungame Co.

L-15a

LANGUAGE: LATER PRAGMATIC–FUNCTIONAL USES

STUDENT: _____ AGE: _____ SCHOOL: _____ GRADE/LEVEL: _____ SPEECH–LANGUAGE CLINICIAN: _____

Date: _____

GOAL: The student will use effective linguistic communication skills in personal, school and vocational activities of daily living.

DIAGNOSTIC: Motor _____
Cognitive _____
Affective _____
Communicative _____

Formal Lang. Test Scores/Test _____
Audiological Assessment _____
Other _____

LONG–RANGE OBJECTIVE: The student will use appropriate communication skills in at least three adult living activities (such as obtaining a social security number, opening a checking account, applying for a charge account, etc.) first in role–play with clinician or teacher until judged appropriate, and then in real life or role–play situation with person unfamiliar to student.

SHORT–TERM OBJECTIVES THE STUDENT WILL:	Date In.	DESCRIPTION OF STIMULI AND RESPONSES	Date Accom.	COMMENTS TECHNIQUES EVALUATION
1. provide multiple pieces of personal information (including first and last name, address, age, school, grade, birthdate, brothers, sisters, pets) in response to questioning by at least two different adults (clinician, teacher, parent) with no prompting (8 of 10 correct over three consecutive occasions).				
2. demonstrate discrimination of appropriate amounts of information to provide spontaneously in casual conversation (at least two role–play contexts with clinician, teacher or friend; and at least two real or contrived contexts with person new to student) by just providing name when first introduced, and waiting to provide more personal information until asked by conversational partner, or until conversation calls for it. (No more than 1 of 5 pieces of information inappropriately volunteered over five consecutive occasions.)				
3. initiate casual conversation appropriately (in at least two role–play contexts with clinician, teacher or friend; and at least two real or contrived contexts with person new to student) by asking questions about the *other person's* interests before stating own. (No more than 1 of 5 pieces of information inappropriately volunteered over five consecutive occasions.)				
4. discriminate appropriate occasions for engaging in conversation with strangers by stating in which situations described by the clinician the student would interact and will role–play appropriate things to do and say (appropriate responses and role–play in 4 of 5 situations presented by clinician over five consecutive sessions).				

This form may be reproduced as often as necessary. / Copyright © 1979 by Communication Skill Builders, Inc.

L-15b

LANGUAGE: LATER PRAGMATIC–FUNCTIONAL USES

Date: _____

Student: _____

SHORT-TERM OBJECTIVES THE STUDENT WILL:	Date In.	DESCRIPTION OF STIMULI AND RESPONSES	Date Accom.	COMMENTS TECHNIQUES EVALUATION
5. demonstrate ability to use telephone to place an outgoing call (by listening for dial tone, dialing, waiting at least six rings for answering, asking, " Is ____ there?" and concluding conversation appropriately with statements such as "I have to go now," before saying "goodbye") and answering an incoming call (by saying, "Hello," waiting for request of caller, saying "This is he/she; Just a moment, I'll go get her/him/my mom, etc.; I'm sorry, he/she's not here right now," and concluding conversation appropriately). (At least two role–play outgoing and incoming calls completed at home and reported by parent.)				
6. provide complete and appropriate personal information in oral (and written if possible) form as would be required for a basic job interview in at least four consecutive role–play situations with clinician followed by at least three contrived situations role–played with persons new to student (no more than two pieces of unknown, incomplete or inappropriately presented information in each interview).				
7. list and/or describe at least five items recalled from list presented (orally or written) by clinician, teacher, or parent in placing an order in a retail store (at least three role–play and two real life situations), and will ask and/or answer appropriate questions of role–play and real life store workers in filling the order (no more than two pieces of inappropriate or omitted information in each situation).				
8. demonstrate appropriate uses of humor by: a. looking at a simple one–frame cartoon and reading the caption with the appropriate inflection (4 of 5 correct over three consecutive sessions). b. telling what is humorous about a one–frame cartoon or simple comic strip (4 of 5 correct over three consecutive sessions). c. retelling a simple riddle or two–line joke to two new people (three different occasions). d. reducing inappropriate laughter to no more than one instance per observation period (4 of 5 observation periods; define duration and context).				

This form may be reproduced as often as necessary. / Copyright © 1979 by Communication Skill Builders, Inc.

L-15c

LANGUAGE: LATER PRAGMATIC–FUNCTIONAL USES

Date: _____

Student: _____

SHORT-TERM OBJECTIVES THE STUDENT WILL:	Date In.	DESCRIPTION OF STIMULI AND RESPONSES	Date Accom.	COMMENTS TECHNIQUES EVALUATION
9. when displaying an emotion, state the emotion he is feeling and explain why and how he intends to deal with it to clinician, teacher, parent or friend (on at least five occasions).				
10. retell a personal experience, well-known story, T.V. program, newspaper item, etc. in appropriate temporal sequence, organized from major topic to fine detail, with no more than two elements out of sequence, to at least two separate listeners (clinician, teacher, parent, friend) on 4 of 5 consecutive occasions).				
11. LONG–RANGE: The student will use appropriate communication skills in at least three adult living activities (such as obtaining a social security number, opening a checking account, applying for a charge account, etc.) first in role-play with clinician or teacher until judged appropriate, and then in real life or role-play situation with person unfamiliar to student.				

L-16 LANGUAGE:
SEMANTIC ACQUISITION OF ABSTRACT/ CATEGORICAL USES

The objectives for this sequence to develop abstract/ categorical uses of language are written so that they can be applied to a number of cognitive levels. The planning of instructional activities for this area is rather controversial, since most normal developmental theorists, particularly those who follow in the tradition of Jean Piaget, insist upon an orderly unfolding of stages which is relatively resistant to "teaching," or being hurried. In addition, language and cognitive development are typically viewed as separate phenomena, particularly in the very early stages, by Piagetian psychologists. This second viewpoint has been historically questioned by the Russian psychologist Vygotsky (1962), and more recently has been receiving a lot of attention from psycholinguists, many of whom are experimenting with application of the cognitive theories of *adaptation* and *assimilation* to the language acquisition process itself, and are tending to view language acquisition as one aspect of cognitive development. The complex interactions of language and cognition at the later developmental stages, and particularly in the operations of formal thought and logical reasoning, are far less controversial, but certainly not totally understood.

Planning activities for developing abstract/categorical uses of language does make sense if one views the "teaching" process of speech and language intervention to be primarily one of assessing a child's readiness level, arranging the linguistic and nonlinguistic aspects of the environment so that the critical features stand out, and encouraging the child to engage in hypothesis testing and concept formation with the help of specific modeling and feedback. Language-impaired children who have excessive difficulty with semantic and cognitive processing may even be led to use their expressive syntactic abilities to code verbal directions to themselves, first vocally and then subvocally, and thus increase their selective attention for perceptual-motor and problem-solving tasks (Douglas *et al.* 1976; Miechenbaum 1977). Other resources for suggestions on techniques for facilitating active learning by children are Blank's (1973) *Teaching Learning in the Preschool,* and Wiig and Semel's (1976) chapter entitled, "Remediation of Cognitive Processing Deficits."

Successful intervention in this area requires an awareness by the clinician of the child's current level of cognitive functioning, since only those concepts which represent a slight stretching of the child's current level of functioning are likely to be learned. Speech-language pathologists are not cognitive psychologists, but it is possible for them to acquire an understanding of the basic outline of the Piagetian stages of development using a source, such as Beard (1969), and the notes included with this sequence. Recent attempts have also been made by several in the field of speech-language pathology to structure the fundamentally informal nature of Piagetian assessment tasks to be more clinically useful with language-impaired students (Chappell and Johnson 1976; Yates 1977; Dihoff 1976).

Some of the cognitive tasks which might be incorporated into this sequence of objectives would be those designed to develop abilities in the areas of:

1. *Classification.* The child groups pictures or objects together based upon some common trait. Classification based upon perceptual attributes seems to be acquired first.

2. *Multiple classification.* The child groups a set of objects in more than one fashion; for example, first based upon shape, then upon color, and finally upon size. Later, the child selects an item to fit into a matrix so that it corresponds by one shared feature with other items in its vertical column and by another shared feature with other items in its horizontal row.

3. *Class inclusion.* The child views an array, such as fruit, and labels the similarity, such as "all fruit." Later the child answers questions from an adult by stating that there is more fruit than oranges, and that if the adult took all of the fruit and the child took the rest, the adult would have more — since all of the objects were fruit in the first place.

4. *One-to-one correspondence.* The child states that two sets of objects are still equal in number if their one-to-one correspondence has been established, even if the members of one set are spread farther apart after the members of the two sets have been matched.

5. *Conservation.* The child observes a demonstration wherein one of two items equal in *mass, weight, length* or *liquid quantity* is made

to appear perceptually different, and states that the quantity remains the same (i.e., neither the adult nor the child has "more" now) even though (a) one ball of clay has been flattened, or (b) divided into smaller portions, or (c) one set of sticks has been laid in crooked fashion rather than end–to–end, or (d) the liquid from one glass has been poured into a taller, thinner glass. Later, the child explains the conservation of quantity using concepts of:

Invariant quantity. The child states that nothing has been added or taken away.

Compensation. The child states that something being done to one part of the material is compensated for in another dimension.

Reversibility. The child states that if the substance were returned to its original form, it would be the same.

6. *Seriation.* The child looks at a series of sticks, cylinders, rings, etc., of graduated length or size, and reproduces the sequence in correct order after it has been scrambled.

7. *Class inclusion, with grouping by ascending hierarchy.* The child groups picture cards under ascending category labels, such as *duck, bird and animal,* or *dog, mammal and animal,* and answers questions about the appropriateness of stacking pictures of different types of birds under the *bird* label, but not under the *duck* label, etc.

In addition to maintaining an awareness of the cognitive functions children must acquire, the speech–language clinician needs a strategy for organizing the abstract linguistic processes with which they are so closely intertwined. In fact, this is an area in which linguistic production is sometimes thought to precede cognitive comprehension. For example, normal children may be observed to ask "why" questions before they can answer them (Blank 1975) and to use the tools of logical thought (such as abstract conjunctions) before they can think logically. Intervention in this area should be closely coordinated with that of sequence L–8, *Semantic Acquisition of Conceptual Vocabulary.* Wiig and Semel (1976) additionally provide both an outline of component linguistic relationships and some specific suggestions for remediation in their chapter on cognitive processing deficits.

Major categories which should be considered, particularly for older students, include:

1. Comprehension of the subtle differences between vocabulary items representing different parts of speech:

    a. *Verbs,* including fine distinctions between verbs which are close in meaning (e.g., "cut," "slice," "carve").

    b. *Adjectives,* including use of contrastive stress to signify meaning, order of sequence for multiple attributes used to describe a noun, identification of a selected attribute in answer to Wh–questions, use of comparative morphemes —er and —est, etc.

    c. *Pronouns,* both personal and demonstrative, including recognition of the effects of shift of emphatic stress upon meaning (Maratsos 1973), as in the examples:

    John hit Harry and then *Brynn* hit him.
    (Harry is hit by Brynn.)

    John hit Harry and then Brynn hit *him.*
    (John is hit by Brynn.)

    d. *Prepositions,* especially including later developing idiomatic uses (of which there are many — Fries 1952; Streng 1972), such as:

    Mabel is in the circus.
    Susan is at the circus.
    That act came from the circus.
    The investigator is looking into the circus.

2. Comprehension of abstract word relationships among:

    a. *Antonyms.*
    b. *Synonyms.*
    c. *Homonyms.*
    d. *Multiple-meaning words.*

3. Semantic classification, including a progression of abilities, such as:

    a. *Functional word definitions.*

    b. *Multifaceted word definitions.*

    c. *Comparing and contrasting* related and unrelated words on a concrete level.

    d. *Comparing and contrasting* related and unrelated words on a more abstract level.

    e. *Placing labels* in a hierarchical relationship according to their superordinate/subordinate status.

4. Processing verbal analogies. Wiig and Semel (1976, p. 181) provide 16 categories of relationship and suggest strategies for ordering the remediation process.

5. Processing logico–grammatical relationships. Wiig and Semel (1973, 1974) report the following order of difficulty:

    a. *Comparative relationships.* ("John is bigger than Stewart.")

b. *Passive relationships.* ("The girl was introduced by Claire.")

c. *Spatial, age or other multiple ordering relationships.* ("Mindy is younger than Ali, and Ali is younger than Brandy. Who is in the middle?")

d. *Temporal–sequential relationships* signified by using such qualifiers and conjunctions as:
   (1) when, while, after, before, during, since, etc. (signifying temporal relationships);
   (2) all, none, some, any, all except, all but, not, neither . . . nor, etc. (signifying inclusion/exclusion); and
   (3) if . . . then, because, so, etc. (signifying cause/effect).

6. Comprehension of semantic transformation devices, such as:

a. *Idioms.* ("The price of meat is skyrocketing.")

b. *Metaphors.* ("She felt as high as a kite.")

c. *Proverbs and platitudes.* (Aesops Fables, morals of stories.)

7. Comprehension of semantic relationships in sentences and paragraphs which include:

a. *Inconsistencies and absurdities.* ("He was so cold, he took off his jacket.")

b. *Ambiguities.* ("John hates shooting guns.")

c. *Hyperbole.* ("She's the best runner in the whole world.")

Additional resources for this area of remediation are Semel's (1973) *Sound Order Sense* program and the *Semel Auditory Processing Program* (1976). The Boning (1976) *Specific Skills Series,* and Worthley's (1978) *Sourcebook of Language Learning Activities* also include some good practice material. Inhelder, Sinclair and Bovet (1974) suggest intervention strategies from a Piagetian point of view, and Bereiter and Englemann (1966) have developed a procedure for leading students to draw logical conclusions about relationships by using concrete materials which are multiply classified by shape, size and color.

A Summary of Piaget's Developmental Stages

I. SENSORI-MOTOR (Birth–2 Years)	II. CLASSES, RELATIONS & NUMBERS (2–12 Years) A. Pre-Operational (2–7 Years)		B. Concrete Operations (7–12 Years)	III. FORMAL OPERATIONS (12–15 Years)
	1. Pre-Conceptual 2–4 Years)	2. Receptive (4–7 Years)		
		MAJOR CHARACTERISTICS		
Equipped with a few innate reflexes and innate tendencies to organize actions into SCHEMAS. Does not INTERNALIZE – rather, behavior is based on actions and transient perceptions. No evidence of MEMORY as adults experience it. LATE: begins to recognize resemblances between actions in situations; prerequisite to the development of REPRESENTATIVE SCHEMAS. Development of LANGUAGE at the end of the period partially replaces ACTION both by speed and flexibility.	Though thinking is REPRESENTATIONAL, it is not yet conceptual. There are gains in ability to represent one thing by another. Verbal signs are individually catalogued and vary in meaning, depending on setting. (Daddy may be anyone who lights a pipe.) Imitation is largely unconscious: Q. Who told you that? A. I just thinked of it. TRANSDUCTIVE (disconnected) reasoning – child sees resemblances, but does not understand how to make classes and see their interrelationships. EGOCENTRIC. Schemas still derive from his own actions.	Children begin to give reasons for their beliefs and to form some concepts, but thinking is still not operational (i.e., they still cannot make comparisons mentally but must build them up one at a time in action. ACTION is not yet INTERNALIZED). Thinking depends on PERCEPTUAL judgments and may not always lead to the same conclusion (in time or person; i.e., it is non-reversible). The child is unable to keep more than one relationship in mind at a time. Child remains EGOCENTRIC. Relative terms are given absolute meanings.	Children begin to internalize ideas of classes and series. They can explain classes and understand relationships between them. Thinking still depends on ACTION, though they can now use OPERATIONS in imagination – these will depend on imagery at first. Operations are logical – REVERSIBLE. Problem-solving continues by TRIAL & ERROR. EGOCENTRICITY decreases and is replaced by cooperative play. Content with partial explanations of environment.	This period begins through increased collaboration with others. Thinking is more abstract. Can use elements alone, with dealing with object imagery of objects. Considers many viewpoints. Able to survey many possibilities, form theories and conceive imaginary worlds. Problem-solving by hypothesis testing probabilities. Seeks global explanations and general laws.

I. SENSORI-MOTOR (Birth–2 Years)	II. CLASSES, RELATIONS & NUMBERS (2–12 Years) A. Pre-Operational (2–7 Years)		B. Concrete Operations (7–12 Years)	III. FORMAL OPERATIONS (12–15 Years)
	1. Pre-Conceptual (2–4 Years)	2. Receptive (4–7 Years)		
	MAJOR CHARACTERISTICS			
	EGOCENTRIC SPEECH USED TO: (1) direct action; (2) replace actions in imaginary play. Also uses SOCIAL SPEECH in giving information, asking and answering questions, argument, criticism, commands and requests.			
	OBSERVATIONAL EVIDENCE			
First evidence of acquired ADAPTATION is ability to suck thumb at will. 6 mos.: looks at hand that drops falling object. 8 mos.: looks to floor if sees start of fall. CAUSALITY – uses body actions to produce continuation of unconnected events. Amuses self by putting things repeatedly in and out of box, dropping objects and finding them again. Begins to study reversible displacement. Moves objects away from face and back again. Begins to recognize constancy of objects – will look for ball that has rolled in new place. CAUSALITY – now sees that adult may cause activity. Places adult hand in position to snap fingers.	Child's sense of identity changes depending on age, clothes, situation; does not recognize self in mirrors, photos. Animistic – attributes life to inanimate objects (this may be culture-bound trait). Play – imitates animate and inanimate objects. Uses EGOCENTRIC SPEECH. *At first* of period will put colored shapes that "go together" into a design that interests him. Late in period will arrange by shape *or* color but not both. Thinks shapes of objects change, depending upon his point of view. By 3½ years: copy a short line of beads by matching individual items but fail to put them in correct order, getting only adjacent pairs correct, regardless of overall sequence.	Still have NO concept of CONSERVATION. ooo ≠ o o o Cannot keep account of both length and number. ⊟⊟ ≠ ⊟ Can describe dimensions, but cannot see how they compensate for one another (e.g., with clay balls). o ≠ ⌒o On "draw the largest and smallest square," intuitive children draw successively large squares. By 6 or 7 years: begin to have concept of 1:1 correspondence and permanence of the relationship, BUT will still say beads put into tube would make longer necklace than beads in dish because "it is tall." ▯ ≠ ⬭ In *series* (as in stick length) compares only 2 items at a time. ‖ıl‖ıl	Puts series of sticks in order by surveying, then ordering according to length. ‖ılıı Can classify on more than one relationship simultaneously – CONSERVATION. Fewer attempts at imaginary play and greater desire to model reality. Limitations in verbal reasoning: "Edith is fairer than Susan; Edith is darker than Lily; who is the darkest of the three?" – up until 12 years child considers one statement at a time. Difficulty in explaining proverbs – instead of seeing symbolism, relates to own experience. Language may exceed conceptual development.	Begins to understand relative values. Moral judgments look extreme. Begins to reason in propositions: If _____ , you would_____ . Develops concepts of infinity (e.g., believes line can be subdivided an infinite number of times).

References and Other Resources

Beard, R. M. *An Outline of Piaget's Developmental Psychology for Students and Teachers.* New York: Basic Books, 1969.

Blank, M. *Teaching Learning in the Preschool: A Dialogue Approach.* Columbus: Charles E. Merrill Publishing Company, 1973.

Blank, M. Mastering the intangible through language. In Aaronson, D. and R. Rieber (eds.). Developmental psycholinguistcs and communication disorders. *Annals of the New York Academy of Sciences, 263,* 44-58, 1975.

Bereiter, C. and S. Englemann. *Teaching Disadvantaged Children in the Preschool.* Englewood Cliffs, N.J.: Prentice-Hall, Inc., 1966.

Boning, R. A. *Specific Skill Series* (2nd edition). New York: Barnell Loft, Ltd., 1976.

Chappell, G. E. and G. A. Johnson. Evaluation of the cognitive behavior of the young nonverbal child. *Language, Speech and Hearing Services in Schools, VII,* 17-27, 1976.

Developmental Learning Materials (publ.). *Concepts for Communication, Treesorts, Classification Cards — People and Things,* etc. Niles, Ill.: Developmental Learning Materials.

Dihoff, R. Standard and nonstandard applications of Piagetian assessment procedures. Unpublished paper, University of Wisconsin — Madison, 1976. To appear in Miller, J. F. (ed.), *Assessing Children's Language Behavior: A Developmental Process Approach.*

Dobbs, S. S. *Homonym Puzzles.* Woburn, Mass.: Curriculum Associates, Inc.

Douglas, V. I., P. Parry, P. Marton and C. Garson. Assessment of a cognitive training program for hyperactive children. *Journal of Abnormal Child Psychology, 4,* 389-410, 1976.

Englemann, S. *The Basic Concept Inventory: Pupil's Test and Scoring Booklet* (Field Research Edition). Chicago: Follett Educational Corporation, 1967.

Forest, R. G. *Collective Nouns, Antonyms and Synonyms.* Woburn, Mass.: Curriculum Associates, Inc.

Fries, C. C. *The Structure of English: An Introduction to the Construction of English Sentences.* New York: Harcourt, Brace, Jovanovich, 1952.

Furbush, P. M., E. A. Ross and D. D. Durrell. *Thirty Lessons in Outlining — Level I, Organization Skills: More Lessons in Outlining.* Woburn, Mass.: Curriculum Associates, Inc.

Hill, H. D. and M. J. McKenna. *Outline-Building.* Woburn, Mass.: Curriculum Associates, Inc.

Inhelder, B., H. Sinclair and M. Bovet. *Learning and the Development of Cognition.* Cambridge: Harvard University Press, 1974.

Johnson, D., F. DiGiammarino, M. Bradley and C. Corcoran. *Word Analysis: Levels 1, 2, 3 & 4.* Woburn, Mass.: Curriculum Associates, Inc.

Johnson, D. J. and H. R. Myklebust. *Learning Disabilities: Educational Principles and Practices.* New York: Grune & Stratton, Inc., 1967.

Karnes, M. B. *GOAL I* and *GOAL II: Language Development Programs.* Tucson, Ariz.: Communication Skill Builders.

Laird, S. *Reading Skills Practice Kit — I, Reading Skills Practice Kit — II,* and *Laird Comprehension Skills Program.* Woburn, Mass.: Curriculum Associates, Inc.

Maratsos, M. B. The effects of stress on the understanding of pronominal co-reference in children. *Journal of Psycholinguistic Research, 2,* 1-8, 1973.

Meichenbaum, D. *Cognitive-Behavior Modification: An Integrative Approach.* New York: Plenum Press, 1977.

Modern Education Corporation (publ.). *Cognitive Development Workbooks, 40-Fours, Problem-Solving Cards.* Tulsa, Okla.: Modern Education Corporation.

Moore, G. N. and G. W. Woodruff. *Elaborative Thinking Sets.* Woburn, Mass.: Curriculum Associates, Inc.

Morley, S. A. *Dimensions of a Word.* Woburn, Mass.: Curriculum Associates, Inc.

Scinto, J. *Homonym Tales.* Woburn, Mass.: Curriculum Associates, Inc.

Semel, E. M. *Semel Auditory Processing Program* (SAPP). Chicago: Follett Publishing Corp., 1976.

Smith, F. *Comprehension and Learning: A Conceptual Framework for Teachers.* New York: Holt, Rinehart & Winston, 1975.

Streng, A. *Syntax and Hearing: Applied Linguistics for Teachers of Children with Language and Hearing Disabilities.* Washington, D.C.: Alexander Graham Bell Association for the Deaf, 1972.

Teaching Resources (publ.). *Association: Sets 1 and 2, Categories, Functions, Parts and Wholes,* etc. Boston: Teaching Resources.

Vygotsky, L. S. *Thought and Language.* Cambridge, Mass.: The M.I.T. Press, 1962.

Wiig, E. H. and E. M. Semel. Comprehension of linguistic concepts requiring logical operations. *Journal of Speech and Hearing Research, 16,* 627-636, 1973.

Wiig, E. H. and E. M. Semel. Development of comprehension of logico-grammatical sentences by grade school children. *Perceptual and Motor Skills, 38,* 171-176, 1974.

Wiig, E. H. and E. M. Semel. Logico-grammatical sentence comprehension by adolescents with learning disabilities. *Perceptual and Motor Skills, 38,* 1331-1334, 1974.

Wiig, E. H. and E. M. Semel. *Language Disabilities in Children and Adolescents.* Columbus, Ohio: Charles E. Merrill Publishing Company, 1976.

Worthley, W. J. *Sourcebook of Language Learning Activities.* Boston, Mass.: Little, Brown and Company, 1978.

Yates, J. Piagetian interview activities. Handout from short course presented at the annual conference of the American Speech and Hearing Association, Chicago, 1977.

L-16

LANGUAGE: SEMANTIC ACQUISITION OF ABSTRACT/CATEGORICAL USES

Date: _____

STUDENT: _____ AGE: _____ SCHOOL: _____ GRADE/LEVEL: _____ SPEECH–LANGUAGE CLINICIAN: _____

GOAL: The student will be able to use language as a tool for thinking at a level commensurate with his/her cognitive development.

DIAGNOSTIC: Speech Characteristics _____
    Audiological _____
    Cognitive: Psych. Assess. _____
    Piagetian Level _____
    Other _____

    Language: General Characteristics _____
      Formal Testing _____
      (ITPA subtests/Basic Concept. Inv./etc.) _____
      Other _____

LONG–RANGE OBJECTIVE: The student will verbally explain the target conceptual relationship or cognitive function using two different sets of materials.

*SHORT–TERM OBJECTIVES FOR THE STUDENT WILL:	Date In.	DESCRIPTION OF MATERIALS, COGNITIVE TASK, VERBAL TASK	Date Accom.	COMMENTS TECHNIQUES EVALUATION
1. demonstrate the target cognitive ability by reproducing an example activity demonstrated by the clinician using clear–cut concrete materials (using at least two different sets of materials).				
2. reverse the teacher/student role by instructing the clinician in the same manner the student was instructed under step 1 to manipulate material/perform an action/etc.				
3. demonstrate extension of the concept/cognitive function by manipulating new sets of materials with less obvious demonstration of the conceptual relationship (two new sets of materials).				
4. verbally explain the conceptual relationship or cognitive function performed by using appropriate conjunctions, ordering morphemes, etc. while actually manipulating the materials (at least three of the sets used earlier).				
5. verbally explain the conceptual relationship/cognitive function or answer questions about it without actually manipulating the materials (this skill appears during the period of concrete operations and beyond, 7–12 years plus).				
6. LONG–RANGE: The student will verbally explain the target conceptual relationship or cognitive function using two different sets of materials.				

* Lists of developmental cognitive skills (based on Piagetian stages) related to communicative competence have been compiled by Dihoff (1976) and Yates (1977).

AP–17 AUDITORY PROCESSING: DISCRIMINATION

Auditory discrimination problems and other auditory processing deficits often go hand–in–hand with language disorders and learning disabilities. Many diagnostic tools and remediation approaches have been constructed on the theory that skills such as auditory discrimination, temporal sequencing and short-term memory are necessary prerequisites to the development of language, and that remediation of the component skills will often improve overall language ability. However, Bloom and Lahey (1978) provide a critical summary of much of the research designed to assess the relationships of language ability and auditory skills and conclude that (1) although an association has been demonstrated, (2) there is more evidence that generalized language disability, or some common basic deficit, "causes" reduced auditory sequential memory, for example, than vice versa, and that (3) there is no body of evidence to support the practice of remediation of specific abilities (Bortner 1971).

Such cautionary statements make it questionable whether a speech–language pathologist should ever select sequences AP-17, *Discrimination,* or AP-18, *Short-Term Sequential Memory.* The sequences are included primarily for their usefulness in assessing a student's development along the dimensions, and for the contribution they make to the intervention programs of children with hearing deficits. However, Katz (1978) also summarizes recent research on the role such supposedly peripheral problems as intermittent hearing loss caused by otitis media may play in the etiology of learning disabilities. He points out that "Stimulating a deprived ear or one with conductive hearing loss seems to improve hearing function" (p. 885). The other major reason for including the auditory processing sequences is to assist children who have severe reading and speaking disabilities in developing the sound-symbol association skills necessary to assist in the complex process of learning to read and to articulate difficult words.

A number of years ago, Myklebust (1954) suggested a hierarchical model for the successive acquisition of language processing in the modalities: first in listening, then speaking, then reading, and finally writing. However, evidence suggests that the model should not be viewed as totally unidirectional. Most of us can relate to the experience of becoming able to pronounce an unusual name

better when we know how it is spelled, and of observing first graders who have had /f/ and /θ/ confusions sort them out spontaneously in the process of learning to read. The motor theory of speech perception (e.g., Lane 1965) can partially account for such phenomena, and the contribution that production ability can make to the development of discrimination is discussed in relation to sequence A–7, *Articulation: Phoneme Acquisition.*

A model which recognizes the bidirectional nature of language acquisition in the four major modalities provides a better theoretical basis for remediating some of the higher level reading and speaking problems some children exhibit. The *Auditory Discrimination in Depth* program (Lindamood and Lindamood 1969) can serve as an effective way of teaching the analytical components of the reading process and helping children with phonological sequencing problems develop strategies for decoding and encoding complex sound combinations as well. The *Goldman–Lynch Sounds & Symbols Development Kit* (1971) is designed to develop similar abilities in younger children, and the Semel (1970) *Sound-Order-Sense* materials and *Semel Auditory Processing Program* (1976) provide multi-level activities for application to this and broader language areas.

Subobjectives one and two with this auditory processing sequence are designed using the principles of the McGinnis (1963) Association Method. The Association Method has been widely criticized as a total language program because of its synthetic approach (and often synthetic products). However, it can yield excellent results in developing reading ability in older children with some —although restricted — language ability who have been unable to learn to read using traditional methods. It can also assist children with severe misarticulations to sort out the complicated process of sequencing sounds and syllables in difficult-to-pronounce words. This method should not be used alone, but in combination with other, experience–based, meaningful learning opportunities. Smith (1975) and Kavanagh and Mattingly (1972) provide models for understanding the interrelationships of speaking and reading, and emphasize the complex strategies employed by competent readers, who use multiple cueing systems, phonics, structure and context to derive meaning from what they read.

The form and function principles discussed in relation to sequence L-9, *Morphological and Syntactic Rule Acquisition,* apply in this area as well.

Most of the objectives of the subobjective sequences are reasonably self-explanatory and adaptable to different approaches, but if they are to be used in the style of the Association Method, Monsees (1972) and DuBard (1974) should be consulted for a further explanation of the more recent techniques. The original version and DuBard's encourage the use of cursive writing because it (a) reduces common reversals, (b) assists children who have spatial relationship problems, (c) develops the concepts of words and word boundaries, and (d) transfers easily to the ability to read manuscript later. Monsees (1972) suggests a modified manuscript method, and *D'Nealian Handwriting* (Thurber and Jordan 1978), a similar modification, is being suggested for regular education students.

The primary visual arrays used to present activities at the various instructional levels are:

1. *Scatter drills* — used with single sound-symbol combinations (with consonants written in one color; vowels in another).

p   t

o-e

m   a

2. *Drop drills* — used to practice CV and VC syllable combinations (consonants and vowels are written with different colors of chalk).

pa

pa

pa

3. *Blending drills* — used to help students begin to blend isolated phonemes into smooth syllables, moving the finger gradually from consonant to vowel as each is produced.

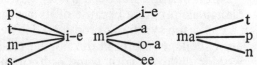

4. *Cross drills* — used to introduce alternate spellings and meaningful words.

ba-e	bay	bai
bote	boat	bowt
bi-e	by	bigh
ba-e	bay	bai

In cross drills, the children first learn by example that all elements in a row are pronounced the same. Then they are introduced to alternate spellings, still pronounced in the same way as the already learned primary spellings used in that row. Finally, word meanings are associated with sound

patterns. The children come to know that pictures turned backwards during the cross drill represent at least one of the units on the board which is a real word. Suspense builds up and it becomes a game to determine which of the sound patterns is meaningful.

In the original version of the McGinnis method, this process is used simply to introduce words for the first time, and spontaneous attempts by the children at higher levels are generally discouraged. When the approach is used as suggested here — to develop reading and speaking skills upon a preexisting, though restricted, language foundation — children can be allowed to work at as high a level as possible without reducing program effectiveness. Although the association activities themselves work best when they are tightly structured and attention is kept directly on the task at hand, spontaneity and meaningfulness can be encouraged in the total language program. In fact, competence with meaningful uses of language provides a good pathway to the successful decoding of the more structural aspects of its oral and written forms.

References and Other Resources

Bloom, L. and M. Lahey. *Language Development and Language Disorders.* New York: John Wiley & Sons, 1978.

Bortner, M. Phrenology, localization, and learning disabilities. *Journal of Special Education, 5,* 23-29, 1971.

Developmental Learning Materials (publ.). *Auditory Perception Training* and other auditory skills materials. Niles, Ill.: Developmental Learning Materials.

DiSimoni, F. *The Token Test for Children.* Boston: Teaching Resources.

DuBard, E. *Teaching Aphasics and Other Language Deficient Children: Theory and Application of the Association Method.* Hattiesburg, Miss.: University Press of Mississippi, 1974.

Goldman, R. and M. E. Lynch. *Goldman-Lynch Sounds & Symbols Development Kit.* Circle Pines, Minn.: American Guidance Service, 1971.

Incentives for Learning (publ.). *Sound Matching.* Chicago: Incentives for Learning.

Johnson, D. J. and H. R. Myklebust. *Learning Disabilities: Educational Principles and Practices.* New York: Grune & Stratton, Inc., 1967.

Katz, J. The effects of conductive hearing loss on auditory function. *Asha, 28,* 879-886, 1978.

Kavenagh, J. F. and I. G. Mattingly. *Language by Ear and by Eye: The Relationships Between Speech and Reading.* Cambridge, Mass.: The M.I.T. Press, 1972.

Lane, H. The motor theory of speech perception: A critical review. *Psychological Review, LXXXII,* 275-309, 1965.

Lee, D. M. and R. V. Allen. *Learning to Read Through Experience* (2nd edition). Englewood Cliffs, N.J.: Prentice-Hall, Inc., 1963.

Lindamood, C. H. and P. C. Lindamood. *Auditory Discrimination in Depth.* Boston: Teaching Resources, 1969.

McGinnis, M. A. *Aphasic Children: Identification and Education by the Association Method.* Washington, D.C.: Alexander Graham Bell Association for the Deaf, 1963.

McNeil, M. R. and T. E. Prescott. *Revised Token Test.* Baltimore: University Park Press, 1978.

Modern Education Corporation (publ.). *Auditory Perceptual Enhancement Program (PEP), Perceive and Respond: Auditory Discrimination Program.* Tulsa, Okla.: Modern Education Corporation.

Monsees, E. K. *Structured Language for Children with Special Language Learning Problems.* Washington, D.C.: Children's Hearing and Speech Center, 1972.

Myklebust, H. R. *Auditory Disorders in Children: A Manual for Differential Diagnosis.* New York: Grune & Stratton, 1954.

Myklebust, H. R. *The Psychology of Deafness: Sensory Deprivation, Learning and Adjustment* (2nd edition). New York: Grune & Stratton, 1964.

Proff, J. *Speed Spelling.* Tigard, Ore.: C. C. Publications, Inc.

Rees, N. Auditory processing factors in language disorders: The view from Procrustes' bed. *Journal of Speech and Hearing Disorders, 38,* 304–315, 1973.

Semel, E. M. *Sound-Order-Sense: A Developmental Program in Auditory Perception.* Chicago: Follett Educational Corporation, 1970.

Semel, E. M. *Semel Auditory Processing Program (SAPP).* Chicago: Follett Educational Corporation, 1976.

Smith, F. *Psycholinguistics and Reading.* New York: Holt, Rinehart and Winston, 1973.

Thurber, D. N. and D. R. Jordan. *D'Nealian Handwriting.* Glenview, Ill.: Scott, Foresman and Company, 1978.

Wiig, E. H. and E. M. Semel. *Language Disabilities in Children and Adolescents.* Columbus, Ohio: Charles E. Merrill Publishing Company, 1976.

Yale, C. A. *Formation and Development of Elementary English Sounds.* Northampton, Mass.: Clark School for the Deaf, 1946.

AP-17a

AUDITORY PROCESSING: DISCRIMINATION*

STUDENT: _____ AGE: _____ SCHOOL: _____ GRADE/LEVEL: _____ SPEECH–LANGUAGE CLINICIAN: _____

Date: _____

GOAL: The student will be able to discriminate sufficient intensity, frequency and duration of sound patterns to enable accurate perception, production and self-monitoring of speech.

DIAGNOSTIC:
Visual–Motor _____
Cognitive _____
Phonetic Analysis _____
Audiological Assessment _____
Auditory Discrimination Score/Test _____

MLU _____
Language Age/Test _____
Morphological _____
Overall Language _____
Other _____

LONG-RANGE OBJECTIVE: Given an identical word pair or minimal pair (the same except for one sound), spoken by the clinician the child will state whether they are the "same" or "different" (19 of 20 correct over three consecutive sessions).

SHORT–TERM OBJECTIVES THE STUDENT WILL:	Date In	DESCRIPTION OF STIMULI AND RESPONSES	Date Accom.	COMMENTS TECHNIQUES EVALUATION
1. demonstrate ability to localize sound by pointing, with eyes closed, in direction from which sound comes (9 of 10 correct over three consecutive sessions).				
2. demonstrate ability to discriminate *gross* sound differences by selecting a picture from a set of five to match a recorded environmental or animal noise (at least three different sets, with 4 of 5 correct on each over three consecutive sessions).				
3. demonstrate ability to discriminate *loudness/softness* by performing and labeling actions (beating rhythm instrument; shouting/whispering; etc.) to correspond to intensity dimension of clinician/teacher/parent model (9 of 10 correct over three consecutive sessions).				
4. demonstrate ability to discriminate *fast/slow* auditory tempo by performing and labeling actions (beating rhythm instruments; clapping; etc.) to correspond to rate of clinician/teacher/parent model (9 of 10 correct over three consecutive sessions).				
5. demonstrate ability to discriminate *long/short* sound duration by performing and labeling actions (blowing toy instruments, voicing stop or continuant phonemes, etc.) to correspond to duration dimension of clinician/teacher/parent model (9 of 10 correct over three consecutive sessions).				

*See note on page 139.

This form may be reproduced as often as necessary. / Copyright © 1979 by Communication Skill Builders, Inc.

137

AP-17b

AUDITORY PROCESSING: DISCRIMINATION

Date: _____

Student: _____

SHORT-TERM OBJECTIVES THE STUDENT WILL:	Date In.	DESCRIPTION OF STIMULI AND RESPONSES	Date Accom.	COMMENTS TECHNIQUES EVALUATION
6. demonstrate ability to discriminate *high/low* pitch by performing and labeling actions (standing on tiptoe/squatting down; playing the xylophone, etc.) to correspond to frequency dimension of clinician/teacher/parent model (9 of 10 correct over three consecutive sessions).				
*7. demonstrate ability to make sound–symbol associations in all modalities (three sessions correct with no prompting for each sound):				
a. *Listening* and pointing to one symbol out of many choices when clinician/teacher says, for example, "Show me /t/."				
b. *Saying* the sound correctly in imitation of the clinician/teacher, who says, for example, "Say /i/."				
c. *Reading* the sound when its symbol (presented with many choices) is pointed to by the clinician/teacher, who says, "Read this."				
d. *Writing* the symbol for the sound produced by the clinician/teacher, who says, for example, "Write /k/."				
*8. demonstrate ability to analyze and synthesize phonological sequences by (4 of 5 correct in novel contexts over two sessions):				
a. *Reading* (i.e., *saying*) words written by the clinician/teacher using increasing complexity: CV (consonant–vowel), VC, CVC, CCVC, CVCC, multisyllabic.				
b. *Writing* (or arranging symbols for) words spoken by the clinician/teacher using increasing complexity.				
9. state "yes" or "no" correctly when asked whether two words presented by clinician/teacher/parent rhyme (8 of 10 correct over three consecutive sessions).				
10. LONG–RANGE: The student will state whether two words in an identical pair, or minimal pair (alike except for one phoneme, e.g., "bear/pear"), spoken by clinician/teacher/parent, are the "same" or "different" (19 of 20 correct over three consecutive sessions).				

*Children who experience major difficulties in this area affecting speaking and reading development may benefit from the *Auditory Discrimination in Depth* (A.D.D.) program by Lindamood and Lindamood (1969). Suboblective sequences are provided for assisting with objectives 7 and 8. Modified Yale charts (see AP-17e) provide a way of organizing traditional orthography into phonetic categories. Use of the Initial Teaching Alphabet (i.t.a.) or the *High Hat Program* (Goldman and Lynch 1971) provides other options.

AP-17c

AUDITORY PROCESSING: DISCRIMINATION

Date: _____

STUDENT: _____ AGE: _____ SCHOOL: _____ GRADE/LEVEL: _____ SPEECH–CLINICIAN: _____

SUBOBJECTIVE ONE – SOUND/SYMBOL ASSOCIATION

SHORT-TERM OBJECTIVES THE STUDENT WILL:	Date In.	LISTING OF PHONEMES FOR WHICH OBJECTIVE IS MET	Date Accom.	COMMENTS TECHNIQUES EVALUATION
1a. demonstrate appropriate attending behaviors of sitting and listening, and will perform simple imitative tasks for three sessions without anticipating an instructional command (e.g., "stand up, come to the board, do this, go back, sit down").				
1b. perform the tasks below to demonstrate associations for each of the phonemes listed, without prompting, in three successive sessions.				
(1) *Attend* to the sound and symbol as they are introduced and *articulate* the sound (one at a time; clinician/teacher prompts as necessary; this step is for introducing a new sound and shaping its articulation).				
(2) *Say* the sound in imitation of the clinician/teacher while pointing to its symbol in a scattered array (e.g., "Say /t/.").				
(3) *Trace* the symbol (in a scattered array) for the sound produced by the clinician/teacher, and say the sound at the beginning of the tracing motion (e.g., "Trace /p/.").				
(4) *Lip read* the sound, by saying it while pointing to its symbol in a scattered array, following its silent production by the clinician/teacher (e.g., "Show me /o/.").				
(5) *Listen* to the sound without seeing it produced (i.e., clinician's/teacher's hand over mouth, or child's back turned) and say it while pointing to its symbol in a scattered array (*auditory only step*; e.g., "Show me /m/.").				
(6) *Read* the sound while pointing to the visual symbol written in a scattered array (*recognition step*; e.g., "Read this.").				
(7) *Write* the symbol for the sound produced by the teacher/clinician as one of several being practiced and saying it at the beginning of the writing motion (*writing from memory*; e.g., "Write /I/.").				

*See footnote, page 143.

This form may be reproduced as often as necessary. / Copyright © 1979 by Communication Skill Builders, Inc.

AP-17d

AUDITORY PROCESSING: DISCRIMINATION

Date: _____

Student: _____

SUBOBJECTIVE ONE – SOUND/SYMBOL ASSOCIATION

SHORT-TERM OBJECTIVES THE STUDENT WILL:	Date In.	LISTING OF PHONEMES FOR WHICH OBJECTIVE IS MET	Date Accom.	COMMENTS TECHNIQUES EVALUATION
*(8) *Recognize* the symbol with eyes closed and say it after his/her finger is put through the tracing motion by the clinician/teacher (*motor memory* step; "What's this?").				
1c. perform the tasks listed (as described above) to demonstrate associations for each of the CV (consonant–vowel) and VC (vowel–consonant) syllables presented three at a time in a "drop drill" or "blending" written array:				
(1) Attention and articulation (a) Separated production (b) Blended production				
(2) Tracing				
(3) Lip reading				
(4) Listening (auditory only)				
(5) Reading				
(6) Writing				

*The first seven steps of objectives 1b are those outlined by McGinnis (1963) for the Association Method. Step eight of objective 1b was added by teacher Pamela Clifford (1978) for its effectiveness with her language and learning disabled students. This method's high degree of repetition, multiple associations (developed one at a time), and over-learning, help severely impaired students learn to speak and read sounds, and write symbols with success. Cursive writing is used in the Association Method as presented by McGinnis (1963) and DuBard (1974). All of these steps should be followed only for children who seem unable to learn and retain sound/symbol associations in more traditional ways.

Phonemes can be written into the space provided as they are introduced in the step, and circled when the criterion is met for that phoneme and step. Production of the schwa vowel following consonants should be avoided where possible and deemphasized when avoidance is impossible. The phonemes with their primary and secondary spellings (Yale, 1946; Monsees, 1972) are listed on AP-17e. Where the same spelling may be pronounced in two different ways a superscript ^{1} indicates primary pronunciation, and superscript ^{2} indicates secondary pronunciation.

This form may be reproduced as often as necessary. / Copyright © 1979 by Communication Skill Builders, Inc.

143

AP-17e   AUDITORY PROCESSING: SUBOBJECTIVE ONE – SOUND/SYMBOL ASSOCIATION

PHONEMIC NOTATION SYSTEM

Date: _____

VOWELS

Phonemic Spelling	Primary Spelling	Secondary Spelling	Example
/u/	oo¹		pool
/ʊ/	oo²		look
/oʊ/	o-e	oa, ow²	home
/ɔ/	aw		law
/a/	o		mom
/i/	ee	ea¹	bee
/eɪ/	a-e	ai, ay	make
/e/	e	ea	red
/æ/	a		cat
/ʌ/	u		up
/ɝ/	ur	er, ir	fur
/aɪ/	i-e	igh	write
/aʊ/	ou	ow¹	house
/ɔɪ/	oi	oy	oil

CONSONANTS

Phonemic Spelling	Primary Spelling	Secondary Spelling	Example
/h/	h		he
/w/	w		we
/p/	p		pie
/b/	b		boy
/m/	m		my
/t/	t		tie
/d/	d		do
/n/	n		no
/l/	l		lip
/r/	r		run
/k/	k	c, ck	key
/g/	g		go
/ŋ/	ng		rang
/ŋk/	nk		think

CONSONANTS

Phonemic Spelling	Primary Spelling	Secondary Spelling	Example
/f/	f	ph	fish
/v/	v		very
/θ/	th¹		think
/ð/	th²		that
/s/	s	c (e)	see
		c (i)	
		c (y)	
/z/	z	s²	zoo
/ʃ/	sh		she
/tʃ/	ch	tch	chew
/dʒ/	j		juice
/j/	y		you
/ks/	x		box
/kwɪ/	qu		quick

AUDITORY PROCESSING: DISCRIMINATION

STUDENT: _____ AGE: _____ SCHOOL: _____ GRADE/LEVEL: _____ Date: _____

SPEECH–LANGUAGE CLINICIAN: _____

SUBOBJECTIVE TWO – PHONOLOGICAL ANALYSIS AND SYNTHESIS

SHORT-TERM OBJECTIVES / THE STUDENT WILL:	Date In.	LISTING OF EXAMPLE SOUND COMBINATIONS AND WORDS		Date Accom.	COMMENTS TECHNIQUES EVALUATION
		CV (e.g., "bee"), VC (e.g., "it") and CVC (e.g., "pat")	CCVC (e.g., "stop") CVCC (e.g., "books")		
2a. perform the tasks listed to demonstrate association for each of the word types listed (two times without prompting for each new word):					
(1) *Attention and articulation.* Child imitates teacher's production of sounds written in a three or four "cross drill": (a) Separated Articulation (b) Blended Articulation					
(2) *Association with meaning.* Child sounds out written word and produces it while looking at the picture.					
(3) *Writing from immediate memory.* Child copies word (sounding as he/she writes) and then rewrites it from memory (with model covered).					
(4) *Listening.* Child points to each sound in sequence as it is produced by the teacher.					
(5) *Tracing and copying.* Child says and writes word several times on paper.					
(6) *Lip reading.* Child repeats word sounded out by teacher, finds the written word, and articulates it as he/she points to the letters.					
(7) *Auditory.* Child repeats word spoken by teacher with mouth covered, selects the picture, matches picture to the written word, and reads the word.					
(8) *Recall.* Child produces word to correspond with picture only and writes (or forms the letter chips) word from memory.					
2b. articulate, read and write more complex, multisyllabic words.					
2c. read words in sentences and demonstrate comprehension by matching to pictures or verbal descriptions or by answering questions.					

AP–18 AUDITORY PROCESSING:
SHORT-TERM SEQUENTIAL MEMORY

All of the comments in sequence AP–17 regarding the efficacy of designing remediation strategies based upon a specific disability model of language disorders apply here as well. As the footnote with this sequence emphasizes, the applicability of the objective to improvement of overall language ability is highly suspect.

Short–term sequential memory has no proven causal relationship to general psycholinguistic ability. Bloom and Lahey (1978) report on the literature which shows a correlation between many aspects of perceptual dysfunction and language disorder. However, they also emphasize that recall of auditory sequential information may be more a sensitive index of an individual's familiarity with a linguistic code than a processing ability on which language learning is dependent — since material already organized some way in a subject's knowledge about language and the world is more easily recalled. For example, Bloom and Lahey's summary shows that meaningful words are recalled better than nonsense words, concrete words better than abstract words, and words coded syntactically are recalled best. It has also been found that inaccuracies occurring during sentence imitation provide a more reliable index of true linguistic processing ability than a completely accurate echoing of the sentence does, and a number of diagnostic tools in the area of syntax are built upon this principle (e.g., *Detroit Tests of Learning Aptitude* (Baker and Leland 1959), *Northwestern Syntax Screening Test* (Lee 1969, 1971), *Carrow Elicited Language Inventory* (Carrow 1974), *Test of Language Development* (Hammill and Newcomer 1977), and *Oral Language Sentence Imitation Screening Test* and *Diagnostic Inventory* (Zachman *et al.* 1976, 1977, 1978).

Wiig and Semel (1976) do see some value in designing remediation strategies to improve short–term auditory memory, not with the objective of expanding the number of words — such as digits, which can be repeated in a measurement task — but rather with the objective of increasing the size of perceptual–conceptual "chunks" that can be retained. They summarize research which has identified a number of variables that affect immediate recall and that should be kept in mind when designing remediation strategies, including: (1) word frequency, (2) associative strength, (3) linguistic structure, (4) logical relationship, (5) length, (6)

suprasegmental features, (7) salience, and (8) serial position. The question remains, however, whether working directly on the interacting complex of syntactic–semantic–pragmatic–cognitive rule systems might not be a better way to achieve the same ends.

Semel's programs, *Sound–Order–Sense* (1970) and *Semel Auditory Processing Program* (1976), do, in fact, provide activities for this area of intervention in the context of a more global approach. The main drawback to some of those activities is the metalinguistic decision–making demands they place upon children who cannot use the rules spontaneously, let alone reflect upon them. For such children, clinicians should avoid procedures which require students to rearrange scrambled sentences, or to assess correct usage in others. It is generally more fruitful to work directly on the child's competence with the restricted structures themselves by using procedures outlined with sequence L–9, *Morphologic and Syntactic Rule Acquisition.* Reflective activities, and other procedures which were originally developed for research on normal language processing, can then be used with older children and adolescents as they learn to deal with the more abstract demands of studying English as an academic subject. For younger children, specific short–term memory tasks can be useful in stretching the ability to handle the multiple requests of home and school. Parents, classroom teachers, and paraprofessionals can often assist in the implementation of such activities *(objectives five, eight* and *eleven),* leaving the speech-language pathologist time to work on other aspects of the problem. The same holds true for *objectives three, six* and *nine.*

References and Other Resources

Baker, H. J. and B. Leland. *Detroit Tests of Learning Aptitude.* Indianapolis: Test Division of Bobbs-Merrill, 1959.

Bloom, L. and M. Lahey. *Language Development and Language Disorders.* New York: John Wiley & Sons, 1978.

Carrow, E. *Carrow Elicited Language Inventory.* Austin, Tex.: Learning Concepts, 1974.

Developmental Learning Materials (publ.). *Auditory Perception Training (APT),* and other auditory skills materials. Niles, Ill.: Developmental Learning Materials.

Kessler, R. and J. Friedland. *Following Directions: Advanced.* Woburn, Mass.: Curriculum Associates.

Lee, L. L. *Northwestern Syntax Screening Test.* Evanston, Ill.: The Northwestern University Press, 1971.

Lindamood, C. H. and P. C. Lindamood. *Auditory Discrimination in Depth.* Boston: Teaching Resources, 1969.

Newcomer, P. L. and D. D. Hammill. *Test of Language Development.* Austin, Tex.: Empiric Press, 1977.

Pirie, J. and A. Pirie. *Following Directions — Primary* and *Intermediate.* Woburn, Mass.: Curriculum Associates.

Rush, M. L. *The Language of Directions: A Programmed Workbook.* Washington, D.C.: Alexander Graham Bell Association for the Deaf, 1977.

Semel, E. M. *Sound-Order-Sense: A Developmental Program in Auditory Perception.* Chicago: Follett Educational Corporation, 1970.

Semel, E. M. *Semel Auditory Processing Program (SAPP).* Chicago: Follett Educational Corporation, 1976.

Wiig, E. H. and E. M. Semel. *Language Disabilities in Children and Adolescents.* Columbus, Ohio: Charles E. Merrill Publishing Company, 1976.

Zachman, L., R. Huisingh, C. Jorgensen and M. Barrett. *Oral Language Sentence Imitation Screening Test (OLSIST)* and *Oral Language Sentence Imitation Diagnostic Inventory (OLSIDI).* Moline, Ill.: Linguisystems, Inc.

AP-18a

AUDITORY PROCESSING: SHORT–TERM SEQUENTIAL MEMORY*

STUDENT: _____ AGE: _____ SCHOOL: _____ GRADE/LEVEL: _____ SPEECH–LANGUAGE CLINICIAN: _____

Date: _____

GOAL: The student will demonstrate ability to recall and reproduce, in sequence, information of a length appropriate to his/her age and level.

DIAGNOSTIC:
Visual–Motor _____
Cognitive _____
Phonetic Analysis _____
Audiological Assessment _____
Auditory Discrimination Score/Test _____
MLU _____
Language Age/Test _____
Morphological _____
Overall Language _____
STM for Digits _____
Other _____

LONG–RANGE OBJECTIVE (last in sequence): The student will carry out a series of four commissions in the order presented by the clinician.

SHORT–TERM OBJECTIVES (leading to objective stated above) THE STUDENT WILL:	Date In	DESCRIPTION OF STIMULI AND RESPONSES	Date Accom.	COMMENTS TECHNIQUES EVALUATION
1. demonstrate ability to discriminate a sequenced pair of loud/soft; fast/slow; long/short; high/low sounds produced in random sequence by clinician/teacher/parent, by naming which member of the pair came first (3 of 4 correct of each dimension over three consecutive sessions).				
2. match a patterned three–unit sequence of long and short tones on a toy horn or other instrument by reproducing the clinician's model (8 of 10 correct over three consecutive sessions).				
3. repeat a series of three words belonging to the same semantic category (e.g., "six, five, eight"; "dog, cow, horse"; "run, hop, swim") in the same sequence as the clinician/teacher/parent's verbal model (4 of 5 sequences correct on the first trial over three sessions).				
4. repeat a five–morpheme sentence of appropriate grammatical complexity following the clinician's model with no omissions (9 of 10 correct for two sessions).				
5. carry out a series of two commissions in the order presented by the clinician in the sentence type, "V the N (Prep the N)" (4 of 5 correct for three consecutive sessions).				
6. repeat a series of five words belonging to the same semantic category in the same sequence as the clinician/teacher/parent's model (4 of 5 different sequences correct on the first trial over three sessions).				

*See note on page 153.

This form may be reproduced as often as necessary. / Copyright © 1979 by Communication Skill Builders, Inc.

AP-18b

AUDITORY PROCESSING: SHORT-TERM SEQUENTIAL MEMORY*

Date: _____

Student: _____

SHORT-TERM OBJECTIVES THE STUDENT WILL:	Date In.	DESCRIPTION OF STIMULI AND RESPONSES	Date Accom.	COMMENTS TECHNIQUES EVALUATION
7. repeat an eight-morpheme sentence of appropriate grammatical complexity following the clinician's model with no omissions (9 of 10 correct for two sessions).				
8. carry out a series of three commissions in the order presented by the clinician in the sentence type, "V the N (Prep the N)" (4 of 5 correct for three consecutive sessions).				
9. repeat a series of five words belonging to different semantic categories (e.g., "shoe, ladder, run, pie, mother") in the same sequence as the clinician/teacher/parent's verbal model (4 of 5 different sequences correct on the first trial over three consecutive sessions).				
10. repeat a ten-morpheme sentence of appropriate grammatical complexity following the clinician's model with no omissions (9 of 10 correct for two consecutive sessions).				
11. carry out a series of four commissions in the order presented by the clinician/teacher/parent in the sentence type "V the N (Prep the N)" (4 of 5 correct for three consecutive sessions).				

*IMPORTANT: The applicability of this sequence to improvement of overall communication skills is highly suspect. The ability to repeat sequences of digits has no proven causal relationship to general psycholinguistic ability; the ability to follow commands is largely determined by comprehension of prepositional concepts; and inaccuracies occurring during sentence imitation provide a more reliable index of true linguistic processing ability than a completely accurate echoing of the sentence does. When a child experiences difficulty in the area of short-term auditory memory, it is generally more fruitful to work directly on the morphological and syntactic problems which tend to co-occur, and to use the sound/symbol association and phonological analysis and synthesis tasks of the Discrimination Sequence (AP-17) to assist the child whose auditory processing deficit is affecting speech and reading. Short-term memory tasks are easily administered by parents and paraprofessionals and their aid can be enlisted in helping the child stretch his or her short-term memory, leaving the professional time to work on the higher level problems often associated with restricted auditory memory.

AP-19 AUDITORY PROCESSING AND RECALL:
WORD RETRIEVAL

The inability to retrieve appropriate words accurately and quickly can be a great hindrance to fluent expression and effective communication. Wiig and Semel (1975), in a study of word retrieval by learning disabled students, found that both perseverative errors and substitutions of words within the same grammatic and semantic class were common. Response delay and overuse of such all-purpose words as "thingamajig" and "whatchamacallit" can also be suggestive of dysnomia, as can consistent reluctance to respond to direct questions at all. Formal evaluation of word retrieval is difficult since so many variables are involved, but the "Visual Confrontation Naming" subtest of the *Boston VA Aphasia* test (Goodglass and Kaplan 1972) can be used (see Wiig and Semel 1975), and parents and teachers will often confirm a clinician's suspicion that word finding problems are occurring by immediately recognizing the child as one who "has problems coming up with words that (they know) he or she knows."

As in other "auditory processing" areas, students' abilities in this area should be viewed in the context of their more global linguistic facility. Retrieval ability depends upon the manner in which information is stored as much as upon the cueing system used to locate elusive items. Wiig and Semel (1975) suggest that remediation efforts focus on developing *accuracy, fluency, flexibility* and *speed* in word recall, and emphasize, based upon Luria (1973), that the child must learn, not only to retrieve the target word from within a related set of words, but also to inhibit retrieval of related words from a set with similar probabilities.

The objectives of sequence AP-19 are designed to help children both with their internal organization systems and with their self-cueing strategies for retrieving desired words. The objectives of sequence L-16, *Semantic Acquisition of Abstract and Categorical Uses,* may also be useful in assisting children to develop organized storage systems for linguistic information. Johnson and Myklebust (1967) and Wiig and Semel (1976) both offer techniques for this area of remediation. For example, internal imagery for recall and retrieval can be facilitated by having a child close his or her eyes and practice picturing and naming items one might find together in a grocery store.

Many children with severe word finding problems are also excessively sensitive to communicative pressures and often become so dysfluent that they may be classed as stutterers — and even enter into the learning spiral of stuttering behavior. Therefore, a major objective of the intervention process should be to prevent the development of unhealthy stalling and avoidance devices by encouraging the development of healthy search strategies. Speed of retrieval is an important part of the process, and gradual increments of temporal and propositional pressure can be built into the remediation plan using the objectives of sequence F-28, *Fluency: Transfer and Maintenance.*

References and Other Resources

Goodglass, H. and E. Kaplan. *Boston Diagnostic Aphasia Examination.* Philadelphia: Lea & Febiger, 1972.

Johnson, D. J. and H. R. Myklebust. *Learning Disabilities: Educational Principles and Practices.* New York: Grune & Stratton, Inc., 1967.

Luria, A. R. *The Working Brain.* New York: Basic Books, 1973.

Wiig, E. H. and E. M. Semel. Productive language abilities in learning disabled adolescents. *Journal of Learning Disabilities, 8,* 583-586, 1975.

Wiig, E. H. and E. M. Semel. *Language Disabilities in Children and Adolescents.* Columbus, Ohio: Charles E. Merrill Publishing Company, 1976.

AUDITORY PROCESSING AND RECALL: WORD RETRIEVAL

Date: _____

STUDENT: _____ AGE: _____ SCHOOL: _____ GRADE/LEVEL: _____ SPEECH–LANGUAGE CLINICIAN: _____

GOAL: The student will be able to recall and produce words in his/her vocabulary without abnormal delay during spontaneous communication with others in the environment.

DIAGNOSTIC:
Visual–Motor _____
Cognitive _____
Phonetic _____
Audiological _____
General Auditory Processing _____
MLU _____

Language Age/Test(s) _____
Overall Language _____
PPVT _____
Average Number Retrieval Problems in 10-minute conversation _____
Other _____

LONG–RANGE OBJECTIVE: The student will self–cue with no more than five seconds delay on all but two word-finding problems occurring in a 10-minute taped conversation about a familiar subject with someone other than the clinician (three different occasions).

SHORT–TERM OBJECTIVES THE STUDENT WILL:	Date In.	DESCRIPTION OF ACTIVITIES/ VOCABULARY/MATERIALS	Date Accom.	COMMENTS TECHNIQUES EVALUATION
1. rapidly produce words with no more than one delay greater than five seconds in each type of the activities (two consecutive sessions each):				
a. Roundabout fill–in				
b. Stimuli pictures in categories				
c. Category named by clinician				
d. Words in series				
e. Synonyms				
f. Opposites				
g. Rhyming or sound association tasks				
h. Other common word associations				

AUDITORY PROCESSING AND RECALL: WORD RETRIEVAL

Date: _____

Student: _____

SHORT-TERM OBJECTIVES THE STUDENT WILL:	Date In	DESCRIPTION OF ACTIVITIES/ VOCABULARY/MATERIALS	Date Accom.	COMMENTS TECHNIQUES EVALUATION
2. rapidly name series of unrelated pictures/objects, with self-cueing only, and no more than one delay greater than five seconds in each group of 10 (4 of 5 groups, two consecutive sessions).				
3. rapidly respond to direct questions in one topic area with subvocal self-cueing only, and no more than one delay greater than five seconds for 4 of 5 questions in each topic area (three topic areas, two consecutive sessions).				
4. rapidly respond to direct questions about mixed topics, with subvocal self-cueing only, and no more than one delay greater than five seconds (10 to 15 questions, two consecutive sessions).				
5. demonstrate ability to self-cue with no more than a five-second delay on all but two word finding problems occurring in a 10-minute taped conversation about a familiar subject with the clinician in the speech room (three different occasions).				
6. demonstrate ability to self-cue with no more than five-second delay on all but two word finding problems occurring in 10-minute conversation in speech room with slightly increased propositionality (additional people in room, unfamiliar topic with someone other than the clinician outside the speech room) (three different occasions).				
*7. LONG-RANGE: The student will self-cue with no more than a five-second delay on all but two word finding problems occurring in a 10-minute taped conversation about a familiar topic with someone other than the clinician outside the speech room (three different occasions).				

*The major goal for students with word finding difficulties is to prevent the development of potentially unhealthy stalling and avoidance devices by encouraging the development of healthy search devices. If a student has many signs of frustration related to communication propositionality, it may be necessary to desensitize him to time pressure gradually and it may be useful to combine this sequence with objectives for transfer and maintenance of fluent speech.

AP–20 AUDITORY PROCESSING AND RECALL:
LONG-TERM MEMORY

Older children who have acquired brain damage as the result of head trauma or other cerebral insult seem to have the greatest need for the objectives of this sequence. The abilities required are integrally tied to those in the semantic and functional–pragmatic areas and may best be remediated using those objectives. However, since difficulty in remembering one's past actions or upcoming responsibilities can be an especially debilitating aspect of brain damage, and since deficits in this area can greatly inhibit academic functioning, this separate sequence of objectives is also provided.

Activities which are applicable to this area of intervention are available in Johnson and Myklebust (1967), Wiig and Semel (1976) and Worthley (1978). Materials devised for the remediation of problems associated with adult aphasia can also be of use (e.g., Keith 1972) but some of the best practice material can be obtained from a diary kept by the student and his or her parents, and from the educational assignments and materials of the regular curriculum. Extensive parent and teacher counseling programs are also important when helping a child with difficulty in this area learn to cope with the communicative demands of the environment.

References and Other Resources

Johnson, D. J. and H. R. Myklebust. *Learning Disabilities: Educational Principles and Practices.* New York: Grune & Stratton, Inc., 1967.

Keith, R. L. *Speech and Language Rehabilitation: A Workbook for the Neurologically Impaired.* Danville, Ill.: The Interstate Printers & Publishers, Inc., 1972.

Traendly, C. A. *Aphasia Rehabilitation.* Tigard, Ore.: C. C. Publications, Inc.

Wiig, E. H. and E. M. Semel. *Language Disabilities in Children and Adolescents.* Columbus, Ohio: Charles E. Merrill Publishing Company, 1976.

Worthley, W. J. *Sourcebook of Language Learning Activities.* Boston, Mass.: Little, Brown and Company, 1978.

AP-20a

AUDITORY PROCESSING AND RECALL: LONG–TERM MEMORY

STUDENT: _____ AGE: _____ SCHOOL: _____ GRADE/LEVEL: _____ SPEECH–LANGUAGE CLINICIAN: _____

Date: _____

GOAL: The student will be able to recall and communicate events which occurred a week or more in the past.

DIAGNOSTIC:
Visual–Motor _____
Cognitive _____
Phonetic Analysis _____
Audiological Assessment _____
General Auditory Processing _____
_____

MLU _____
Language Age/Test(s) _____
Overall Language _____
Word Retrieval _____
Other _____

***LONG–RANGE OBJECTIVE:** The student will retell in sequence, at least five points of an interesting activity in which he/she participated a week or more earlier (three different occasions).

SHORT–TERM OBJECTIVES THE STUDENT WILL:	Date In.	DESCRIPTION OF ACTIVITIES/ EXPERIENCES/MATERIALS	Date Accom.	COMMENTS TECHNIQUES EVALUATION
1. remember and name three of five objects/people/places involved in activities performed *earlier in session* with teacher/clinician (three consecutive sessions).				
2. remember and name three of five objects/people/places involved in activities performed *earlier in day* with teacher/clinician/parent in response to question prompts (three consecutive sessions).				
3. place three or four picture cards in correct sequence and tell the accompanying story using ordering connectors such as first, second, next, and then, last, etc. (at least one sentence about each picture for three of four sets of picture cards, three consecutive sessions).				
4. verbally list own activities in a typical day in sequence with minimal visual prompts (two consecutive sessions with no more than one omission from the sequence prepared earlier with clinician/parents).				
5. tell which activities and attributes are associated with days of the week, and seasons and months of the year (two consecutive sessions with no more than two errors in each activity).				

*See note on page 165.

This form may be reproduced as often as necessary. / Copyright © 1979 by Communication Skill Builders, Inc.

163

AUDITORY PROCESSING AND RECALL: LONG–TERM MEMORY

Date: _____

Student: _____

SHORT–TERM OBJECTIVES THE STUDENT WILL:	Date In.	DESCRIPTION OF ACTIVITIES/ EXPERIENCES/MATERIALS	Date Accom.	COMMENTS TECHNIQUES EVALUATION
6. verbally list specific detail in sequence for a particular activity on a given day to match description written by parents (no more than one prompt by clinician, two consecutive sessions).				
7. retell at least five major characters and plot elements in sequence from an assigned TV program viewed the night before with no more than one prompt by clinician (student can self–prompt with cues prearranged with clinician, two consecutive sessions).				
8. LONG–RANGE: The student will retell, in sequence, at least five points of an interesting activity in which he/she participated a week or more earlier (three different occasions).				

*The abilities required for this sequence are integrally tied to those in semantic and functional–pragmatic areas.

V–21 VOICE:
AWARENESS AND MODIFICATION OF ENVIRONMENTAL INFLUENCES ON VOCAL ABUSE

When a student has a voice disorder as a result of improper vocal habits, the two primary goals of remediation are: (1) reduction of vocal abuse, and (2) easier initiation of phonation (Burk 1971). Sequence V–21 is designed to assist with the first goal when misuse of the voice has been identified as a major causative factor in the development of such medically diagnosed conditions as vocal nodules, polyps or contact ulcers.

Accurate diagnosis by the speech–language pathologist is an especially critical part of voice remediation, and yet we have few formalized tools for the process. Perhaps the major reason so many clinicians feel insecure when dealing with voice disorders in children is that the concept of "voice quality" is a confusing one. Voice quality is determined by the complex interaction of a number of physiological and acoustic variables, but the most important distinction the clinician must make is the one between the *phonatory* and *resonatory* components of voice production. Disorders of phonation (e.g., hoarseness) and resonation (e.g., nasality) may, of course, co–occur, and resonation is determined not only by the openness of the passageway through the nasal cavity, but by the configuration of the oral and pharyngeal cavities and tongue. However, by far the majority of problems of laryngeal and velopharyngeal functioning are separate and should be managed differently in the intervention process.

Wilson's (1971) St. Louis Jewish Hospital Scales have provided us with one tool for sorting out the components of voice quality for individual children. In addition to the two major scales for rating laryngeal and resonatory behavior separately, minor scales are provided for assessing speaking rate, vocal intensity, and tonal variation. The rating scale for laryngeal behavior has two dimensions. The vertical scale is used for rating pitch, and the horizontal scale is used for rating the degree of tension and/or breathiness associated with phonation. Children who have vocal nodules, for example, often show three symptoms: (1) tension associated with vocal hyperfunctioning, "+2," (2) breathiness associated with excessive air escape, "–2," and (3) pitch which is noticeably low for the person's age and sex, "–2." The second major scale for rating resonance is explained in the notes for the sequence on velopharyngeal functioning (V–24). For clinicians who feel

somewhat insecure about their abilities to judge voice quality variables, the calibration tapes and explanation of Wilson and Rice's (1977) *Voice Disorders* kit provide an excellent resource.

It is helpful for the child and his or her parents to identify environmental factors which have contributed to misuse of the voice. If the child is six or older, it may be best to give him or her primary responsibility for identifying and changing those conditions. With children younger than age six, Boone (1973) cautions that efforts to alter vocal abuse are rarely successful. In such cases, it may be better to enlist major parental support and to concentrate on parent–child and sibling interactions. Patterson and Gullion's (1971) *Living with Children* may show parents ways to modify their children's behaviors, as well as help them to see how their own behavior is affected. Many parents find that children yell less when the whole family attempts to adopt gentler speaking habits.

Special considerations for dealing with the objectives of this sequence follow.

1. One way students learn to appreciate the harmful effects of yelling — and banging their vocal folds together — is through clapping their hands very hard and fast. This helps them to discover that hands become red and sore during even brief periods of abuse, and that the same kind of thing happens to their vocal folds.

2. Boone (1971, 1977) cautions against group therapy for children with voice disorders because of broad individual differences. Connelly, Wilson and Leeper (1968) and Burk and Lynch (1969), however, have described methods for working with voice disordered children in groups, and found that group therapy can even offer some advantages. An important part of the process is making the outstanding features of disordered voice quality, and each child's unique identifying voice characteristics, apparent via group discussion. Children can listen to tapes of each other's voices and develop their own labels and representative drawings of the features of voice quality. Some examples (Burk 1971) are: "the hitting voice" (for abrupt vocal attack), "the air voice" (for aphonic episodes), and "the gravel voice" (for vocal fry).

3. A specific listing of personal vocal abuse factors generated by the child is the most meaningful way to identify harmful conditions of voice production. One approach is to suggest general types of abusive behaviors and then let the child list those, and others, which are pertinent. A detailed diary of a few days will help make the child and the parents aware of instances of vocal abuse. Blonigen (1978) describes a process of constructing a voice scrapbook with two lists. One could be labeled "These are things that hurt my voice," and the other could be labeled "These are the things I can do when I feel like yelling." The second list is important and can be further developed in conjunction with *objective five.* After the lists have been developed, the child can go over the list with the clinician at the beginning of subsequent sessions so that the major elements are remembered and practiced.

4. Once the child has compiled his or her listing of categories of abuse, counts can be made for specified situations (e.g., before school, playing with friends, playing with brother, watching T.V., etc.) and types of behaviors (e.g., yelling, throat clearing, funny voices, etc.). It is better to break the day down into types of activities and rate those separately than to try to rate the whole day. Charts should be kept simple at first and complexity added gradually to increase the likelihood that they actually will be used by children and their parents.

   Older children can keep their own "yelling charts," and the experience of counting yelling instances will tend to make them do less yelling without thinking. Leather wrist counters and knitting counters tied to belt loops can be used to keep track of the counts. Younger children may need help to count their vocal abusive behaviors. Crain and Reaves (1977) have suggested "good" and "bad news" notes passed among parent, teacher and clinician with such headings as:

   (a) "Yea! Quiet Clear Cord is happy because..."

   (b) "Uh oh! Nasty Nodule is happy because..."

   (c) "Yea! Nasty Nodule is getting smaller because..."

   (d) "Uh oh! Nasty Nodule feels stronger today because..."

   A tally chart for rating the behaviors of the day just before bedtime could be posted on the refrigerator, with two columns, one headed with a sandpaper monster, "Nasty Nodule," and the other with a soft fuzzy caricature of "Quiet Clear Cord."

5. After vocal abusive behaviors have been identified, it is important to discover: (a) how the environment can be shaped to elicit less yelling or other abusive behaviors, (b) which abusive instances can be eliminated entirely, and (c) what better alternatives can be substituted in situations not likely to be controlled in other ways. Developing family hand signals for "talking" over loud noises, such as motorcycles, snowmobiles, or workshop equipment, can be a fun alternative, as can whistling with the fingers or other play noises not produced with the larynx. Blonigen's (1978) list entitled "These are the things I can do when I feel like yelling" can be especially helpful.

6. Rarely would the vocal rest objective be implemented by a speech–language pathologist, unless in conjunction with a medical procedure. Occasionally, however, a few days of minimal talking (especially with *no whispering*) will provide the impetus needed to show a child with a long–standing problem and associated vocal nodules that changing vocal habits can make a difference.

7. The use of a chart to illustrate the actual decline of vocal abuse instances is a most powerful tool in helping the process become concrete for a child and his or her family. Boone (1973, 1977) provides examples.

References and Other Resources

Blonigen, J. Management of vocal hoarseness caused by abuse: An approach. *Language, Speech and Hearing Services in Schools, IX,* 142-150, 1978.

Boone, D. R. Voice therapy for children. *Human Communication,* Winter, 30-43, 1973.

Boone, D. R. *The Voice and Voice Therapy* (2nd edition). Englewood Cliffs, N.J.: Prentice-Hall, Inc., 1977.

Burk, K. W. Diagnosis and clinical management: Voice disorders in the school-age child. Paper presented at a public school clinician meeting, Bloomington, Ind., 1976.

Burk, K. W. and M. Lynch. Group or individual therapy for children with vocal nodules. *Clearinghouse, 1,* 5-6, 1969.

Connelly, M. K., F. B. Wilson and H. A. Leeper. A group voice therapy technique for decreasing vocal abuse in children with vocal nodules. Unpublished paper, The Jewish Hospital of St. Louis, St. Louis, Missouri, 1968.

Crain, J. W. and S. B. Reaves. Vocal abuse in school-age children: Therapy can be fun. Paper presented at the annual conference of the American Speech and Hearing Association, Chicago, 1977.

Greene, M. C. C. *The Voice and Its Disorders.* Philadelphia: J. B. Lippincott Company, 1975.

Moore, G. P. *Organic Voice Disorders.* Englewood Cliffs, N.J.: Prentice-Hall, Inc., 1971.

Patterson, G. R. and M. E. Gullion. *Living with Children* (revised edition). Champaign, Ill.: Research Press Company, 1971.

Polow, N. G. and E. D. Kaplan. *Symptomatic Voice Therapy.* Tulsa, Ok a.: Modern Education Corporation.

Wilson, D. K. Children with vocal nodules. *Journal of Speech and Hearing Disorders, 26,* 19-26, 1961.

Wilson, F. B. The voice disordered child: A descriptive approach. *Language, Speech and Hearing Services in Schools, 4,* 18-22, 1971.

Wilson, F. B. and M. Rice. *Voice Disorders.* Boston: Teaching Resources, 1977.

VOICE: AWARENESS AND MODIFICATION OF ENVIRONMENTAL INFLUENCES ON VOCAL ABUSE

STUDENT: _____ AGE: _____ SCHOOL: _____ GRADE/LEVEL: _____ SPEECH–LANGUAGE CLINICIAN: _____

Date: _____

GOAL: The student and his/her parents and siblings will work together to create an environment which will encourage normal use of voice.

DIAGNOSTIC: Oral Structures and Function _____
Otolaryngolical: Date _____ Physician _____
Results _____
Audiological _____
Types of Abusive Uses: yelling ____ singing ____ crying ____ coughing ____
throat clearing ____ inapprop. pitch ____ inapprop. loudness ____
talking over loud noises (snowmobile, motorcycle, etc.) ____

making funny noises (describe) _____
other _____

Laryngeal Functioning:
Tension _____ Sites _____
Breathiness _____ Periodic Aphonia _____
Glottal Attacks _____
Other _____
Ability to Imitate:
Pitch Change _____
Loudness Change _____
Onset of Phonation: smooth _____ rough _____
Termination of Phonation: smooth _____ rough _____
Respiration: Type _____
Count on one Breath: _____ sustain /s/ _____ /z/ _____
Other _____

LONG–RANGE OBJECTIVE: The student will not abuse his/her voice more than five times per week as tallied by parents on a chart each day over a two–week period.

SHORT–TERM OBJECTIVES THE STUDENT WILL:	Date In.	DESCRIPTION OF SPECIFIC STIMULI, SETTINGS AND RESPONSES	Date Accom.	COMMENTS TECHNIQUES EVALUATION
1. demonstrate awareness of laryngeal functioning (appropriate to age level)* by describing how voice is produced and the effects of using the vocal folds roughly (two separate sessions at least one week apart with minimal prompting).				
2. use appropriate vocabulary and/or abstract drawings to represent desirable and undesirable features of voices on tape or produced by clinician/class-mates/self (three consecutive sessions with no prompting).				
3. list all the ways he/she abuses own voice and at least five different situations where he/she tends to do so (three consecutive sessions with no prompting).				
4. count and chart the number of abusive instances (with parental assistance if necessary) on each of five out of seven days for two successive weeks.				

*See note on page 173.

v–21b

VOICE: AWARENESS AND MODIFICATION OF ENVIRONMENTAL INFLUENCES ON VOCAL ABUSE

Date: _____

Student: _____

SHORT–TERM OBJECTIVES THE STUDENT WILL:	Date In.	DESCRIPTION OF SPECIFIC STIMULI, SETTINGS AND RESPONSES	Date Accom.	COMMENTS TECHNIQUES EVALUATION
5. demonstrate or describe alternative behaviors which can be used to replace old instances of vocal abuse in response to situations suggested by the clinician (e.g., whistling to call friends; telling siblings, "No matter what you do, I won't use my yelling voice.").				
6. keep silent under conditions outlined for a _____ day period. (This vocal rest objective would not be used with children except in extreme cases where no improvement occurs with traditional methods, or in rare cases, following surgical treatment by a physician.)				
7. reduce the number of abusive instances counted and charted to no more than five times per week (for two successive weeks).				

*Boone (1973) cautions that efforts to alter vocal abuse are rarely successful before age six. A number of other authors have suggested ways to make this part of the process more motivating. Connelly, Wilson and Leeper (1968) describe a group voice therapy technique. Burk (1971) suggests having the children draw representations of their own and other voices. Crain and Reaves (1977) use clever labeling of homework activities; students are asked to become "super sleuths" in tracking down vocal abuse and discovering alternatives to yelling, and to describe (as appropriate) whether "Quiet ClearCord" or "Nasty Nodule" had a better day. When charting abuse instances, parents might help children characterize the day by posting pictures to represent either the villain or hero(ine) on the refrigerator door as appropriate.

V–22 VOICE:
ESTABLISHMENT AND TRANSFER OF INCREASED LARYNGEAL HYPOFUNCTIONING TO REPLACE VOCAL ABUSE

When a child has been placed in a voice intervention program because of vocal hyperfunctioning and vocal abuse, the first major goal of therapy is to reduce the abusive instances (see sequence V–21) and the second is to teach an easier manner of phonation. The attributes to be encouraged are: (1) speaking with adequate respiration from a generally relaxed condition, (2) appropriate pitch, and (3) a breathy approach to phonation.

Children who are tense or who have inefficient respiratory habits for speech are likely to show excessive laryngeal hyperfunctioning and resulting vocal pathology. Improving posture, retraining breathing habits when clavicular components are present, and encouraging coordinated thoracic and abdominal movement, can assist children to have more air with which to power the voice. Gross motor activity followed by relaxation, techniques of progressive relaxation (Jacobson 1957), and simple instructions for "letting go" can help children learn how to become aware of, and reduce, tension in the laryngeal area.

Vocal pathologies such as vocal nodules affect phonatory quality by changing the weight, compliance and smooth approximation of the vocal folds (Moore 1971). Many children seem to increase their vocal difficulties inadvertently when they shift pitch levels and work harder at voice production to overcome the first symptoms of breathiness or roughness associated with a beginning voice problem or a bad cold. While such strategies may lead to a temporarily clearer voice quality, in the long run they aggravate the problem. One of the major counseling objectives of voice intervention is for a child to accept a breathy voice, at his or her optimal pitch, as a desirable transition to a healthy, clear voice.

Moncur and Brackett (1974) and Wilson and Rice (1977) provide detailed suggestions for planning voice intervention programs and Boone (1971, 1977) describes 24 facilitating approaches for voice therapy. One of the most effective, particularly with school-age children, is the yawn–sigh technique. Blonigen (1978) has further developed the technique and provides lists of stimulus /h–/ words, and phrases as well as a data-keeping procedure for charting progress. Basically, the procedure consists of teaching children to produce a sigh or a yawn, and then to initiate phonation in each of the following contexts with a soft, breathy approach: (1) /h–/ plus vowel monosyllables, (2) one-syllable /h–/ words, (3) two-syllable /h–/ words, (4) three-syllable /h–/ words, (5) four-syllable /h–/ words, (6) sentences of six-syllable length, (7) sentences of eight-syllable length, (8) breathy sentences of varying syllable length, (9) speech with breathiness in self-composed sentences, (10) sentences read from past classroom textbooks, (11) sentences read from current classroom textbooks (which will tend to elicit more tension), and finally (12) soft glottal approach speech in conversation with the clinician and others.

References and Other Resources

Blonigen, J. Management of vocal hoarseness caused by abuse: An approach. *Language, Speech and Hearing Services in Schools, IX,* 142-150, 1978.

Boone, D. R. *The Voice and Voice Therapy* (2nd edition). Englewood Cliffs, N.J.: Prentice-Hall, Inc., 1977.

Jacobson, E. *You Must Relax.* New York: McGraw-Hill Book Co., 1957.

Moncur, J. P. and I. P. Brackett. *Modifying Vocal Behavior.* New York: Harper & Row, Publishers, 1974.

Moore, G. P. *Organic Voice Disorders.* Englewood Cliffs, N.J.: Prentice-Hall, Inc., 1971.

Wilson, F. B. and M. Rice. *Voice Disorders.* Boston: Teaching Resources, 1977.

v-22   VOICE: ESTABLISHMENT AND TRANSFER OF INCREASED LARYNGEAL HYPOFUNCTIONING TO REPLACE VOCAL ABUSE

STUDENT: _____   AGE: _____   SCHOOL: _____   GRADE/LEVEL: _____   SPEECH–LANGUAGE CLINICIAN: _____

Date: _____

GOAL: The student will use a clear voice, free from tension and with appropriate pitch and loudness in all settings.

DIAGNOSTIC: This sequence is appropriate when the child shows laryngeal hyperfunctioning and other behaviors as described in the vocal abuse diagnostic summary.

LONG–RANGE OBJECTIVE: The student will demonstrate maintenance of target voice in one full session of conversation with clinician following a four–week interval with no therapy.

SHORT–TERM OBJECTIVES THE STUDENT WILL:	Date In.	DESCRIPTION OF SPECIFIC STIMULI, SETTINGS AND RESPONSES	Date Accom.	COMMENTS TECHNIQUES EVALUATION
1. demonstrate ability to relax extrinsic laryngeal muscles following gross motor activity or push–pull exercise or during head–rolling exercise (two consecutive sessions with verbal stimulus to relax only).				
2. demonstrate ability to produce easy onset of voice using yawn, sigh, /h/–initiated vowels, or other structured practice of breathy voice quality with appropriate loudness and pitch (4 of 5 trials of each type for three consecutive sessions).				
3. demonstrate ability to discriminate target voice (relaxed and with increased breath flow) from old voice by counting to three in either voice when asked by clinician (negative practice) (three trials each over two consecutive sessions).				
4. demonstrate ability to control laryngeal functioning (pitch, loudness, intonation patterns) in vowels, words or short phrases by imitating clinician's model (4 of 5 trials correct on each type using target voice over three consecutive sessions).				
5. use target voice (relaxed; with extra breath flow; appropriate pitch and loudness) while reading short paragraph or in other structured conversation (self–correcting all misuses of voice; two consecutive sessions).				
6. use target voice in unstructured conversation for one entire session with clinician/classmate.				
7. use target voice during entire session following two–week interval with no therapy.				
8. use target voice during entire session following four–week interval with no therapy.				

This form may be reproduced as often as necessary. / Copyright © 1979 by Communication Skill Builders, Inc.

V-23 VOICE:
ESTABLISHMENT AND TRANSFER OF INCREASED LARYNGEAL HYPERFUNCTIONING TO REPLACE BREATHY VOICE

School-age children rarely require therapy to increase the strength with which the vocal folds adduct. In the cases where there is, however, bowing due to excessive fatigue, or tissue reduction as a result of removal of multiple juvenile papilloma, the objectives of sequence V-23 can be of use.

Wilson and Rice (1977) encourage exercises to improve general physical conditioning, and suggest the progression from exaggerated, forced voice production, "talking hard," to more natural production of a clear speaking voice. Boone (1971, 1977) provides additional detail about using pushing to obtain vocal fold adduction. The most subtle way of using pushing, and one which can also be employed in class without being noticed, is for the student to grab the edges of the chair on which he or she is sitting and to push as if to lift his or her body from the chair, without actually doing so. The technique can be timed to correspond with natural phasing and can be gradually faded as the voice becomes stronger.

Sequence V-23 could also be adapted for use with students who have functional aphonia. *Objectives one* and *two* would then perhaps require further breakdown. Steps would need to be provided to ease the student from reflexive to voluntary voice production. An important part of such a program would be to avoid placing blame on the student for failure to produce voice and to elimi- nate any such implicit or explicit accusations by parents, siblings and peers (Boone 1977). It can be explained that the problem is related to having learned to keep the vocal folds apart (perhaps following a period of true laryngitis) and that the student will now have to relearn how to bring the vocal folds together to produce voice. Such a rationale will enable the student to begin to phonate and still "save face." Gargling and other gimmicks as well as a great expression of confidence in the child's ability to produce voice with the "new approach" can often provide the necessary impetus for the return to normal speaking behavior. If the problem is identified and handled early, children may only occasionally require referral for psychotherapy, but the clinician should always be aware of signs indicating that referral may be warranted.

References and Other Resources

Boone, D. R. *The Voice and Voice Therapy* (2nd edition). Englewood Cliffs, N.J.: Prentice-Hall, Inc., 1977.

Green, M. C. C. *The Voice and Its Disorders.* Philadelphia: J. B. Lippincott Company, 1975.

Van Riper, C. and J. V. Irwin. *Voice and Articulation.* Englewood Cliffs, N.J.: Prentice-Hall, Inc., 1958.

Wilson, F. B. and M. Rice. *Voice Disorders.* Boston: Teaching Resources, 1977.

v-23a   VOICE: ESTABLISHMENT AND TRANSFER OF INCREASED HYPOFUNCTIONING TO REPLACE BREATHY VOICE

Date: _____

STUDENT: _____ AGE: _____ SCHOOL: _____ GRADE/LEVEL: _____ SPEECH–LANGUAGE CLINICIAN: _____

GOAL: The student will use a clear voice with appropriate pitch and loudness in all settings.

DIAGNOSTIC: Oral Structures and Function _____
Otolaryngological: Date _____ Physician _____
Results _____ Allergies _____
Audiological _____
Other _____

Laryngeal Functioning:
Breathiness _____
Loudness _____
Variability _____
Habitual Pitch _____
Respiration: Type _____
Count on one Breath _____
Sustain /s/ _____ Sustain /z/ _____

LONG–RANGE OBJECTIVE: The student will demonstrate maintenance of target voice in one full session of conversation with clinician following a four–week interval with no therapy.

SHORT–TERM OBJECTIVES THE STUDENT WILL:	Date In.	DESCRIPTION OF SPECIFIC STIMULI, SETTINGS AND RESPONSES	Date Accom.	COMMENTS TECHNIQUES EVALUATION
*1. demonstrate voicing of reflexive type, vowels or the word "how," during physical activity (coughing/throat-clearing/pushing-pulling/lifting self off chair with arms) on first attempt (9 of 10 trials each over two consecutive sessions).				
2. demonstrate intermittent voice with sufficient clarity and loudness while reading short paragraph over white noise played through earphones (three consecutive sessions).				
3. demonstrate target voice with exaggerated tension (in vowels, consonant-vowel syllables with /m,n/, words, short phrases) following clinician's instruction to "talk hard," with physical straining (4 of 5 phrases over three consecutive sessions).				
4. accurately judge acceptability of tape-recorded segments of own voice during various practice activities (9 of 10 correct over three consecutive sessions).				
5. demonstrate target voice with reduced signs of overt tension and sufficient air volume in vowels, syllables, words, short phrases (4 of 5 trials each over three consecutive sessions).				

*See note on page 183.
This form may be reproduced as often as necessary. / Copyright © 1979 by Communication Skill Builders, Inc.

181

v-23b   VOICE: ESTABLISHMENT AND TRANSFER OF INCREASED HYPOFUNCTIONING TO REPLACE BREATHY VOICE

Date: _____

Student: _____

SHORT-TERM OBJECTIVES THE STUDENT WILL:	Date In.	DESCRIPTION OF SPECIFIC STIMULI, SETTINGS AND RESPONSES	Date Accom.	COMMENTS TECHNIQUES EVALUATION
6. use target voice in social speech with someone other than clinician (three separate occasions outside clinic room).				
7. use target voice with clinician for one full session following two-week interval with no therapy.				
8. use target voice with clinician for one full session following four-week interval with no therapy.				

*See Wilson and Rice (1977) for further suggestions. They emphasize the need for general physical conditioning. See also *Royal Canadian Air Force Exercise Plans for Physical Fitness*.

This form may be reproduced as often as necessary. / Copyright © 1979 by Communication Skill Builders, Inc.

V–24 VOICE:
ESTABLISHMENT AND TRANSFER OF VELOPHARYNGEAL RESONATORY FUNCTIONING

Resonatory problems seem particularly difficult to manage because of the complex interrelationships between structural and functional variables. Much time has been wasted, and frustration generated, in futile attempts to correct a problem of hypernasality with speech therapy when the structures were simply not sufficient to achieve closure. Similarly, problems of hyponasality (cold in the nose quality or *cul de sac* resonance) are far more likely to be remediated by following appropriate medical referral techniques and procedures than by any amount of speech training. However, speech intervention in coordination with other treatment approaches, or when the structural components are adequate, is often the necessary element to achieve the desired results in voice quality and articulatory clarity.

As always, accurate diagnosis is a critical part of the process. Van Hattum (1974) summarizes diagnostic considerations for speakers with cleft palate speech and emphasizes the need to sort out problems which are (1) unrelated, (2) indirectly related, and (3) directly related to the physical deficits. In diagnosing the directly related components of the problem, Van Hattum recommends that one analyze the client's ability to use the eight musculoskeletal valves appropriately to control, phonate, and articulate the flow of air for speaking. The eight constrictor positions are:

the lower lip and the teeth in the maxillary arch, the lower lip and the upper lip, the tongue and the teeth, the tongue and the alveolar ridge, the tongue and the hard palate, the posterior portion of the tongue and the velum, the velopharyngeal port, and the glottis. Although it is not a valve, the patent egress from the nasal cavity at the nares is a terminal boundary of the speech mechanism (p. 300).

Children with insufficient ability to achieve closure at the level of one of these valves (particularly the velopharyngeal port) are likely to substitute inappropriate valving at one or more of the other constrictor points. It is helpful then for the clinician to be aware of the multiple valving points so that children who have learned to substitute glottal stops for /k/ and /g/, for example, can be taught to eliminate such inappropriate compensatory behaviors.

A number of instruments are available for analyzing the structure and function of the velopharyngeal mechanism; for example, cinefluorographic films (Moll 1965), the Hunter Oral Manometer (Van Hattum 1974), the Taub Oral Panendoscope (Willis 1972), and the Tonar II (Fletcher 1972). However, since the technology and expertise for using such equipment are not generally available in school speech–language intervention programs, a team approach to diagnosis and remediation is particularly critical for dealing with problems of this nature. Even when an Oral Cleft Clinic is available in a reasonable vicinity, it is often the responsibility of the school speech–language pathologist to make good decisions about children to be referred.

The best tool most clinicians possess is the ability to judge the student's speaking behavior itself, both in single words and connected speech. Wilson's (1971) St. Louis Jewish Hospital Scale, explained first in the notes with sequence V–21, also includes a major scale for rating resonation which provides an excellent system for making the observation process more objective. Normal resonance is characterized as "0," denasality as "–2," assimilated nasality (progressive and retrograde influence of nasal consonants upon neighboring vowels) as "+2," severe assimilated nasality (but with consonants still relatively pure) as "+3," and pervasive nasality (involving both consonants and vowels) as "+4."

The *Iowa Pressure Articulation Test* (Morris, Spriesterbach and Darley 1961) also helps to assess articulation errors and permits inferences regarding intraoral pressure and velopharyngeal difficulty associated with specific types of articulatory errors. Hypernasality can, in fact, be viewed as an articulation disorder, with the position of the velum creating the distinctive feature difference between /b/ and /m/ and between /d/ and /n/. Rapid transitions between the alternating syllables, "be me be me, etc." and "no do no do, etc.," can help the clinician to assess a child's ability to achieve appropriate timing and degree of closure (Willis 1977). Willis also suggests having students count from 55 to 65 as a means of obtaining multiple examples of the ability to achieve closure for the production of fricatives.

A number of nonspeech behaviors have been explored as well for their applicability for determining whether a client can obtain sufficient velopharyngeal valving to produce speech with normal

186   *Voice*

resonance. Students can be asked questions about the frequency with which they get water in their noses at the drinking fountain and other problems of that nature. Although "there is general agreement that blowing, sucking, swallowing, gagging, and puffing do not parallel speech production sufficiently to offer useful diagnostic information" (Van Hattum 1974, p. 316), a TOM (tongue-tip outside mouth, puffed cheek) procedure was described by Hess (1970) and reported by Van Hattum (1974) for assessing the ability to achieve a seal between the oral and nasal cavities without using the posterior portion of the tongue as a valve. Sprintzen, McCall and Skolnick (1975) also review the research evidence regarding blowing and other nonspeech behaviors and conclude that the similarities between blowing and speaking are sufficient to justify the development of a special remediation technique, based upon simultaneous blowing and phonating, shown to be an effective means of reducing hypernasality.

As always, a child's individualized program should be designed to meet his or her multiple needs. Cleft palate children, in particular, frequently have language delays associated with their speaking difficulties, and the articulatory nature of the degree and timing of velar movement should also be considered. Many apraxic children, for example, have nasality problems associated more with their motor planning, timing and sequencing difficulties than with structural insufficiency.

Suggestions for using the short–term objectives of sequence V–24 follow.

1. Children with hypernasality frequently adopt abnormal articulatory patterns and habits, such as facial grimacing, in misguided attempts to compensate for nasal escape. Such behaviors usually make the speech sound worse and are visually distracting. The general functioning of the articulators should be a consideration in planning therapy for such problems. Van Riper and Irwin (1958) and Van Hattum (1974) offer suggestions for tongue and other oral exercises.

2. *Objective two* would be used only briefly to amplify sensory feedback from the velopharyngeal activity for children whose palates are habitually sluggish. The velum can be gently stimulted with a tongue blade or applicator as the student phonates on /ɑ/ and a verbal cue, such as "up," can be spoken by the clinician at the moment of stimulation. Such a cue can then become a conditioned stimulus, in a classical conditioning paradigm, for increased movement without tactile stimulation (the unconditioned stimulus).

3. Children should be encouraged to become aware of nasality as a distinctive articulatory feature, and developing their own labeling system seems to help.

4. For some students, a certain amount of negative practice helps develop kinesthetic and auditory feedback and control.

5. Appropriate posture, broad oral openings and forward positioning of the tongue increases the likelihood that speech will be produced with more oral than nasal breath flow. Van Hattum (1974) suggests the use of continuant consonants (/w/, /l/, /r/, /j/ and /h/) plus vowels (e.g., "awa,") in the early efforts to shape articulatory behavior, because of the minimal intraoral pressure required for such combinations. Gradually, the student is led to bring the lips together in progressive shaping of "awa" syllables into "apa" syllables, for example, and other phonemes are included in the process as well. These combinations are eventually shaped into words with initial vowels followed by stop consonants (e.g., "opera," "opposite") and lists of such words can be written into students' speech notebooks for practice at home as well as at school.

6. Since fricative consonants require more intraoral pressure than stop consonants, *objective six* is not likely to be successful unless *objective five* has already been met. If several months have been spent on *objective five* with no appreciable results, the clinician should plan to refer the child for further medical–structural evaluation. If *objective six* is implemented, production can be shaped from sounds requiring less, to those requiring more, intraoral pressure (e.g., "ata" to "atsa" to "at Sally's," etc.).

7. Since *speaking rate* is a major variable in determining articulatory accuracy for children who have marginal ability to achieve velopharyngeal closure, gradual increments of speaking rate, with continued emphasis upon clarity, can help a child improve the quality of conversational speech, *if* the structures are adequate.

8. Production of rapidly alternating syllables with oral and nasal consonants adds another element of complexity to the process.

9. *Objectives nine*, *ten* and *eleven* are presented to assist in the generalization process to new people and settings.

References and Other Resources

Boone, D. R. *The Voice and Voice Therapy* (2nd edition). Englewood Cliffs, N.J.: Prentice-Hall, Inc., 1977.

Fletcher, S. G. Contingencies for bioelectronic modification of nasality. *Journal of Speech and Hearing Disorders, 37,* 329–346, 1972.

Hess, D. A. The TOM puffed cheeks test of velopharyngeal competence. Unpublished manuscript, 1970.

Moll, K. L. A cinefluorographic study of velopharyngeal functions in normals during various activities. *Cleft Palate Journal, 2,* 112–122, 1965.

Morris, H. L., D. C. Spriestersbach and F. L. Darley. An articulation test for assessing competency of velopharyngeal closure. *Journal of Speech and Hearing Research, 4,* 48–55, 1961.

Sprintzen, R., G. McCall and M. L. Skolnick. A new therapeutic treatment of velopharyngeal incompetency. *Journal of Speech and Hearing Disorders, 40,* 69–83, 1975.

Van Hattum, R. J. Communication therapy for problems associated with cleft palate. In Dickson, S. (ed.), *Communication Disorders: Remedial Principles and Practices.* Glenview, Ill.: Scott, Foresman and Company, 298–355, 1974.

Van Riper, C. and J. Irwin. *Voice and Articulation.* Englewood Cliffs, N.J.: Prentice-Hall, Inc., 1958.

Willis, C. R. and M. L. Stutz. The clinical use of the Taub oral panendoscope in the observation of velopharyngeal function. *Journal of Speech and Hearing Disorders, 37,* 495–502, 1972.

Willis, C. R. Personal demonstration. 1977.

Wilson, F. B. The voice disordered child: A descriptive approach. *Language, Speech and Hearing Services in Schools, 4,* 18–22, 1971.

v-24a

VOICE: ESTABLISHMENT AND TRANSFER OF VELOPHARYNGEAL RESONATORY FUNCTIONING*

STUDENT: _____ AGE: _____ SCHOOL: _____ GRADE/LEVEL: _____ SPEECH–LANGUAGE CLINICIAN: _____

Date: _____

GOAL: The student will use speech with normal nasal resonance in all settings.

DIAGNOSTIC:

Oral Structures and Function _____

Otolaryngological: Date _____ Physician _____

Results _____ Allergies _____

Surgical History _____

Audiological _____

Other Speech–Language _____

Laryngeal Functioning _____

Other _____

Velopharyngeal Functioning:

Denasal _____ Assimilated Nasality _____

Severe Assimilated Nasality (Cons. Still Relatively Pure) _____

Pervasive Nasality (Involving Both Consonants and Vowels) _____

Ability to Produce Seal for Non-Speech Activities _____

Rapid Alternation Between Nasal/Non-Nasal Syllables (me/be; no/do) _____

LONG–RANGE OBJECTIVE: The student will use appropriate resonation in spontaneous conversation with someone other than the clinician outside the clinic room (two different recorded conversations with no more than two nasal/oral substitutions).

SHORT–TERM OBJECTIVES THE STUDENT WILL:	Date In.	DESCRIPTION OF SPECIFIC STIMULI, SETTINGS AND RESPONSES	Date Accom.	COMMENTS TECHNIQUES EVALUATION
1. demonstrate correct placement of articulators for all phonemes in consonant–vowel (CV) syllables produced in imitation of clinician with no facial grimacing or distorting (4 of 5 trials each over three consecutive sessions).				
2. indicate awareness of velopharyngeal movement by raising finger to correspond to movement of velum stimulated tactilely by clinician during production of /a/ phoneme (4 of 5 trials; two consecutive sessions).				
3. use special vocabulary appropriate to age level to describe movement of velum ("back door") to make some sounds nasal (m, n, n̞) and others not (two consecutive sessions).				
4. indicate abilities to control velar movement by going from nasal (negative practice) to oral productions of /a/ to correspond to clinician's verbal cues (4 of 5 trials; two consecutive sessions).				

See note on page 191.

This form may be reproduced as often as necessary. / Copyright © 1979 by Communication Skill Builders, Inc.

V–24b

VOICE: ESTABLISHMENT AND TRANSFER OF VELOPHARYNGEAL RESONATORY FUNCTIONING*

Date: _____

Student: _____

SHORT–TERM OBJECTIVES THE STUDENT WILL:	Date In.	DESCRIPTION OF SPECIFIC STIMULI, SETTINGS AND RESPONSES	Date Accom.	COMMENTS TECHNIQUES EVALUATION
5. produce VCV "words," moving gradually from medial continuant consonants /w/l/r/j/h/, to medial stop consonants /p/b/t/d/k/g/, with broad oral openings on vowels and appropriate resonance (9 of 10 words with plosive stops over three consecutive sessions), e.g., "awa" to "apa" to "operate."				
6. produce single syllable words with initial fricative /s/, /z/, /ʃ/, /ʒ/ and affricative /tʃ/dʒ/ consonants (9 of 10 words with no nasal emission over three consecutive sessions).				
7. produce rapidly alternating sequences of five or more CV syllables having no nasal consonants (18 of 20 syllable groups with appropriate oral resonance over three consecutive sessions).				
8. produce CV syllables beginning with alternating oral and nasal consonants (be me be me; no do no do) rapidly, in groups of five with accurate timing of resonatory shifts (18 of 20 syllable groups over three consecutive sessions).				
9. produce structured sentences having a mixture of oral and nasal consonants slowly and with posture, breath flow and oral opening sufficient to encourage normal resonance (no more than five nasal/oral substitutions in each of five consecutive sessions).				
10. produce mixed sentences with appropriate resonation in less structured settings with clinician/teacher/parent (no more than five nasal/oral substitutions in each of five separate settings).				
11. use appropriate resonation in spontaneous conversation with someone other than the clinician outside the clinic room (two different recorded conversations with no more than five nasal/oral substitutions).				

*Though labeled as a voice intervention sequence, the objectives presented here are integrally tied to phoneme articulation and, as always, should be coupled with other appropriate program objectives. It is also important to note that in no other area is physiological assessment and medical treatment more critical to the success of modification procedures than this one. In instances where the child is waiting for velopharyngeal surgery or the fitting of a prosthetic appliance, the first three objectives in this sequence would still be applicable.

F–25 FLUENCY:
MODIFICATION OF ENVIRONMENTAL INFLUENCES

The objectives of sequence F–25 are written to be implemented primarily with parents and teachers, and with students who are at an awareness stage of stuttering. Very young children who seem to have excessive difficulty speaking, but who are not overly aware of the difficulty, may benefit most from a program which involves their parents, using the objectives of sequence F–25. An indirect approach can be designed to desensitize them to communicative frustration, perhaps using the objectives of sequence F–26, *Fluency: Establishment Using Gradual Increase in Length and Complexity* (Ryan and Van Kirk 1971; Ryan 1974). Older children, and those who seem to be especially aware of their speaking difficulties, should be given more responsibility for changing their own behaviors.

Some factors which may help a clinician determine whether to involve students directly in the process of changing their communication behaviors are those suggested by Casteel and McMahon (1978):

1. The presence of struggle behavior.

2. Avoidance manifested in reading or other oral activities requiring class participation.

3. Ongoing environmental pressure and punishment.

4. Strong evidence of emotional upset directly related to stuttering behavior (p. 7).

During the initial interview process with parents, it is often best to separate the "information gathering" and "information giving" sessions (Luper and Mulder 1964; Burk 1975). Parents who have had reason to become concerned about their child's speaking behaviors are likely to need time to express their own concerns before they are ready to listen to new ideas about their child's problem and how they can help. A traditional problem of school speech–language and hearing programs has been the lack of direct contact between parents and clinician. Although the mandates of P.L. 94–142 are intended to remedy this situation somewhat, it is doubtful that the usual I.E.P. meeting could effectively meet the information gathering and giving objectives of sequence F–25. School administrators can be involved in the process of seeking appropriate avenues for interacting with parents, and as administrators' understanding of the problems of the school speech–language pathologist increases, so

does their willingness to help us seek solutions to those problems. When one of the parents is able to attend meetings on school time, but the other is not, Burk (1975) suggests taping the counseling sessions so that the absent parent can obtain more first-hand information about the problem.

At the information giving stage, Robinson (1964) and others at the Western Michigan University Speech and Hearing Clinic have found that it is better not to give parents a set of "Do's and Don'ts" on a handout. Rather give "prior absolution" for any guilt feelings the parents may have and enlist their aid in locating the fluency disruptors and facilitators for their own child and environment. Some examples are:

Fluency Disruptors	Fluency Facilitators
Interruptions; finishing sentences; speaking for him; misunderstanding	(Fill in the gaps with others)
Complaining; reproaching; accusing; scolding; criticizing; nagging	Affectionate utterances; expressions of approval and appreciation
Hurrying; anticipatory head-nodding; impatient listening; token listening	
Demanding; forbidding; rejecting; sarcasm; angry speech; verbal taboos	
Labeling; branding; correcting; say-it-agains; showing distress	
Overstimulating; tickling; exciting	
Questioning!!!	Making statements; reflecting what child says in other words
Requiring confession of wrong-doing or requesting the verbalization of hurtful or unpleasant experiences.	
Talking too swiftly, too complicatedly! Failing to provide good fluency models.	Simple self-talk; speaking in short sentences to child; having plenty of pauses; casual slowness
Unpleasant parental or sibling talk; anger; anxiety; frustration; worry; etc.	
Interfering; thwarting; refusing; rejecting; too many No's and Don'ts.	

Implemented with older students who are at an awareness level, the objectives of sequence F–25 can be used to compile a personalized list of communicative situations with graduated stress, from those in which speaking is easy and stuttering rarely occurs, to those in which speaking is difficult and stuttering almost always occurs. Then, as the student learns new ways to approach the task of speaking — perhaps using the objectives of sequences F–26, F–27 and F–28 — results for the remaining objectives of sequence F–25 can be entered into the "student" column as appropriate. For this transfer process to new speaking situations, the hierarchy which has been generated by the student and clinician using *objective two* of sequence F–25 can be coordinated with the objectives of sequence F–29, *Fluency: Transfer and Maintenance.* In this way, the student will be provided with a tailor-made program for maintaining fluency in situations which he or she has found to be increasingly stressful in the past.

Objectives three through *six* can then be implemented with older students using various speaking assignments in situations drawn from the hierarchical list. Students can be encouraged to enter into speaking situations which they have been avoiding and to report more objectively on the events of those assignments (Van Riper 1978 and previous editions). The major goal is for students to discover that to a large degree they can, by their own attitudes and actions, determine how much they will allow the manner in which they speak to be affected by environmental influences. Webster and Brutten (1974) provide some specific suggestions for influencing the relearning of alternative responses to environmental pressures.

References and Other Resources

Burk, K. W. Workshop on stuttering: Diagnosis, therapy and parent programs for the pre-school and early school age stuttering child. Lancaster, South Carolina, 1975.

Casteel, R. L. and J. McMahon. The modification of stuttering in a public school setting. *Journal of Childhood Communication Disorders, 2,* 6-17, 1978.

Cooper, E. B. *Personalized Fluency Control Therapy.* Boston: Teaching Resources.

Luper, H. and R. Mulder. *Stuttering: Therapy for Children.* Englewood Cliffs, N.J.: Prentice-Hall, Inc., 1964.

Mowrer, D. E., C. Ausberger and M. Kaiser. *Stuttering: Counting Dysfluencies, Charting and Applying Consequences.* Salt Lake City, Utah: Word Making Productions.

Robinson, F. B. *Introduction to Stuttering.* Englewood Cliffs, N.J.: Prentice-Hall, 1964.

Ryan, B. P. *Programmed Therapy for Stuttering in Children and Adults.* Springfield, Ill.: Charles C. Thomas, 1974.

Ryan, B. P. and B. Van Kirk. *Programmed Conditioning for Fluency: Program Book.* Monterey: Monterey Learning Systems, 1971.

Stocker, B. *The Stocker Probe Technique for Diagnosis and Treatment of Stuttering in Young Children.* Tulsa, Okla.: Modern Education Corporation.

Tanner, D. C. and N. A. Cannon. *Parental Diagnostic Questionnaire* (PDQ). Tulsa, Okla.: Modern Education Corporation.

Van Riper, C. *The Nature of Stuttering.* Englewood Cliffs, N.J.: Prentice-Hall, Inc., 1971.

Van Riper, C. *Speech Correction: Principles and Methods* (6th edition). Englewood Cliffs, N.J.: Prentice-Hall, Inc., 1978.

Webster, L. M. and G. J. Brutten. The modification of stuttering and associated behaviors. In Dickson, S. (ed.), *Communication Disorders: Remedial Principles and Practices.* Glenview, Ill.: Scott, Foresman and Company, 195-236, 1974.

Wingate, M. E. *Stuttering: Theory and Treatment.* New York: Irvington Publishers, Inc., 1976.

Mulder (1964) and Van Riper (1978).

F-25

FLUENCY: MODIFICATION OF ENVIRONMENTAL INFLUENCES

STUDENT: _____ AGE: _____ SCHOOL: _____ GRADE/LEVEL: _____ SPEECH–LANGUAGE CLINICIAN: _____

Date: _____

GOAL: The student, parents and teacher will work together to create an environment which will encourage fluent speech.

DIAGNOSTIC:
Articulation _____
Voice _____
Language _____
Word Retrieval _____

Dysfluency: Stuttered Words/Minute _____
Description _____
Contributing Factors _____

Others _____

LONG-RANGE OBJECTIVE: The parents, teacher and/or student will report that the student has shown progressively less speech difficulty over a period of six weeks or more.

SHORT–TERM OBJECTIVES THE PARENT(S)/TEACHER/STUDENT WILL:	PARENT		TEACHER		STUDENT*		COMMENTS TECHNIQUES EVALUATION
	Date In.	Date Accom.	Date In.	Date Accom.	Date In.	Date Accom.	
1. present background information about the problem and possible contributing factors in initial interview.							
2. indicate lay level knowledge of normal speech and language development and normal dysfluencies in interview format with clinician and assist in developing list of fluency disruptors and facilitators for student.							
3. keep diary style account of student's dysfluencies over a period of _____ days, and comment appropriately on observations.							
4. report on ways in which attention is shifted from the student's dysfluencies to his/her abilities, particularly in non-speech areas.							
5. report on the effects of reducing fluency disruptors and on occasions when plenty of talking opportunity was provided while the student was being fluent.							
6. report that the student has shown progressively less difficulty over a period of six weeks or more.							

*The objectives in this sequence are rarely used with students in the early or transitional stages of stuttering. The suggestions follow those presented by Burk (1975), Luper and Mulder (1964) and Van Riper (1978).

This form may be reproduced as often as necessary. / Copyright © 1979 by Communication Skill Builders, Inc.

F–26 FLUENCY:
ESTABLISHMENT USING GRADUAL INCREASE IN LENGTH AND COMPLEXITY

Young dysfluent children not visibly aware of their problems have often presented speech–language pathologists with a clinical dilemma — whether to chance that the child really is aware of the problem and bring the behaviors to his or her attention in order to work on them directly, or to avoid any direct reference to speaking and work indirectly to control the home and school environments and to desensitize the child gradually to communicative pressure.

The objectives of sequence F–26 provide an option for working directly on speaking behavior, but without drawing attention to the stuttering itself. This approach works well with young children and others who are able to achieve communicative competence and fluency when the length and complexity of the speaking task is taken down to a minimal level and then built up again gradually. It can also be the method of choice when dysnomia seems to have led to some of the child's dysfluencies. For a full explanation of how to use Gradual Increase in Length and Complexity of Utterances (GILCU) to establish fluency, see Ryan and Van Kirk (1971) and Ryan (1974).

Unlike some of the sequences, this one is designed for all of the objectives to be implemented with all children for whom it is selected. Each child should move through the entire sequence, first in reading, then in monologue, and finally in conversation, and then should move on to sequence F–29, *Fluency: Transfer and Maintenance.* Children who are too young to read can imitate the clinician during the reading phase. Topics for monologue can be written on slips of paper and drawn from an envelope as they are required. If merely reducing the length and complexity of the speaking task itself does not give the child the necessary assistance to produce words without tension and stoppages, the objectives of sequence F–27, *Fluency: Establishment and Transfer Using Control of Speaking Rate and Breath Flow,* can be used to help a child discriminate additional dimensions of making the task of speaking easier.

References and Other Resources

Ryan, B. P. Operant procedures applied to stuttering therapy for children. *Journal of Speech and Hearing Disorders, 36,* 264-280, 1971.

Ryan, B. P. *Programmed Therapy for Stuttering in Children and Adults.* Springfield, Ill.: Charles C. Thomas, 1974.

Ryan, B. P. and B. Van Kirk. *Programmed Conditioning for Fluency: Program Book.* Monterey: Monterey Learning Systems, 1971.

F-26a

FLUENCY: ESTABLISHMENT USING GRADUAL INCREASE IN LENGTH AND COMPLEXITY**

STUDENT: _____ AGE: _____ SCHOOL: _____ GRADE/LEVEL: _____ SPEECH–LANGUAGE CLINICIAN: _____

Date: _____

GOAL: The student will speak in all situations with no more than normal dysfluencies.

DIAGNOSTIC:

Articulation _____
Voice _____
Language _____
Word Retrieval _____
Other _____
Contributing Factors _____

Types of Struggle (Sec. Char.) _____

Dysfluency:

	TIME	TOT. WDS.	WHOLE WD. REP.	PART. WD. REP.	PROLONG.	STRUGGLE	% STTD. WORDS	Total Sttd. Words/Min.
Reading								
Monologue								
Conversation								

LONG–RANGE OBJECTIVE: The student will speak fluently in conversation for five minutes with no stuttered words.

SHORT–TERM OBJECTIVES THE STUDENT WILL:	I. (R) IN READING* (I) IMITATION		II. (M) MONOLOGUE		III. (C) IN CONVERSATION		COMMENTS TECHNIQUES EVALUATION
	Date In.	Date Accom.	Date In.	Date Accom.	Date In.	Date Accom.	
1. produce one word slowly and fluently in reading (imitation)/monologue/conversation, with clinician saying "good" after each fluent word (five minutes with no stuttered words).							
2. produce two words slowly and fluently in R(I)/M/C, with clinician saying "good" after each two fluent words (five minutes with no stuttered words).							
3. produce three words slowly and fluently in R(I)/M/C, with clinician saying "good" after each three fluent words (five minutes with no stuttered words).							
4. produce four words slowly and fluently in R(I)/M/C, with clinician saying "good" after each four fluent words (five minutes with no stuttered words).							
5. produce five words slowly and fluently in R(I)/M/C, with clinician saying "good" after each five fluent words (five minutes with no stuttered words).							
6. produce six words slowly and fluently in R(I)/M/C, with clinician saying "good" after each six fluent words (five minutes with no stuttered words).							

* In phase one, imitation may be substituted for reading if the child's reading level dictates such a choice.

**See note on page 201.

FLUENCY: ESTABLISHMENT USING GRADUAL INCREASE IN LENGTH AND COMPLEXITY**

Date: _____

Student: _____

SHORT-TERM OBJECTIVES THE STUDENT WILL:	I. (R) IN READING* (I) IMITATION		II. (M) MONOLOGUE		III. (C) IN CONVERSATION		COMMENTS TECHNIQUES EVALUATION
	Date In.	Date Accom.	Date In.	Date Accom.	Date In.	Date Accom.	
7. read (imitate)/speak one sentence fluently with clinician saying "good" after each fluent sentence (five minutes with no stuttered words).							
8. read (imitate)/speak two sentences fluently with clinician saying "good" after each fluent pair (five minutes with no stuttered words).							
9. read (imitate)/speak three sentences fluently with clinician saying "good" after each fluent three (five minutes with no stuttered words).							
10. read (imitate)/speak four sentences fluently with clinician saying "good" after each fluent four (five minutes with no stuttered words).							
11. read/speak fluently with clinician saying "good" after each 30 seconds of fluent speech (five minutes with no stuttered words).							
12. read/speak fluently with clinician saying "good" after each 45 seconds of fluent speech (five minutes with no stuttered words).							
13. read/speak fluently with clinician saying "good" after each minute of fluent speech (five minutes with no stuttered words).							
14. read/speak fluently with clinician saying "good" after each 90 seconds of fluent speech (five minutes with no stuttered words).							
15. read/speak fluently with clinician saying "good" after every two minutes of fluent speech (five minutes with no stuttered words).							
16. read/speak fluently with clinician saying "good" after every three minutes of fluent speech (five minutes with no stuttered words).							
17. read/speak fluently with clinician saying "good" after every four minutes of fluent speech (five minutes with no stuttered words).							
18. read/speak fluently for five minutes with no stuttered words.							
19. LONG-RANGE OBJECTIVE: The student will speak fluently in conversation with the clinician for five mintues with no stuttered words.							

**The GILCU Program (Ryan and VanKirk, 1971) of which a modification is presented here has been shown to be particularly advantageous for use with young children who are not yet aware of their stuttering since the program places little or no attention on the act of stuttering and it is seldom necessary to discuss stuttering behavior (Ryan, 1974). Children too young to read can imitate the clinician during the reading phase. All steps should be completed in order in each phase. If the child begins to show difficulty, previous steps should be repeated.

*See note on page 199.

F-27 FLUENCY:
ESTABLISHMENT AND TRANSFER USING CONTROL OF SPEAKING RATE AND BREATH FLOW

The objectives of sequence F-27 have been suggested by Casteel and McMahon (1978) as a means of teaching school-age children to make gradually finer discriminations between what one does to be fluent and what one does to be dysfluent. The basic assumptions of their program are:

(1) excessive muscle tension is used when a child stutters; (2) the frequency and severity of stuttering varies with the amount of stress or pressure in the speaking situation; (3) the child who stutters has made incorrect choices in the way he talks; (4) he has made these incorrect choices because he is not aware of what he is doing with his speech mechanism when he stutters or when he is fluent; (5) the child has not taken nor been given responsibility for choosing his speech behavior; and (6) he is capable of learning to be an efficient talker rather than only learning to be an efficient stutterer (p. 7).

The "stages" of this approach are used to control the normal speaking variables of fluency, rate, loudness, pitch, quality and articulation. At first, task complexity is reduced to a level where fluency can almost be guaranteed, by shifting each of the other variables to an undemanding level. Then expectations are reinstated, one at a time, for normal rate, loudness, pitch, quality and articulation. A difference between using this sequence for establishing fluency and either of the others (F-26 or F-28), is that transfer of newly learned skills is built into the steps rather than after completion of the entire sequence. However, if necessary, the clinician can elect to synchronize the objectives of this sequence with those of sequence F-29, *Fluency: Transfer and Maintenance*.

Specific suggestions for using the short-term objectives of this sequence follow.

STAGE I: Stretch and Flow

1. Progressive relaxation (Jacobson 1957) is suggested as the method to help children learn to identify the locus of tension if it begins to interfere with air flow at any time during Stage I, or subsequent stages, of the program. Clinicians may also wish to review the eight constrictor points mentioned in the explanatory notes with sequence V-24, since any of them may potentially impede the air flow if it is closed with abnormal tenseness during speaking.

Schwartz (1976) has emphasized that the larynx is the critical constriction point in triggering stuttering blocks, and has designed his therapy approach around that principle. His suggestions, which are primarily aimed at helping adult stutterers, can also be reviewed for their application to helping children with *objective two* of this stage.

2. The "stretch" of this objective is speech which is prolonged as if it is being produced in slow motion, and the "flow" is exaggerated breathiness, with air flowing through the entire phrase without pauses between words. Similar effects can be obtained by using delayed auditory feedback (Curlee and Perkins 1969; Ryan 1971), but the "stretch" method requires no expensive equipment. Demonstration is provided and instructions are given to the child to "sound like a ghost," or to "string all of your words together as if they are one giant word." Relative monotone and loose articulation are also used. The rationale for this type of speaking, in addition to ensuring fluency, is to enable the student to make fine discriminations of air flow and the motor act of speaking (Casteel and McMahon 1978).

3. *Objective three* of Stage I is a transfer objective which is designed to stabilize the new talking behavior. All of the objectives of Stage I are implemented in the speech room, but subsequent stages include objectives for transferring the new behavior to other situations, with increasing stressfulness, which have been identified using the objectives of sequence F-25.

STAGE II: Increased Breath

1. Relaxation continues to be an important component of the speaking process.

2. The identifying feature of Stage II is the maintenance of fluency with normal rate reinstated, but with continued exaggerated breathiness, monotone, and loose articulation.

3. *Objectives three* and *four* are used in the transfer process, now to outside situations, but still with low stress characteristics, and in the presence of the clinician. Some examples are short conversations with the school secretary, cook or

custodian, or interacting with a friend in the speech room. Peters (1977) presents two case studies where periods of fluency were effectively reinforced by allowing students to invite friends to therapy.

STAGE III: Reduced Breath

1. In this stage, normal rate is maintained, and loudness and vocal variety are reinstated, but the voice is still somewhat breathy and articulation is consciously loose.

2. Reading, monologue and conversation can be used with the clinician in the speech room to stabilize the new talking style of Stage III.

3. Casteel and McMahon (1978) suggest first bringing the child's classroom teacher into the speech room for a brief session, as a gradual transition step to using the new talking style in outside settings. When the new behavior does transfer to the classroom, it should at first be monitored in reading alone. Teachers are far more likely to actually assist with assignments if the assignments work well in the usual routine, if they are brief, and if they are thoroughly explained and demonstrated.

4. Similar procedures can be used for transferring the new speaking style to monologue and conversation as to reading, and to home and other settings as to the classroom.

STAGE IV: Easy Talking

1. By Stage IV, the child should be capable of making the fine discriminations of motor control and air flow which will allow him or her to speak fluently and normally, using free air flow and effortless articulation, but without the exaggeration of previous stages. Casteel and Mc-Mahon (1978) reemphasize the point made by Williams (1957) and others (Shames *et al.* 1969; Sander 1970) that children must assume the responsibility for not only "easy talking," but also for the interferences *they* create in the easy flow of speech. Comments such as, "I held my tongue tight against the roof of my mouth so I should let go and touch easy," are encouraged because they (a) describe the behavior objectively, (b) demonstrate acceptance of the responsibility for the behavior, and (c) suggest a solution.

2. During Stage IV, additional increments can be made in the communicative demands of outside speaking situations.

3. If the child experiences difficulty at any time, or expects to, he or she should return to the speaking style of Stage II or III until control can be reestablished without the "stretchy speech."

4. The objectives of sequence F–29 can be used to supplement sequence F–27 at this point, if necessary.

5. As the child enters this "self-maintenance" objective of the program, contact frequency may be gradually reduced over a period of a year or more until the student is being formally seen only once every three months. Covert monitoring (on the playground, in the cafeteria, via tape recordings, etc.) should continue until the clinician is certain that fluency will be maintained.

References and Other Resources

Casteel, R. L. and J. McMahon. The modification of stuttering in a public school setting. *Journal of Childhood Communication Disorders, 2,* 6-17, 1978.

Curlee, R. F. and W. H. Perkins. Conversational rate control for stuttering. *Journal of Speech and Hearing Disorders, 34,* 245-250, 1969.

Jacobson, E. *You Must Relax.* New York: McGraw-Hill Book Co., 1957.

Peters, A. D. The effect of positive reinforcement on fluency: Two case studies. *Language, Speech and Hearing Services in Schools, VIII,* 15-22, 1977.

Ryan, B. P. Operant procedures applied to stuttering therapy for children. *Journal of Speech and Hearing Disorders, 36,* 264-280, 1971.

Schwartz, M. F. *Stuttering Solved.* Philadelphia: J. B. Lippincott Company, 1976.

FLUENCY: ESTABLISHMENT AND TRANSFER USING CONTROL OF SPEAKING RATE AND BREATH FLOW

STUDENT: _____ AGE: _____ SCHOOL: _____ GRADE/LEVEL: _____ SPEECH-LANGUAGE CLINICIAN: _____

Date: _____

GOAL: The student will speak in all situations with no more than normal dysfluencies.

DIAGNOSTIC:

Articulation _____
Voice _____
Language _____
Word Retrieval _____
Other _____
Contributing Factors _____

Types of Struggle (Sec. Char.) _____

Dysfluency:

	TIME	TOT. WDS.	WHOLE WD. REP.	PART WD. REP.	PROLONG.	STRUGGLE	% STTD. WORDS	Total Sttd. Words/Min.
Reading								
Monologue								
Conversation								

LONG-RANGE OBJECTIVE: The student will speak fluently in conversation for five minutes with no stuttered words.

SHORT-TERM OBJECTIVES THE STUDENT WILL:	Date In.	DESCRIPTION OF STIMULUS MATERIALS AND CONTEXTS	Date Accom.	COMMENTS TECHNIQUES EVALUATION
STAGE I: "Stretch and Flow"				
1. demonstrate gross and fine muscle relaxation without instruction from the clinician.				
2. maintain reduced rate achieved through "stretch," appropriate breathiness through excessive air "flow," low intensity, pitch monotone, and loosely articulated speech.				
3. talk using Stage I style with fluency; i.e., without interferences, during timed observations of reading, monologue and dialogue (three minutes each) on two different days.				
STAGE II: "Increased Breath"				
1. continue using appropriate relaxation.				
2. increase the rate of speech while maintaining excessive breathiness, low intensity, relative monotone, and loose articulation when instructed to talk using Stage II style.				

F-27b

FLUENCY: ESTABLISHMENT AND TRANSFER USING CONTROL OF SPEAKING RATE AND BREATH FLOW

Date: _____

Student: _____

SHORT–TERM OBJECTIVES THE STUDENT WILL:	Date In.	DESCRIPTION OF STIMULUS MATERIALS AND CONTEXTS	Date Accom.	COMMENTS TECHNIQUES EVALUATION
3. demonstrate the use of fluent Stage II speech in at least three low stress situations outside of the clinic room on three different days.				
4. talk using Stage II style without interferences during timed observations of reading, monologue and dialogue (three minutes each on two different days).				
STAGE III: "Reduced Breath" 1. utilize normal rate, loudness and vocal variety while maintaining some breathiness and a slight degree of loose articulation when instructed to talk using Stage III style.				
2. achieve complete fluency in the clinical setting using Stage III style (based upon informal observation by the clinician).				
3. talk using Stage III style without interferences during timed observations of reading, monologue and dialogue (three minutes each) on two different days.				
4. demonstrate the use of fluent Stage III speech in middle and high stress situations in the classroom and at home.				
STAGE IV: "Easy Talking" 1. maintain fluency in the speech room by reducing tension in the speech mechanism using free air flow and effortless articulation.				
2. talk using Stage IV style outside the clinic room on a routine basis.				
3. use adjustive techniques (relaxation and use of Stage II or III) outside the clinic room in order to maintain fluency.				
4. routinely cope with high stress situations.				
5. continue to maintain fluency while the frequency of visits to the clinician are reduced by one-third.				

F–28 FLUENCY:
ESTABLISHMENT USING THE TRADITIONAL APPROACH

For some older children, the clinician may wish to plan a program of speech management using Van Riper's (1971, 1978) traditional techniques of motivation, identification, desensitization, variation, approximation, and stabilization (MIDVAS). Specific suggestions for using the objectives of sequence F–28, and previous sequences, are presented below. The objectives of this particular sequence are presented in the manner suggested by Ryan (1974) and are intended to be used in the order 1 through 10: first with reading, second during monologue, and last in conversation.

1. *Motivation.* The student is led to become an objective observer of his or her own behavior and to take responsibility for it. The suggestions of sequence F–25 and F–27 can be particularly useful in this process.

2. *Identification.* The identification of people, places, things and feelings associated with periods of dysfluency and fluency can also be accomplished using the objectives of sequence F–25, and can be written into the diagnostic heading of F–29. The first three objectives of this sequence are also designed to assist in the processs.

3. *Desensitization.* An ongoing and follow–up desensitization program can be coordinated with the objectives of sequence F–29.

4. *Variation.* Van Riper (1978) describes the purpose of the variation phase as attaching new responses to old cues. The cancellations of *objective four* of this sequence help students to change their response to word and sound fears, and assignments in conjunction with sequence F–25 can also be used for varying responses to situation fears. Webster and Brutten (1974) provide additional suggestions for helping students learn to vary their reactions to communicative stress.

5. *Approximation.* The approximation techniques which are used with the objectives of sequence F–28 are prolonged cancellations, pull–outs, preparatory sets and light contact. The suggestions for using adjusted speaking rate and free air flow in conjunction with sequence F–27 should also be helpful in this phase.

6. *Stabilization.* Taking the student through all 10 objectives, first in reading, then in speaking, and finally in monologue, helps to stabilize the new behaviors. The suggestions of Peters (1977) for using positive reinforcement for fluency, and the reward of bringing a friend to speech sessions, are especially pertinent with *objective ten.* The transfer and maintenance objectives of sequence F–29 can then be used to stabilize the fluent speech further.

References and Other Resources

Peters, A. D. The effect of positive reinforcement on fluency: Two case studies. *Language, Speech and Hearing Services in Schools, VIII,* 15-22, 1977.

Ryan, B. P. *Programmed Therapy for Stuttering in Children and Adults.* Springfield, Ill.: Charles C. Thomas, 1974.

Van Riper, C. *The Nature of Stuttering.* Englewood Cliffs, N.J.: Prentice-Hall, Inc., 1971.

Van Riper, C. *Speech Correction: Principles and Methods* (6th edition). Englewood Cliffs, N.J.: Prentice-Hall, Inc., 1978.

Webster, L. M. and G. J. Brutten. The modification of stuttering and associated behaviors. In Dickson, S. (ed.), *Communication Disorders: Remedial Principles and Practices.* Glenview, Ill.: Scott, Foresman and Company, 195-236, 1974.

F-28a

FLUENCY: ESTABLISHMENT USING THE TRADITIONAL APPROACH*

Date: _____

STUDENT: _____ AGE: _____ SCHOOL: _____ GRADE/LEVEL: _____ SPEECH–LANGUAGE CLINICIAN: _____

GOAL: The student will speak in all situations with no more than normal dysfluencies.

DIAGNOSTIC:

Articulation _____
Voice _____
Language _____
Word Retrieval _____
Other _____
Contributing Factors _____

Types of Struggle (Sec. Char.) _____

Dysfluency:

	TIME	TOT. WDS.	WHOLE WD. REP.	PART WD. REP.	PROLONG.	STRUGGLE	% STTD. WORDS	Total Sttd. Words/Min.
Reading								
Monologue								
Conversation								

LONG–RANGE OBJECTIVE: The student will speak fluently in conversation with the clinician for five minutes with no stuttered words.

SHORT–TERM OBJECTIVES

THE STUDENT WILL:	I. (R) IN READING		II. (M) MONOLOGUE		III. (C) IN CONVERSATION		COMMENTS TECHNIQUES EVALUATION
	Date In.	Date Accom.	Date In.	Date Accom.	Date In.	Date Accom.	
1. produce speech in reading/monologue/conversation with the clinician saying "there" every time student stutters on a word (one minute).							
2. produce speech in R/M/C with the clinician saying "there" and the student raising hand every time student stutters on a word (one minute).							
3. produce speech in R/M/C with the student raising hand every time he/she stutters on a word (one minute, 90 percent correct identification).							
4. produce speech in R/M/C and repeat each stuttered word with clinician saying "good" for every stuttered or fluent cancellation (five minutes, 90 percent correct identification).							
5. produce speech in R/M/C and repeat each stuttered word in a prolonged manner with clinician saying "good" for every prolonged cancellation (five minutes, 90 percent correct identification).							

*See note on page 213.

This form may be reproduced as often as necessary. / Copyright © 1979 by Communication Skill Builders, Inc.

F–28b

FLUENCY: ESTABLISHMENT USING THE TRADITIONAL APPROACH*

Date: _____

Student: _____

SHORT–TERM OBJECTIVES THE STUDENT WILL:	I. (R) IN READING		II. (M) MONOLOGUE		III. (C) IN CONVERSATION		COMMENTS TECHNIQUES EVALUATION
	Date In.	Date Accom.	Date In.	Date Accom.	Date In.	Date Accom.	
6. produce speech in R/M/C and repeat each stuttered word, prolonging the first sound, with clinician saying "good" every time for cancellation (five minutes, 90 percent correct identification).							
7. produce speech in R/M/C and interrupt each stuttered word by prolonging the first sound with clinician saying "good" every other time for pull-out (five minutes, 90 percent correct identification).							
8. produce speech in R/M/C and interrupt each stuttered word as soon as the block begins with a prolongation and with the clinician saying "good" every other time for pull-out (five minutes, 90 percent correct identification).							
9. produce speech in R/M/C and prolong the first sound of any word student thinks he/she might stutter on which clinician saying "good" every other time for prolongation (five minutes, 90 percent correct identification).							
10. read/speak for five minutes without stuttered words following clinician's instructions to "read/speak as fluently as you can," and with clinician saying "good" for every 10 fluent sentences (five minutes at no stuttered words per minute).							
11. LONG–RANGE OBJECTIVE: The student will speak fluently in conversation with the clinician for five minutes without stuttered words.							

*For information on programmed application of Van Riper's traditional approach (1971), see Ryan (1974). These objectives should all be used and should be used in the order 1 through 10 first while reading, second during monologue, and last in conversation.

F-29 FLUENCY:
TRANSFER AND MAINTENANCE

The objectives of sequence F-29 include a hierarchy of activities designed to gradually desensitize the student to communicative pressure (Van Riper 1971, 1978; Ryan 1974). As such they could be adapted for use in conjunction with any of the previous sequences, but particularly with those for voice and articulation. Children with language delays are also often extra sensitive to communicative pressures which can generate stuttering, and the fluency sequences should be coordinated with appropriate areas of language intervention if necessary.

This transfer and maintenance sequence can be further individualized for a stuttering child by developing a personal list of "places/times/people associated with dysfluency" in the *Diagnostic* column on the left of the recording form, and those "associated with fluency" in the column on the right. The student's personalized list of disruptive and facilitating environmental influences can be constructed in coordination with the objectives of F-25, *Fluency: Modification of Environmental Influences*. The questionnaires developed by Webster and Brutten (1974) and Tanner and Cannon (1977), and the activities and recording forms of Cooper's *Personalized Fluency Control* may also be of use. Stocker's *Probe Technique* can also be coordinated with the objectives of this sequence.

Some may object to the goal for this sequence — "The child will permanently use normally fluent speech" — especially in view of the evidence that, at least in part, stuttering is what one does when trying not to stutter. However, it should be remembered that (1) the "goals" for all of these objective sequences are written to define "normality" for the behavior being trained and are rarely copied directly into the child's I.E.P., and (2) "normal fluency" is not the same as *complete* fluency, since normal speakers are also dysfluent at times. For a review of some of the differences between normal dysfluency and behavior which can be classed as stuttering, see Williams (1957). Factors summarized by Burk (1975), to be emphasized in the process of counseling the parents of the nonstuttering child (perhaps in conjunction with sequence F-25 of these objectives), are that the *nonstuttering* child:

1. Does not repeat or hesitate as often as we find in a child who is stuttering, and when he repeats it tends to be the whole word rather than part of a word. Much of this may be described as an effort on his part to revise what is said.

2. When he does repeat or revise what he wants to say, he does it without any particular effort, and no particular word or words seem to give him difficulty.

3. He does not give any indication of being aware or concerned about his speech. One good indication is that he watches his listener when he is talking.

4. There seem to be no particular times when what he does is more noticeable than at other times. You report also that he never seems to mind talking in any situation.

Strong evidence also suggests that, if handled properly, the goal of fluency is not an unreasonable one, especially for children who have not had as long as adult stutterers have had to build up frustrations, fears and anxieties. It may well be that stuttering is what one does trying not to stutter when one has no better alternatives. The objectives of sequence F-29 should only be implemented when the student has learned better alternatives, using the strategies of sequences F-25, F-26 or F-27, and perhaps other techniques, such as those suggested by Curlee and Perkins (1969) or Schwartz (1976). The activities of these objectives are designed to then lead children to *enter* situations of gradually increasing communicative stress, not to avoid them. Casteel and McMahon's (1978) view that the dysfluent child "is capable of learning to be an efficient talker rather than only learning to be an efficient stutterer" (p. 7) seems to be not only a clinically useful one, but also a definitely possible goal.

References and Other Resources

Burk, K. W. Workshop on suttering: Diagnosis, therapy and parent programs for the pre-school and early school-age stuttering child. Lancaster, South Carolina, 1975.

Casteel, R. L. and J. McMahon. The modification of stuttering in a public school setting. *Journal of Childhood Communication Disorders, 2*, 6-17, 1978.

Cooper, E. B. *Personalized Fluency Control Therapy.* Boston: Teaching Resources.

Curlee, R. F. and W. H. Perkins. Conversational rate control for stuttering. *Journal of Speech and Hearing Disorders, 34,* 245-250, 1969.

Ryan, B. P. *Programmed Therapy for Stuttering in Children and Adults.* Springfield, Ill.: Charles C. Thomas, 1974.

Schwartz, M. F. *Stuttering Solved.* Philadelphia: J. B. Lippincott Company, 1976.

Stocker, B. *The Stocker Probe Technique for Diagnosis and Treatment of Stuttering in Young Children.* Tulsa, Okla.: Modern Education Corporation.

Tanner, D. C. and N. A. Cannon. *Parental Diagnostic Questionnaire (PDQ).* Tulsa, Okla.: Modern Education Corporation.

Van Riper, C. *The Nature of Stuttering.* Englewood Cliffs, N.J.: Prentice-Hall, Inc., 1971.

Van Riper, C. *Speech Correction: Principles and Methods* (6th edition). Englewood Cliffs, N.J.: Prentice-Hall, Inc., 1978.

Webster, L. M. and G. J. Brutten. The modification of stuttering and associated behaviors. In Dickson, S. (ed.), *Communication Disorders: Remedial Principles and Practices.* Glenview, Ill.: Scott, Foresman and Company, 195-236, 1974.

F–29a

FLUENCY: TRANSFER AND MAINTENANCE*

STUDENT: _____ AGE: _____ SCHOOL: _____ GRADE/LEVEL: _____ SPEECH-LANGUAGE CLINICIAN: _____

Date: _____

GOAL: The student will permanently use normally fluent speech.

DIAGNOSTIC: Places/Times/People Associated with Dysfluency   Places/Times/People Associated with Fluency

_____ _____

_____ _____

_____ _____

LONG-RANGE OBJECTIVE: The student will speak fluently in all home, school, work and play settings with and without the clinician. (Criterion for success: report of at least three 5- to 10-minute conversations in various settings with no stuttered words, following at least a six-week interval with no direct therapy.)

SHORT–TERM OBJECTIVES THE STUDENT WILL:	Date In.	DESCRIPTION OF ACTIVITIES/ PLACES/PEOPLE	Date Accom.	COMMENTS TECHNIQUES EVALUATION
1. converse with the clinician for 5 to 10 minutes with no stuttered words in each of the following *physical settings* (social reinforcement only):				
a. Speech room with door open				
b. Immediately outside speech room				
c. Down the hall from the speech room				
d. Outside the school building				
e. Walking around the school building				
f. In different rooms in different buildings				
2. Speak for 5 to 10 minutes with no stuttered words with each of the following types of audiences:				
a. One additional person in speech room who does not interact				
b. One additional person in speech room who does interact				
c. Two additional people in speech room who do not interact				
d. Two additional people in speech room who do interact				
e.–h. Continue, up to five people				

This form may be reproduced as often as necessary. / Copyright © 1979 by Communication Skill Builders, Inc.

*See note on page 219.

FLUENCY: TRANSFER AND MAINTENANCE*

Date: _____

Student: _____

SHORT-TERM OBJECTIVES THE STUDENT WILL:	Date In.	DESCRIPTION OF ACTIVITIES/ PLACES/PEOPLE	Date Accom.	COMMENTS TECHNIQUES EVALUATION
2. Continued i. Speech to group of five				
j. Speech to group of ten				
k. Speech to group of fifteen				
3. speak for 5 to 10 minutes with no stuttered words in at least three *different situations* of each type: a. With various strangers in different physical settings with clinician close at hand				
b. With various strangers in different physical settings with clinician at a distance				
c. With various strangers in different settings without the clinician				
4. call, answer and converse for 5 to 10 minutes with no stuttered words in each of the following *telephone* activities: a. With clinician, pretending phone is present				
b. Using a fake telephone with the clinician				
c. Using a real telephone with the clinician				
d. Using a real telephone with friends and/or relatives				
e. Using a real telephone with strangers				
5. speak for 5 to 10 minutes with no stuttered words reported in at least three of each of the following natural environment situations (as appropriate): a. At school, with teacher and peers, with and without the clinician				
b. At home, with parent and siblings, with and without the clinician				
c. At work, with boss and fellow employees with and without the clinician				
6. LONG-RANGE: The student will speak fluently for 5 to 10 minutes in at least three different situations with and without the clinician after a six-week interval with no direct therapy.				

*The transfer program presented here (with slight adaptation) is that summarized by Ryan (1974). This form may be reproduced as often as necessary. / Copyright © 1979 by Communication Skill Builders, Inc.

GLOSSARY

Abdominal breathing: inhalation and exhalation controlled primarily by depression and relaxation of the diaphragm resulting in outward and back movements of the abdominal wall

Abduction: spreading apart (e.g., vocal folds in open position)

Absurdity: statement or paragraph within which ridiculous incongruities appear

Acquired brain damage: brain damage that occurs as a result of accident or illness during or after the language acquisition process has begun

Action: semantic function filled by verbs in basic sentences

Acoustic environment: sounds, both speech and non-speech, which are audible to a listener in a situation

Acquisition: process by which children develop the ability to understand and produce an infinite variety of utterances

Adaptation: development of alternative strategies to cope with the environment

Adduction: bringing together (e.g., vocal folds in closed position)

Affricative: type of phoneme produced by stopping airflow and then pushing it through a constricted opening (e.g., ch, j)

Agent: person or thing that is responsible for action; semantic subject of a sentence which may or may not appear in the first noun phrase of the sentence

Analogy: comparison of two relationships which are similar

Antonym: word of opposite meaning

Aphonia: inability to produce voice above a whisper

Approximation: process of becoming closer to a desired outcome

Articulation: production of speech sounds

Articulators: structures used to produce speech sounds — the teeth, tongue, lips, hard and soft palate

Ascending hierarchy: organization of concepts under labels so that each higher label includes everything below it

Assimilated nasality: sounds produced through the nose only when they occur next to sounds which are supposed to be nasal (i.e., m, n, ng)

Assimilation: modifying existing cognitive systems by adding new information

Athetoid: type of cerebral palsy characterized by arhythmic uncontrollable movements

Attribute: descriptive feature of someone or something

Auditory processing: acts of attending, hearing, perceiving, comparing, remembering, etc., which are part of understanding messages

Auxiliary (Aux): verbal components used to specify shades of meaning of the main verb

Auxiliary construction rule: phrase structure rule proposed by Chomsky to account for all options for signifying verbal meaning using the model → tense + (modal) + (have + en) + (be + ing) + V; generating, for example, the deep structure past + can + have + en + be + ing + go → which when transformed becomes the surface structure "could have been going"

Baseline: measurement of behavior prior to training for purposes of defining current levels and documenting progress

Basic sentence: simple active affirmative declarative sentence made up of a Noun Phrase + Verb Phrase + (complement)

Belly breathing: immature pattern seen in normal infants and some cerebral palsied children in which the rib cage may be depressed except for the flared bottom edge while the diaphragm causes the abdomen to expand during inhalation

Binary feature distinction: attribute which is present in one of two items being compared (+) but absent in the other (–)

Bliss board: communicative device using the symbols devised by C. K. Bliss which aids a person who has difficulty with verbal expression

Breathing rhythm: timing of inhalation and exhalation phases of air exchange which is varied for speaking by shortening the inhalation phase and extending the exhalation phase

Cancellation: technique whereby a stuttered word is immediately repeated voluntarily

Cardinal feature: identifying aspect of a phoneme which is constant even when it is produced by different people in different contexts

Carryover: process by which newly taught behaviors are practiced in new contexts until they become spontaneous and consistent

Cerebral palsy: nonprogressive neuromotor condition usually resulting from congenital brain damage which causes problems of muscular control

Class inclusion: members of a group of elements which have common attributes and can be placed in an ascending hierarchy

Classical conditioning: process by which a stimulus which does not elicit a response (conditioned stimulus) is paired with a stimulus which does elicit the response (unconditioned stimulus) until the response occurs to the first stimulus when the second stimulus is no longer present

[221]

Classification: grouping of items based upon a common attribute

Clavicular breathing: abnormal reliance upon muscles which raise the shoulder blades to create negative air pressure in the lungs for inhalation

Coarticulation: influence upon phoneme production and perception by other phonemes which precede and follow it

Coarticulatory variation: acoustic changes in phonemes created by surrounding phonetic context

Cognition: processes of knowing, including sensation, perception, memory, conceptualization, mental operations, thinking, etc.

Cognitive constraints: dependence upon specific thought processes such as logical operations to reach an outcome

Communicative: pertaining to acts and processes for conveying information

Compensation: substitution of one behavior or process for another which is difficult (may be desirable or undesirable)

Compensatory function: serving as replacement for a difficult or impossible behavior or process

Competence: linguistically, knowledge of the rules of language (psycholinguistic competence) and for using language (sociolinguistic or pragmatic competence)

Complexity: interrelated components which may require many underlying processes for understanding

Conceptual vocabulary: words which represent one's knowledge about attributes and relationships among objects rather than names (e.g., colors, numbers, size words, etc.)

Conditioned stimulus: event which comes to elicit a response only after being paired with another stimulus which already elicits the response

Conjoin: to put together for a common purpose (e.g., making two sentences into one with a conjunction, embedding, etc.)

Connected discourse: extended orderly discussion about a topic for a purpose

Consent: agreeing or granting permission; required by P.L. 94-142 for preplacement evaluation and initial placement

Conservation: cognitive process by which one recognizes that essential attribute relationships are maintained even when exemplary form changes

Content: substance; information conveyed via language

Context: surrounding referential, linguistic, sound and/or written information that assists in the interpretation of the direct message

Contractible: permissible to connect with other words (e.g., copula, "He's my friend," and auxiliary, "They're not going.")

Contrastive stress: emphasis placed upon a word to signify that an important distinction is being made with something previously understood

Convention: general agreement about basic principles of operation

Co-occurring: linguistic structures, referential information and/or behaviors which appear within the same time frame

Co-occurring restricted structures: simplification of linguistic rules related to contextual complexity

Copula: verb "to be" when used by itself as a connector ("She is nice. They are policemen.") rather than as an auxiliary

Count noun: can be preceded directly by number words and can have plural endings (e.g., "four spoons" is permissible but not "four breads" since "bread" is a mass noun)

Creative use: novel application of shared knowledge of linguistic rules to communicate

Criterion: specification of manner in which one can decide whether an objective has been reached

Cul-de-sac resonance: nasal quality caused by forward obstruction of the nasal passage, as if holding one's nose

CV, CVC, CCVC, CVCC: shorthand description of the make-up of syllables and words in terms of consonants and vowels

Decoding: process of using information in a message and its context and internalized knowledge of how a system is organized to arrive at the intended meaning

Deep structure: underlying meaning and basic form of a sentence

Definite article or pronoun: indicates a specific referent (the, this, these) rather than a general one (a, some)

Demonstrative (Dem) pronoun: identifies a specific noun which it can appear with or without (e.g., this, that, these, those, etc.)

Desensitization: process of gradually increasing the threshold of response to a particular kind of stimulus by systematically presenting increasingly less muted forms of the stimulus

Determiner (Det): linguistic device that specifies the state of a noun in a noun phrase; articles, demonstratives, possessives, number, etc.

Developing edge of competence: linguistic theories adopted by a child who is in the process of acquiring knowledge of adult rules of language

Disability: specific problem requiring special help for reduction of its effect on overall ability

Discriminative stimuli: features of an event or object which enable one to tell it apart from a similar event or object

Disassociation: in neuromotor dysfunction, the process of reducing "overflow" so that one part of the body can be moved without triggering corresponding movements in other parts

Distinctive features: attributes of phonemes which identify them as being unique (e.g., ± voiced, ± continuant, etc.). Semantic features serve similar functions (e.g., ± count, ± human, etc.)

"Do" question: one which begins with a form of the implied auxiliary "do" and requires a yes/no response (e.g., "Did he want one?")

Due process: all of the procedures required by P.L. 94-142 to protect the rights of children and their parents

Duration: one of three major dimensions (others are frequency and intensity) which define acoustic events, in this case in terms of the time one lasts

Dysfluency: interruption in the smooth flow and rhythm of speech

Dysnomia: abnormal difficulty in recalling specific words and inhibiting related words to express a meaning; also termed "amnesic aphasia" or "word-finding problem"

Early language: stage of beginning development of knowledge about adult rules of language in which children have their own rules for expressing meaning with one-, two- and three-word phrases

Echolalia: nonmeaningful repetition of a statement or question just heard

Educational performance: must be specified in an I.E.P. to define a child's current level of overall ability with detail in the area of disability

Egocentric: based exclusively on one's own orientation

Ellipsis: omission of one or more words from a complete sentence which can be obviously understood; for example, "Who is coming?" "The man . . . (is coming)."

Encoding: using one's knowledge of organizational rules to construct a meaningful symbolic expression

Enhancement: additional communicative modes used to support but not necessarily replace traditional modes

Environmental language intervention: approach which depends heavily upon important people and meaningful experiences to encourage development which has not occurred spontaneously

Environmental pressure: real or perceived expectations of listeners which increase the likelihood of stuttering

Environmental punishment: consequences of dysfluent moments and other events which lower one's self-image and increase the likelihood of stuttering

Evaluation: process of specifying a subject's abilities and disabilities by using formal and informal observation and tests and knowledge of what would be expected from the individual if no disability were present

Evaluation plan: required specification on I.E.P. to identify how progress will be measured

Exemplar: member of a set which provides a "for instance"

Expansion: response of an adult to a child's utterance which amplifies the child's supposed intended meaning and/or structure

Extrinsic laryngeal muscles: those which support and position the cartilages of the voice box and the rib cage

Feature distinction: a difference in attributes of two phonemes or words which allows them to be discriminated

Fluency: talking with normal rhythm and smoothness (normal speech is rarely perfectly smooth)

Fluency disruptor: something which increases the likelihood that a person will have difficulty talking smoothly

Fluency facilitator: something which increases the likelihood that a person will talk smoothly

Foil: false choice used to help ensure that the correct choice is intentional

Form: structural aspects of language and its physical representation

Formal evaluation: establishment of relative abilities and disabilities using standardized tests

Frequency: acoustic quality perceived as pitch which is determined by the number of wave cycles per second

Fricative: speech feature created by forcing air between two closely spaced articulators (e.g., s, z, sh, etc.)

Full evaluation: diagnostic procedures which consider all aspects of behavior

Function: use or purpose of language

Functional communication: use of language for early developmental purposes and meeting basic needs

Generalization: application of a new behavior or linguistic rule in novel and appropriate contexts

Generalization probing: creating novel contexts which can be used to check whether a new rule or behavior will be applied appropriately without further training

Generate: to create an utterance by using psycholinguistic rules

Glottis: opening between the vocal folds

Goal: desired outcome

Goal area: general category of the desired outcome

Grammatical overload: when excessive linguistic and contextual demands reduce a child's ability to use rules

Handicap: condition defined by P.L. 94-142, including speech [and language] impaired, as needing special education and related services

Holophrase: single-word utterance used by young children to communicate different sentence-like meanings in different contexts

Homonym: word which is spelled and pronounced like another but has a different meaning

Horizontal programming: having activities for several goal areas or aspects of one goal area in process at one time

Hyperbole: extravagant exaggeration used as a figure of speech

Hyperextension of mandible: jutting out of the lower jaw related to imbalanced muscle pulls during chewing and other activities

Hyperfunctioning: muscular activity in excess of that required for normal use

Hypofunctioning: muscular activity less than that required for normal use

Idiom: expression which has a meaning which cannot be derived from the conjoined meanings of its elements

Impairment: disability

Indefinite article or pronoun: indicates a general referent (a, some) rather than a specific one (the, these)

Individualization: process of making a program fit a student's specific needs

Individualized Education Program (IEP): written document required by P.L. 94-142 for all handicapped children

Initial IEP: first plan written after a child is determined to need special education services

Informal evaluation: establishment of abilities and disabilities using natural observation and responses to tasks which have not been standardized but can be compared with one's knowledge of normal expectations

Information-gathering session: history taking and question asking exchange aimed at identifying the origins and development of a problem

Information-giving session: clinical exchange for the purpose of helping parents and/or clients deal with a problem area

Instructional objective: further specification of a goal in terms of an observable and measurable behavior

Instructional plan: component of the IEP which provides specific detail as to how goals are to be reached

Intelligible: capable of being understood

Intensity: acoustic quality perceived as loudness which is determined by the amplitude of component wave forms

Intermediate objective: measurement point between instructional objectives and the overall goal

Intervention: process of consciously assisting the development of an ability which normally proceeds without formal attention

Intraoral pressure: build up of air within the closed cavity of the mouth

Invariant quality: property that the equality of two elements does not change even if one is transformed

Jaw stabilization: cupping a child's chin firmly but loosely enough to enable controlled voluntary movement for eating, drinking or speech

Language: shared knowledge of rules for combining spoken and written symbols into words, phrases and sentences via which meaning can be conveyed and understood

Language intervention program: system designed to assist language development in those not acquiring it normally

Language sample: body of recorded and transcribed utterances gathered for the purpose of analysis

Laryngeal: pertaining to use of the vocal folds

Least Restrictive Environment (LRE): optimal learning situation which is as much like regular education as possible; required by P.L. 94-142

Lexicon: one's words and the concepts underlying them which are constantly changing as new experiences add new words and adjust the meaning of others

Lip pursing: excessive puckering of the lips.

Lip retraction: excessive involuntary drawing back of the lips to expose the teeth

Localize: to identify the direction from which a sound originates

Locative: adverb of place

Locus: region or place

Maintenance: procedures designed to enable keeping a behavior in active use after formal training has ceased

Mandible: lower jaw

Matrix approach: systematic combinations of two sets of words into all possible two-word utterances

Maxillary arch: shape of the upper jaw bone structure

Metalinguistic: language used to talk about language

Metaphor: figurative language in which a word or phrase literally denoting one kind of object or idea is used in place of another to suggest a likeness or analogy between them

Minimal pair: two words which are alike except for one phoneme

MLU: abbreviation for "mean length of utterance," computed by adding the total number of morphemes in 100 or more utterances and dividing by the number of utterances

Modal auxiliary: optional component of the verb system — "can" (could), "will" (would), "shall" (should), "may" (might), "must" (must) and "hafta" and "gonna" which serve as modals in early development

Modality: means of communicating, receptive/expressive, written/oral, listening/speaking/reading/writing

Modification: gradual or partial change

Monologue: connected discourse carried on by one person

Morpheme: smallest meaningful unit of language, such that each word consists of at least one *base morpheme* ("inform"), and can also include a *derivational morpheme* to make it a different part of speech ("information") or an *inflectional morpheme* to fit it into the structure of a sentence ("informed")

Morphological: related to morphemes and the rules of their use

Musculoskeletal valves: points of constriction which can impede airflow

Nasal consonants: "m," "n" and "ng" which are all produced with resonation of air in the nasal cavity

Nasal production: allowing air to enter the nose between the soft palate and the posterior wall of the throat and vibrate there

Negative practice: voluntary production of an undesirable behavior with exaggeration to bring it to a conscious level

Negative pressure: density of air molecules which is less than in a neighboring area, creating a semi-vacuum and tendency for other air to rush in to equalize the pressure

Neuromotor dysfunction: muscular use problem based upon abnormal neural impulses being sent from the brain

New information: in conversation, it is the introduction of meaning not previously shared with the other partner (i.e., change of context)

Nomination: process of naming or labeling something, an early function of communication

Nonexistence: early function of communication which identifies the absence or disappearance of something

Nonsense syllable: combination of consonants and vowels which is intended to serve as a sound unit only and not as a meaningful word

Object: acted-upon part of a sentence

Objective case: grammatical case used to signify that a pronoun is acted upon (e.g., "her, him, them," etc.)

Old information: in conversation, it is the understood meaning or context which is shared by two conversational partners and need not be reverbalized

One-to-one correspondence: relationship of elements of two equal sets

Open-ended program: teaching approach designed to allow individualization

Operation: mental activity which can take the place of action to figure out the solution to a problem

Operational: objective written in such a way as to be measurable and observable and to relate directly to teaching activities

Oral consonant: produced with resonation in the mouth rather than the nose; all consonants except "m," "n" and "ng"

Oral production: directing air through the mouth by closing the velopharyngeal opening to the nose

Orienting reflex: natural tendency of an infant to turn in the direction from which a sound originates

Orthography: representation of the sounds of language by written or printed symbols

Overextension: application of words or rules in contexts which are similar to the appropriate ones but beyond acceptable adult usage (e.g., a horse as a "big doggie" or "feets" as a plural)

Overflow: movement of an unintended muscle group when another is stimulated

P.L. 94-142: The Education for All Handicapped Children Act which mandates a free, appropriate public education for all children

Patent egress: open exit from the body (e.g., nostrils)

Paired stimuli technique: teaching method in which an individual is expected to increase the likelihood of producing a correct response when it is coupled with a previously correct response to a similar stimulus

Perceptual saliency: pertaining to attributes which stand out

Perceptual-conceptual "chunks": cognitive units which are recognized and remembered based upon the manner in which previous experiences have been categorized

Periodic aphonia: loss of voice intermittently within sentences and words

Personal pronoun: word which can be substituted for a person once the reference is clear (e.g., he, she, it, they)

Pervasive nasality: inappropriate resonation of all speech sounds in the nose

Pharyngeal: pertaining to the throat

Phonation: production of voice in the larynx

Phonetic analysis: specification of speech sounds and distinctive features used by an individual speaker

Phonetic context: phonemes and transitions between them that surround a particular sound

Phrase structure rule: syntactic organization of the basic elements of a sentence

Plan: organized program of action for reaching a goal

Platitude: trite remark

Polyp: non-malignant growth on the vocal folds which may be attached with a stem-like connection and is related to vocal abuse

Positive pressure: density of air molecules which is greater than that in a neighboring area, creating a tendency for air to rush outward to equalize the pressure

Possession: early communicative function indicating ownership or personal association

Postulate: presupposition or assumption

Postural stabilization: making the body trunk steady to enable movement of individual parts with less overflow

Pragmatic constraints: limitations based upon acceptable uses of language

Pragmatic-functional: related to uses of language to persuade, inform, request, etc.

Pragmatics: social dynamics of language use for an individual

Preoperational: cognitive stage prior to being able to perform mental activities without real objects

Pre/post-test: method of comparing performance before and after training to determine its effectiveness

Preverbal: skills whose development takes place automatically before a child learns to speak, but may be seriously delayed in children with neuromotor dysfunction

Probing: making spot checks to help determine future course of action

Progressive relaxation: systematic tensing and releasing of muscles, from gross to fine, to enhance sensory feedback and voluntary muscular control of tension

Prolongation: word produced with exaggerated duration

Propositionality: perceived importance of a communicative event, related to the necessity for specific accuracy of information, number of listeners and judgment expected from them

Prosody: rhythmic characteristics of speech

Proverb: saying embodying a common observation in a metaphoric form

Pull-out: technique used to gain control in the midst of a stuttering block by loosening contact and extending duration at the point of difficulty

Quantifiable: measurable in exact terms

Referent: object, person or other meaning which a word or utterance is intended to indicate

Reflexive voicing: sound produced by adduction of the vocal folds which requires no voluntary effort (e.g., coughing, laughing, throat-clearing)

Refrigerator word: practice material to be taken home and posted in a prominent spot to remind the family that it is to be produced correctly

Reinforce: to present a consequence for a behavior which increases the likelihood of the behavior reoccurring

Rejection: refusal, an early function of communication

Remediation: process of correcting a problem

Required context: linguistic situation which demands obligatory use of a rule

Restricted structure: limited rule application as a result of incomplete knowledge of a system

Reversed copula question: yes/no question formed by moving the copular (not auxiliary) form of the verb "to be" to the beginning of the sentence (e.g., "Are you happy?")

Reversibility: in cognition, the ability to reconstruct or reorganize; to perform mental operations and return to the original state (e.g., concepts of conservation require reversible operations)

Review and revision of the I.E.P.: required at least annually by P.L. 94-142

Rules and regulations: published in the Tuesday, August 23, 1977, *Federal Register* to explain the required implementation procedures of P.L. 94-142, and also accompanying many state special education codes to further amplify procedures

Schwa vowel: neutral "uh" sound ($/\Lambda/$) sometimes produced as a place holder during conversation or following exaggerated production of stop consonants in isolation (e.g., $/b\vartheta/$; in phonetic transcription $/\Lambda/$ = stressed, $/\vartheta/$ = unstressed)

Selective attention: narrowing or focusing of consciousness or receptivity based upon prior expectations about which aspects of a situation will be meaningful

Self-correct: to alter spontaneously an incorrect response, signifying monitoring of one's own behavior and that a new rule is in the active learning process

Self-cue: to provide oneself with prompts associated with the desired response in an attempt to trigger it

Semantic-categorization: grouping together and contrasting of verbal concepts based upon shared features and hierarchical relationships

Semantic-cognitive: pertaining to the close association of verbal and nonverbal conceptual operations

Semantic-grammatic rules: descriptions of the early structures children use to perform meaningful functions

Semantic-transformation: application of a statement which has one literal meaning for another figurative meaning (e.g., idioms, metaphors, etc.)

Semantically potent word: selected for its frequency and communicative usefulness to an individual child as a vehicle for learning new articulatory behavior

Semantics: domain of linguistics pertaining to meaning

Sensori-integration: coordinated transfer among sense receptors and different components of the brain to enable smooth control of function; a term used frequently by occupational therapists

Sensori-motor: referring to the interaction of receptive and expressive components of neuromuscular functioning

Sensory feedback: information returning to control centers as an expressive function occurs, enabling one to monitor that function and make desired adjustments

Seriation: orderly arrangement of a set of elements based upon the degree to which each represents a common attribute

Shaping: process of gradually eliciting and reinforcing responses which more and more resemble a target response

Shared information: common prior knowledge two or more conversational partners have about a context

Short-term memory (STM): brief storage of information in the brain where it can be retrieved within a few seconds and/or processed further for long-term memory by "chunking" or will be forgotten

Signed language: specialized symbolic gestural system used to communicate linguistic meaning

Social discourse: formal and orderly verbal interchange using learned conventions

Sociolinguistics: domain pertaining to sociological influences on language learning and use

Soft glottal approach: initiation of phonation with gentle approximation of the vocal folds and smooth vibration rather than abrupt attack; sometimes preceded by an /h/

Speech act: multidimensional aspects of a communicative event

Speech-language clinician: term used in this book to refer to one trained in speech-language pathology (see below)

Speech-language pathologist: professional knowledgeable about the normal development and processes of communication, their disorders and procedures of remediation

Speech-language pathology: professional domain pertaining to the study of normal and disordered communicative processes and remediation strategies

Speech-like utterance: vocalization which uses the phonological rules of one's culture but does not signify word meaning

Stabilization: clinical process of ensuring that an individual has the ability to apply a new rule or behavior spontaneously in all and only the appropriate contexts

Stimulus content: information of focus which is expected to incite a desired activity or response directly

Stimulus context: pertinent information surrounding the direct content which assists in its perception and interpretation

Structural insufficiency: physical incapability to produce a desired behavior

Structured conversation: verbal exchange designed by an adult to elicit certain kinds of responses from a child

Structured play: application of a language intervention objective within an experience-based activity, including modeling, expansion and other interaction techniques

Stuttered word: characterized by an abnormal stoppage, prolongation or repetition of a sound, syllable or the whole word, although whole word repetition more often represents normal dysfluency

Subliminal: below threshold; insufficient to incite overt activity

Subvocally: language produced in thought for one's own benefit, but perhaps with subliminal neuromuscular activity

Suckle pattern: immature sucking reflex in which the tongue cups the nipple or straw and rhythmic mandibular depression occurs

Supplementary materials: stimulus items which can assist in the implementation of an instructional program

Support experiences: activities designed to encourage the natural application of a new rule or behavior

Suprasegmental feature: superimposed aspect of verbal behavior (e.g., intonation, stress, pauses, etc.)

Surface structure: actual sentence which is spoken or written

Synonym: word which means the same or nearly the same as another

Syntactic coding: internalized process for generating spoken utterances using structural rules, which are linguistically symbolized with such rewrite rules as:

$$S \longrightarrow \text{sentence}$$
$$NP \longrightarrow \text{noun phrase}$$
$$VP \longrightarrow \text{verb phrase}$$
$$N \longrightarrow \text{common noun}$$
$$Art \longrightarrow \text{article}$$
$$Det \longrightarrow \text{determiner}$$
$$PAdj \longrightarrow \text{predicate adjective}$$
$$PN \longrightarrow \text{predicate noun}$$
$$Dem \longrightarrow \text{demonstrative}$$
$$Prep \longrightarrow \text{preposition}$$
$$(\quad) \longrightarrow \text{optional}$$
$$/ \longrightarrow \text{choice of elements}$$

Syntactic-pragmatic: organizational rules which apply to specific communicative functions

Syntax: domain of linguistics pertaining to the organization of morphemes into connected utterances using phrase structure rules and their transformations

Tactile stimulation: inciting of sensation or activity by touching

Tactile sensitivity: threshold of awareness of being touched

Talk sample: speech production of a specified duration elicited for the purpose of quantifying a feature of spoken language

Target content: information desired to be conveyed

Target phoneme: speech sound stated in the instructional objective as the desired outcome of intervention

Target structure (TS): syntactic or morphological rule stated in the instructional objective as the desired outcome of intervention

Taxonomical categories: labels for grouping common elements

Temporal pressure: perception of being hurried which often tends to disrupt fluency

Terminal objective: final expectation for a structured sequence within a goal area

Therapeutic conversational turn: modeling and expansion device which builds upon a child's spontaneous communication to achieve a specific objective

Thoracic breathing: inhalation and exhalation of air in the lungs by using primarily the muscles of the neck and chest to elevate the rib cage

Topic-comment: linguistic rule used to describe children's semi-grammatical associations of single words into two-word utterances in early language

Topic switching: presentation of new context as well as new content in discourse

Transfer: application of a newly learned behavior or rule in appropriate novel contexts

Transformation: grammatical operation on a basic phrase structure to alter its form (e.g., negatives, questions, passives); in other domains, also refers to a change which maintains the essence of the original element

Turn-taking: learned process of alternatively speaking and listening which is subject to sociolinguistic convention

Ultimate goal: expectation which would be desired if there were no limitations

Unconditioned stimulus: event which automatically elicits a response

Uncontractible: not permissible to be combined; for example, in some contexts, the copula ("Is Jerry hitting?"), and the auxiliary ("No, John is.")

Unintelligible: cannot be understood

Utterance: verbal expression which functions as a unit

Variation: process of making a partial change by altering one attribute or characteristic

VC, VCC: shorthand description of the makeup of syllables and words in terms of vowels and consonants (e.g., "it, eats")

Velopharyngeal: referring to relationship of the soft palate to the posterior and lateral walls of the throat and the opening between them

Velum: soft palate

Vertical programming: completion of activities in one goal area or aspect of a goal area before initiating activities in the next

Vital capacity: volume of air the lungs are capable of inhaling and exhaling for life purposes

Vocal: related to voice production for speaking purposes

Vocal abuse: habitual practices which harm the tissues of the larynx (e.g., yelling, coughing, laughing, singing, frequent throat-clearing, etc.)

Vocal hyperfunctioning: voice production with excessive muscular tension

Vocal hypofunctioning: voice production with insufficient muscular tension

Vocal folds: muscular shelves in the larynx used to produce voice; "vocal cords"

Vocal interplay: alternative speech-like productions by an adult and child for the sake of enjoyment of the sound and social aspects of the event

Vocal nodules: callus-like growths which develop on the vocal folds as a result of vocal abuse

Vocal play: speech-like productions made by a child for his or her own enjoyment

Voice: production of sound by adducting the vocal folds and forcing an airstream between them causing them to vibrate

Wh-question: request for information rather than a yes/no response, beginning with such words as "who," "what," "where," "how," "why," etc.

White noise: mixture of sound waves extending over a broad frequency band which sounds like "shh"

Word retrieval: process of recalling and producing desired words while inhibiting production of associated words